KT-521-631

THE M. & E. HANDBOOK SERIES

AUDITING

AUDITING

Leslie R. Howard, F.C.A.

Principal Lecturer in
Financial and Management Accountancy,
City of London Polytechnic

THIRD EDITION

MACDONALD & EVANS LTD

8 John Street, London W.C.1

1970

First published August 1966
Reprinted September 1967
Second edition June 1968
Reprinted March 1969
Third edition June 1970

©

MACDONALD AND EVANS LTD

1970

S.B.N.: 7121 0120 9

This book is copyright and may not be
reproduced in whole *or in part* (except for
purposes of review) without the express
permission of the publishers in writing.

HANDBOOK *Conditions of Sale*

This book is sold subject to the condition
that it shall not, by way of *trade or otherwise,* be lent, resold, hired out or otherwise
circulated without the publisher's prior
consent in any form of binding or cover
other than that in which it is published
*and without a similar condition including
this condition being imposed on the subsequent purchaser.*

Printed in Great Britain by
UNWIN BROTHERS LIMITED
WOKING AND LONDON
(7566 HCO)

GENERAL INTRODUCTION

The HANDBOOK Series of Study Notes

HANDBOOKS are a new form of printed study notes designed to help students to prepare and revise for professional and other examinations. The books are carefully programmed so as to be self-contained courses of tuition in the subjects they cover. For this purpose they comprise detailed notes, self-testing questions and hints on examination technique.

HANDBOOKS can be used on their own or in conjunction with recommended textbooks. They are written by college lecturers, examiners, and others with wide experience of students' difficulties and requirements. At all stages the main objective of the authors has been to prepare students for the practical business of passing examinations.

P. W. D. REDMOND
General Editor

NOTICE TO LECTURERS

Many lecturers are now using HANDBOOKS as working texts to save time otherwise wasted by students in protracted note-taking. The purpose of the series is to meet practical teaching requirements as far as possible, and lecturers are cordially invited to forward comments or criticisms to the Publishers for consideration.

AUTHOR'S PREFACE TO
THIRD EDITION

A THIRD edition of this book has become necessary owing to the rapid development in auditing techniques, due not only to widening experience in auditing electronic data processing systems, but also to the changing views on auditing procedures brought about by the use of Internal Control Questionnaires and Standard Audit Programmes applied in auditing in depth. These matters have been brought completely up to date to include the latest Recommendations of the Institute of Chartered Accountants. Additional material in a short Appendix to cover the overall change in auditing methods as a result of greater familiarity with computer auditing has also been included.

The relevant case law including the practical application of both the Companies Acts has also been kept fully up to date.

Acknowledgments are due to the various accountancy bodies mentioned below for permission to use their examination questions, and in addition, special acknowledgment must be accorded to the Institute of Chartered Accountants of England and Wales for the extensive use of quotations from their *Statements on Auditing* and other publications, as indicated, and where these have not actually been quoted, for the close following of the techniques outlined, since they constitute authoritative recommendations to the Accountancy profession. The following publications are particularly relevant:

Questions given are those set at final level examinations except where otherwise indicated. Abbreviations used are as follows:

C.C.A.   Association of Certified and Corporate Accountants.

C.A.   Institute of Chartered Accountants of Scotland.

C.A.(E.W.)   Institute of Chartered Accountants of England and Wales (Designated in the text as the Institute of Chartered Accountants).

Leslie R. Howard

April 1970

CONTENTS

TABLE OF CASES

(Where the facts are noted, the page number is in italics)

CHAPTER I

THE NATURE OF AUDITING

NATURE OF AUDITING

1. Introduction. Originally an auditor was one to whom the receipts and payments of an establishment were read (as is signified in the Latin verb *audire*, to hear) and the practice was known to have been exercised by such ancient civilisations as the Egyptians.

The increased complexity of commerce today has greatly widened the scope of the auditor's operations, and calls for a high degree of skill and discernment, but the underlying principle of the examination of completed transactions still exists. With this background in mind we turn to a general definition of the word *audit*.

2. Definition of an audit. An audit may be described as an examination by an auditor of the evidence from which the final revenue accounts and balance sheet of an organisation have been prepared, in order to ascertain that they present a true and fair view of the summarised transactions for the period under review and of the financial state of the organisation at the end date, thus enabling the auditor to report thereon.

Examining the definition a little more closely it will be observed that the auditor examines the evidence, *i.e.* mainly the books, accounts and vouchers of the establishment. But, in certain circumstances it may be necessary for the auditor to go even further in his examination, *e.g.*, to examine actual assets held.

Such definitions often refer to the ascertainment of the true and fair view of the *profit or loss* for the period, but it is felt that the foregoing wording is more inclusive since many organisations, such as those of non-trading bodies, do not use the term profit or loss but rather an excess of income over expenditure (or vice versa). Further, not only are the end figures of a revenue account important in themselves, but the constituent parts of the revenue account must also give a true and fair view of the transactions they represent.

It is important to remember that the examination must be such as to enable the auditor to report thereon.

3. Concomitant features of an audit. It is a common misunderstanding that the purpose of an audit is to detect errors and fraud. This might be the case when an investigation of a set of accounts and their relevant documents is conducted, but this is not the main purpose of an audit.

It is true that an audit may reveal the presence of errors and fraud but this is only a subordinate feature, arising only in the course of the conduct of the normal auditing work and as such is of relevance only as an advantage arising. Likewise, the moral check arising upon the carrying out of the audit does much to prevent error or fraud arising, and so these two vital factors emerge as *subsidiary* to the main purpose of the audit, *viz.*,

(a) The detection of errors and fraud.
(b) The prevention of errors and fraud.

4. Audit and accountancy work compared. The assumption has so far been made that the accounts and balance sheet are submitted to the auditor, but in practice the auditor frequently prepares the accounts and balance sheet himself.

A clear distinction must be drawn, however, between the work of an auditor as such and his work as an accountant. To return to the original definition, the auditor's task is to "audit" the completed work, and although in preparing the accounts he may carry out certain auditing work, this preparatory work is only carried out in his capacity as an accountant.

Frequently in the course of his work the auditor may become aware of weaknesses and inefficiency in the working of the system, and he may bring such matters to the notice of the client or his staff. When so doing, the auditor is again acting in his capacity as an accountant (since as an auditor it is not his duty to advocate certain methods of working). Nevertheless, with his skill and experience, the auditor will be most helpful to those by whom he is engaged but such work must always be considered apart from the work of the audit.

This distinction in the particular nature of the work on which the auditor is engaged is important since various liabilities and duties are inherent in his work which in certain circumstances may be called into question with far-reaching consequences.

5. Complexity of an audit. The complexity of manufacturing and commercial transactions and the methods by which such transactions are recorded for accounting and other purposes has turned the simple "hearing" of the auditor of the miscellaneous receipts and payments into an intricate operation requiring a degree of skill and experience which is commensurate with the work undertaken.

As yet many audits can be conducted by those with no specified qualification, but where the interests of the public at large are affected, statutory requirements have been laid down in respect of those who may undertake such work. These legal requirements are discussed in more detail later (*see* XIV) but at this stage it is emphasised that although auditing may be carried out in most cases by any person requested to do so, such duties may only be carried out efficiently by the exercise of the professional skill and experience of those qualified to do so.

CLASSIFICATION OF AUDITS

The various types of audit which may be undertaken are distinguishable in the first instance by two main classifications:

(a) According to the *nature of the work* undertaken.
(b) According to the *method of approach* to the work.

6. Classification by nature of work undertaken. Under this class can be grouped the following basic types of audit:

(a) Private audits.
(b) Statutory audits.
(c) Internal audits.

7. Private audits. In such cases the auditor will operate according to an *agreed limit of work*. This does not mean that the whole of his work is specifically stated before commencement, but some broad agreement as to what work is required

will have been laid down.   This agreement may be in the form
of an understanding to do all the work the auditor considers
necessary to the issue of a report, the terms of which are
indicated.

> He may for example report on his having received all the
> information and explanations he has required and his satisfac-
> tion as to the accounts and balance sheet concerned giving a
> true and fair view of the financial affairs and position of the
> organisation. Such a report as this would necessitate conducting
> a *full audit*.
>
> On the other hand, it may be specified in the instructions to
> the auditor that he is only required to give a report stating his
> satisfaction as to the accounts and balance sheet being in
> accordance with such work as he has undertaken.   Such a
> report might be in general terms stating that the accounts are in
> accordance with the information and explanations given to him.

The specification of the extent of the work to be carried out
may take different forms; *e.g.* the auditor may be appointed
by a letter giving details of requirements, but where an organisation such as a club or charity is concerned, he may be
employed to complete the audit in accordance with the *rules
and regulations* of the organisation as laid down in the constitution.

In any case, the auditor should always be most particular to
obtain a statement in writing as to the nature and scope of the
work he is to undertake.

8. Statutory audits.   Where statutory audits are to be
conducted, the legal requirements will provide the necessary
information as to the nature of the certificate required, and
here the auditor will carry out the work in whatever manner he
considers necessary and no restriction may be put upon him.
The important factor to consider in this case is that the
auditor's appointment is carried out in accordance with the
legal stipulations, and he should be careful to examine the
minutes of the meeting or any other legal document whereby
he is appointed.

9. Internal audits.   These differ fundamentally from the
types of audit already mentioned in that the foregoing audits
are undertaken by an independent auditor who conducts his

work as apart from the organisation whose books he is auditing. For this reason the auditor is often referred to as an *external* auditor.

The *internal* auditor on the other hand is an employee of a business engaged in work on behalf of the organisation, although the nature of his work requires that he shall be given an element of independence whilst engaged in his work.

As the duties of the internal auditor are closely bound up with the internal check and control of a business, this type of audit is dealt with more fully in Chapter III on the subject of internal control.

10. Classification by method of approach. The method of approach to his work by the auditor will determine under which of the following, often over-lapping, classifications the audit will be designated.

(a) Final or completed audit.
(b) Interim audit.
(c) Continuous audit.
(d) Balance sheet audit.

11. Final or completed audit. By a final or completed audit is implied that the audit is carried through to completion in *one continuous session*. Although the audit may be commenced before the end of the accounting period, by its nature it will have to take place at least partly after the end of the financial period since it is carried through to conclusion on the one occasion.

(a) *Advantages*.

    (i) Work can be carried through to conclusion, so obviating:

        1. The necessity of taking up partially completed work requiring note-taking to indicate to what stage work has been carried;

        2. The possibility of any alteration of figures after work has been carried out.

    (ii) The time-tabling of audit staff to the work is simplified.

(b) *Disadvantages*

    (i) Where work is of an extended nature, delays may occur after the end of the financial period, so retarding the completion of the audit. This is an important factor as it is often desired to call the Annual General Meeting and to publish the accounts as soon as possible after the year end.

(ii) Where, as is often the case, financial periods of various clients end on the same date, difficulties may be experienced in deploying audit staff.

12. Interim audit. This is when an audit is conducted *to a particular date within the accounting period*. Attendance may be to audit the figures for a month or for a quarter, as the work may require. It would differ distinctly from the final audit in the extent of the work carried out; verification of assets, for example, being left until the final audit.

(a) *Advantages*.

(i) This type of audit may fulfil a need where the publication of interim figures is necessary.

(ii) Such interim work can speed the completion of the final audit at the end of the financial period.

(iii) Error and fraud may be discovered more quickly during the accounting period.

(iv) The attendance of staff at intervals imposes a sound moral check as well as doing much to ensure that work is kept up to date.

(b) *Disadvantages*.

Figures may be altered after having been audited, so necessitating additional work in note-taking and otherwise to guard against this.

13. Continuous audit. This method is frequently, but not necessarily, in operation in large organisations. The work is conducted throughout the course of the financial year but *is not taken to a specific accounting period*, as is an interim audit. It might be, that during the course of the continuous work interim figures are being audited, but the significant factor here is that the auditor will be engaged continuously on the audit throughout the financial period. Staff may be in residence throughout the period or may come and go at irregular intervals, but particularised set periods of operation would not apply.

(a) *Advantages*.

(i) The advantages as for interim audits (*see* **12** (i), (ii) and (iii)) above also apply here.

(ii) The moral check mentioned above applies even more so as continuous audit work need not be carried out to any specific date.

(iii) Audit staff may be used more effectively since they may be sent at intervals when other work is slack.

(iv) With the additional time made available, work may be carried out more thoroughly and in greater detail.

(b) *Disadvantages*.

(i) Figures may be altered either fraudulently or misguidedly after audit. This constitutes a real danger and action has to be taken to guard against it.

(ii) It may be inconvenient for a client's staff to be interrupted in the course of their work by auditors requiring their books and documents.

(iii) A tendency may evolve for a client's staff to rely upon the auditors to help them out of difficulties in the course of their work, *e.g.*, to discover errors in figures found when balancing accounts. This may be helpful to the staff but may necessitate further working time on audits, which may not be easily justified by the size of the audit.

(iv) Additional work may be required on such audits by the continual taking up of work not fully completed.

(v) To lessen the effect of (iv) above, extensive note-taking may be necessary to maintain an even flow of work, as well as ensuring no alterations are put through the books after they have been audited.

14. Balance sheet audit. This is of more recent origin than the normal type of audit, and has proved more popular in the USA than in this country. It may be, however, that with the consolidation of industry into larger economic units such audits may become more widely used.

It is convenient here to give an explanation of the operation of a balance sheet audit, although it is appreciated that it may be preferred to return to this after studying the details of work outlined in ensuing chapters.

Unlike the work entailed in the more usual type of audit it is necessary to commence from the balance sheet, working back to the books of prime entry and their documentary evidence. It is essential to ensure, however, that there is a reliable system of internal check and control in operation; assuming this to be the case, the following broad scheme of operation might be suitable for a balance sheet audit:

(a) Examine the minute books of the organisation, taking notes on any matters of importance affecting the accounts and balance sheet items.

(b) Compare the revenue account for the year of audit with that of the previous year, ascertaining the reasons for any material differences.

(c) Compare the increase or decrease of variable expenses in conjunction with the variation in turnover. Unit quantities are important with regard to turnover, and adjustment and allowance should be made for price, purchase tax or other variations.

(d) Carefully investigate any changes in gross profit rates; in conjunction with this examine stock values. The separation of various sales lines for investigation purposes should be made.

(e) Any items of a non-recurring nature should be examined such as losses, or profits incurred on fixed assets. Depreciation charges should be carefully checked in conjunction with the assets concerned. The effect of these and variations in expenses mentioned above should render any change in net profit readily explainable.

(f) The effect of the profit or loss for the period in varying the balance sheet should be explained. Schedules, such, as sources and disposition of funds statements may be usefully applied.

(g) The variation in fixed asset holdings should be examined by means of schedules showing movements since the last balance sheet date.

(h) Examine the variation in current assets as compared with the previous year. Accounting ratios may be most useful together with credit control schedules.

(i) The lists of prepayments and accruals should be scrutinised, any material alterations being investigated.

(j) Examine all remaining balance sheet items, such as share capital, taxation, etc., ascertaining that these are in order as prevails with normal audit requirements, e.g., taxation being fully provided for on current profits.

(k) All assets held and liabilities owed should be verified.

(l) Ascertain whether any capital commitments exist, and that any items on which subsequent losses might arise have been provided for.

Since the foregoing (and often, at the auditor's discretion, even more detailed work) may be required by a balance sheet audit, it may be queried what advantage arises from not performing the more normal full audit. In the balance sheet audit a good deal of such work as vouching and casting, which is normally considered necessary, may be eliminated. It is essential, therefore, in the case of the balance sheet audit, that the internal check and control systems should be sound, and that the auditor carrying out the audit should be highly skilled, as much depends on his detecting any underlying error by his ability in the interpretation of accounts. Consequently, such an audit would be most efficacious in the case of a large organisation employing qualified accounting staff and preferably having an internal audit department.

PROGRESS TEST 1

1. Give a definition of an audit. (1, 2)

2. For what main purpose is the auditor's examination carried out? (2, 3)

3. Does the auditor's examination extend only to the books accounts and vouchers? (2)

4. What are the concomitant features of an audit? (3)

5. Is it the auditor's duty to prepare the accounts and balance sheet? (4)

6. If the answer to 5 above is in the negative, why do auditors frequently do this? (4)

7. If the auditor finds weaknesses and inefficiences in the system, what should he do? (4)

8. Frequently audits are carried out by those who are not qualified accountants. Are there any reasons why this should not be so? (5)

9. Into what main classifications do audits fall? (6–10)

10. Name the various types of audits conducted. (6–10)

11. By what means are the limits of the auditor's work specified? (7–11)

12. By what means should the auditor ensure that the extent of his work is specified? (7)

13. Where the auditor's work is carried out under Statute, who may dictate the extent of his examinations? (8)

14. When appointed under Statute, what should the auditor do on taking up his appointment? (8)

15. What is the fundamental difference between an internal and external audit? (9)

16. In what way does a balance sheet audit differ from a normal audit? (14)

17. State the advantages and disadvantages of:

    (a) Final audits.
    (b) Interim audits.
    (c) Continuous audits.   (11-13)

SPECIMEN QUESTIONS

1. What are the main purposes of an audit and how may these be achieved? *C.C.A.* (*Inter.*)

2. Explain the advantages and disadvantages of a continuous audit and indicate the steps which can be taken to minimise the disadvantages. *C.A.* (*E.W.*)

3. Describe the disadvantages of an interim audit and state the steps you would take to minimise them. *C.C.A.* (*Inter.*)

4. What is meant by a balance sheet audit and give a suggested programme to be followed in such an audit? *C.C.A.*

5. You are required to consider the case of a business whose trading is subject to seasonal variation, and to state the best time in which to set the close of its accounting period, having regard to:

    (a) The preparation of annual accounts, and
    (b) The audit of those accounts.
Give reasons for your answer. *C.C.A.*

CHAPTER II

GENERAL PROCEDURE OF WORK

PROFESSIONAL ETHICS

1. Taking up appointment. On taking up any new audit the requirements as to professional etiquette and proper terms of appointment should be first attended to. (Regarding contractual terms of appointment *see* pp. 212–13.)

Even before receiving official recognition, it was taken as a matter of professional etiquette to communicate with the retiring auditor on taking up a new appointment, in order to enquire whether any objection might be raised. This has now been recognised as a requisite part of professional etiquette by the established accountancy bodies and incorporated into their regulations. This is also now a statutory requirement under the *Friendly* and *Industrial and Provident Societies Act*, 1968.

2. Regulations of accountancy bodies. The regulations laid down by both the Institute of Chartered Accountants in England and Wales and by the Association of Certified and Corporate Accountants state that their members should not accept nomination for replacement of an auditor without first communicating with the previous or existing auditor, such a communication being preferably in writing and enquiring whether the accountant concerned wishes to point out any reason why the nomination should not be accepted. *The rule applies whether the accountant to whom the enquiry is addressed is a member of the same professional body or not.* Where permission is not granted by the client or organisation concerned to make such a communication then the nomination should not be accepted.

Not only is professional courtesy the concern of the accountancy bodies, the purpose is also to give their members opportunity to decide whether they feel they can properly accept the nomination. In the case of companies, it is important to preserve the rights of the shareholders, including their right to change the company's auditor if it is their desire to do so, and at the same time the independence of the existing or previous auditor.   The legal position of the existing auditor who may have to communicate to a proposed new auditor matters damaging to the company depends upon whether the existing auditor has been authorised by the company to discuss the company's affairs with the proposed new auditor.   On receipt of the communication from the existing auditor, the proposed new auditor should request such authorisation, but even if he does not receive this he will still have qualified privilege as a strong measure of protection, provided he states what he believes to be true without malice.   The proposed new auditor should decline to accept nomination if he is informed that the existing auditor has not been given permission to discuss the company's affairs.

NEW AUDITS

The following are the main points to which the auditor should give attention when taking up a new audit.

3. Extent of work. The exact scope and limit of the auditor's duties should be ascertained.   In the case of a statutory audit these will be specified, but in other cases the auditor should ensure that he has been instructed in writing with the limit of his duties clearly stated (*see* p. 212).

4. Additional accountancy work. Any special requests for work outside that which the auditor considers necessary for the purposes of his audit he should bring to the attention of his client, pointing out his right to charge an additional fee for such work.

5. Regulations of the organisation. The auditor should carefully examine these, making notes of matters of particular importance.

6. Officials and records. Lists should be obtained of:

(*a*) Responsible officials and the nature of their office.

(b) List of books with names and designation of those maintaining them.

7. Adequacy of system. This should be examined in conjunction with internal control questionnaires and standard audit programmes, a letter of weaknesses being sent if necessary (*see* p. 23). A tour of the business should be made for the auditor to acquaint himself intimately with its nature and working.

8. Preparation of audit programme (*see* p. 15.)

9. Background information. Previous accounts, balance sheets and any relevant analyses should be examined.

AUDIT WORKING PAPERS

Whilst not specifying any particular form, the Council in *Recommendation U.12* points out that the working papers should be such as will enable the auditors to achieve their object of forming an opinion on the accounts on which they report. For this purpose they should facilitate control of the current year's audit, provide evidence of the work done, provide schedules to support accounts and information on the business including its recent history. The following brief details have been extracted from U.12.

10. Current file. Primarily being concerned with the accounts being audited, it should contain normally:

(a) A copy of accounts or statements on which the auditors are reporting authenticated by directors' signatures or otherwise.

(b) Index (cross-referenced), internal control questionnaires and standard audit programmes duly referenced to one another, plus any flow charts.

(c) A schedule for each item in the balance sheet and statutory profit and loss account, preferably including comparative figures, showing its make-up and how existence, ownership and value or liability have been verified. These schedules should be cross-referenced to documents arising from external verification such as bank letters and the results of circularisation of debtors and attendance at physical stock-taking.

(d) A check-list concerning compliance with statutory disclosure provisions.

(e) A record showing queries raised during the audit and their disposal, with notes where appropriate for attention the following year. Queries not cleared at the time should be entered on to a further schedule for the attention of the person reviewing the audit and for reference to the client if necessary. Material queries, which cannot be settled satisfactorily by immediate reference to the client, may require a qualification of the auditor's report and should be fully documented and supported by a note of all discussions with the client and any explanations given.

(f) A schedule of important statistics or working ratios, comparative figures being included where appropriate.

(g) Extracts of relevant minutes of directors' or shareholders' meetings cross-referenced to working schedules.

(h) Letters of representation, i.e. written confirmation by the client of information and opinions expressed in respect of matters such as stock values and amounts of current and contingent liabilities.

Matters which, while not of permanent importance, will require attention during the subsequent year's audit should be listed, with references to the relevant working papers, and this note should be transferred to the next current file when opened.

11. Permanent file. Matters of continuing importance affecting the company or the audit should be kept in a separate file, suitably indexed, and these should normally include:

(a) Memorandum and Articles of Association and other appropriate statutory or legal regulations.

(b) Copies of other documents and minutes of continuing importance.

(c) A short description of the type of business carried on and the places of business.

(d) Lists of accounting records and responsible officials and plan of organisation.

(e) Statements showing a note of any accounting matters of

importance such as a history of reserves and bases of accounting adopted, *e.g.*, for the valuation of stock and work in progress, depreciation and the carrying forward and writing off of expenditure ultimately chargeable to revenue.

(*f*) The client's internal accounting instructions and internal audit instructions, including where appropriate stock-taking instructions.

Steps should be taken to ensure that the permanent file is brought up to date at the appropriate times.

In the case of a non-statutory audit the permanent file should also contain the client's instructions as to the scope of the work to be performed.

AUDIT PROGRAMMES

12. Doubts as to utility. There used to be some doubt as to the efficacy of audit programmes mainly due to the fact that as they constitute a programme of work to be completed on an audit, such work might be carried out exactly according to the programme, so stifling initiative, and assisting in the possibility of fraud. This latter point may be considered possible, as any interested member of the client's staff, if not actually seeing the programme, could soon become acquainted with the manner in which the work of the audit would be carried out.

However, it is now generally agreed that to work on each audit without a guide to the work involved would necessitate repetitive enquiries wasting valuable time and causing annoyance to the client's staff. Furthermore, it would be possible to overlook part of the audit. (The advantages and disadvantages are summarised below, **24-25**.)

13. Compilation. The programme itself may be compiled as the initial enquiries are made on the commencement of the new audit.

The programme may take different forms but would usually commence with the basic work of the audit, care being taken to see that similar work viewed from two different aspects is not repeated. For example, under the section of work regarding the sales day book postings to the sales ledger, and under the section of work regarding the sales ledger, listing again the necessity of checking the ledger postings against the sales day book.

SUMMARY OF AUDIT WORK PROCEDURES

14. Introduction. Having mentioned above the work to be undertaken at the commencement of an audit with regard to Memorandum and Articles, internal control, etc., the outline of an audit is now given which is generally applicable. At this stage this may serve, not only as an example of the work, but may also afford a brief overall glimpse of the procedures involved in an audit. (Differing points of varying types of audits are shown in chapter XII.)

15. Main cash book.

(*a*) Obtain bank certificates direct from bank.

(*b*) Check bank statements with cash book and paying-in slips, noting dates of lodgements; check direct lodgements with advice notes.

(*c*) Examine periodic reconciliations and check in detail the reconciliation at the closing date.

(*d*) Check transfers to petty cash book.

(*e*) Check postings to nominal ledger.

(*f*) Vouch a number of payments which constitute postings to nominal ledger, especially those of a personal nature, *e.g.* expense payments to members of the organisation.

16. Petty cash book.

(*a*) Ascertain that it is initialled periodically by a responsible official, and note size of float; ensure imprest amount not exceeded.

(*b*) Test a number of vouchers. See that payments in respect of various items appear reasonable.

(*c*) Check cash in hand plus vouchers which may not have been entered and ensure all balances, where more than one, are produced simultaneously. Have any large I.O.U.'s, or old ones, authenticated.

(*d*) Check postings to nominal ledger.

17. Wages and salaries.

(*a*) Vouch net payments in cash book with wages and salaries summaries. Vouch deductions of P.A.Y.E., national insurance, etc., to nominal ledger, and check to wages control account (if kept).

(b) Test payments with time cards, etc., and rates with authorisation lists.

(c) Check variations in salaries with increase lists.

(d) Test with P.A.Y.E. deduction cards if maintained; if not, then with final summaries for submission to Inland Revenue.

(e) Test additions and cross-casts on sheets.

(f) Check that total payments to directors, etc., are in accordance with contracts and minutes passed.

(g) Ascertain that all summaries are initialled by a responsible official.

18. Purchases.

(a) Examine in depth the prevailing system, using a sample number of transactions from:

    (i) Original orders.

    (ii) Goods received book.

    (iii) Entries in stock records.

    (iv) Invoices and statements received, noting whether the stages of invoice checking work are duly initialled. Check analysis.

(b) Examine invoices in period following audit to ensure invoices not put through after date.

(c) Note any purchases made not in nature of trade and any on behalf of staff, ensuring that these are properly charged.

(d) Check postings to nominal ledger.

(e) Vouch capital expenditure and check postings to nominal ledger accounts.

19. Sales.

(a) Examine in depth the prevailing system by using a sample of a number of sales transactions from:

    (i) Customers' orders.

    (ii) Copies of invoices (check with goods outwards book).

    (iii) Deductions from stock.

    (iv) Entries in debtors' accounts.

(b) Check goods outwards book at end of period and ascertain whether sales invoices rendered for goods despatched.

(c) Test goods outwards book with stock records to ensure goods sold not shown as stock where not despatched.

(d) Check system and ascertain all credit notes properly authorised.

(e) Check day book postings to nominal ledger.

(f) Where fixed assets have been sold, vouch these, ensuring proper authorisation and treatment in accounts.

20. Stocks and work in progress.

(a) Observe if possible actual stocktaking and ensure internal check maintained.
(b) Check final sheets with rough stock sheets enquiring into any material differences.
(c) Test-check sheets with stock records maintained in departments.
(d) Check a number of values set on stock, check casts.
(e) Enquire into stock written off or written down.
(f) Compare with previous year's figures.
(g) Compare stock figures with stock control account, if kept.
(h) Check overall position as to gross profit and rate of turnover.
(i) Obtain stock certificate.

21. Bought and sales ledgers.

(a) Check control accounts from books of prime entry.
(b) Test postings.
(c) Examine accounts, noting methods of settlement, discounts, transfers and test additions.
(d) Check balances in and down to next period and with list of balances. Take note of exceptional items—debit balances on purchases ledger, or credit balances on sales ledger. Ensure adequate bad debts provision.
(e) Enquire into bad debts written off.

22. Nominal ledger.

(a) Vouch direct journal entries and transfers between accounts.
(b) Check additions.
(c) Check with trial balance.
(d) Check with prepayments and accruals schedule.
(e) Check depreciation charges.
(f) Examine taxation account, checking items with computations in conjunction with audit notes and correspondence with Inland Revenue, etc.

23. Final accounts and balance sheet.

(a) Check figures from trial balance and schedules.
(b) Compare with previous year's figures, using percentages for comparative purposes where useful; and investigate any inexplicable fluctuations.
(c) Compare with any internal accounts prepared, such as those used for costing purposes.

(d) If cost accounts maintained on a separate basis, reconcile with these.

(e) Check statutory accounts and consult audit records for any items to be shown as special notes.

(f) Obtain directors' signatures and append audit report.

ADVANTAGES AND DISADVANTAGES OF AUDIT PROGRAMMES

24. Advantages.

(a) A permanent record of the work is constantly available. This facilitates:

  (i) The allocation of work between clerks.

  (ii) The resumption of work by those taking up the audit after its commencement.

(b) The chance of work being overlooked is obviated.

(c) Unnecessary enquiries on each attendance as to routine work are avoided so saving time of both clients' and auditor's staff.

(d) Programmes may easily be kept up to date by variation as required.

(e) In the event of any subsequent enquiry the actual audit staff engaged on the work may be ascertained.

(f) As definite instructions are laid down, junior clerks may need less supervision.

(g) A clear perspective of the work involved is made available by the existence of the programme.

25. Disadvantages.

(a) Work may tend to become mechanical, variations in the working system of the organisation being overlooked.

(b) If work is carried out according to a predetermined plan, fraud may be facilitated.

(c) Work may be hurried in order to complete a required schedule, whereas greater concentration on one aspect even to the omission of another might be of advantage on occasions.

With regard to the disadvantages which could arise by the use of audit programmes, these may be overcome by encouraging initiative amongst all levels of staff. Also the recommendation changes in the audit programme should be encouraged.

26. Discretion in use of programmes. As the disadvantage

mentioned in **30** (c) may quite possibly arise, staff should be given to understand that the audit programme should not be completed merely by the inclusion of signatures in all available spaces, but that if for some reason work has been varied to the omission of some aspects, the person in charge should make a qualifying note to this effect.

PROGRESS TEST 2

1. What should an auditor do on first being offered a new audit in the case of a continuing business?   **(1)**

2. For what reasons should an auditor communicate with the previous auditor before taking up his appointment.   **(1, 2)**

3. In what ways should an auditor ascertain the extent of the work he is to do?   **(3, 4)**

4. May any restrictions be put upon the auditor where he is appointed under Statute?   **(3–6)**

5. To what documents should the auditor pay particular attention on first being appointed?   **(6)**

6. Are *internal* check questionnaires of any importance to the statutory auditor?   **(12)**

7. What matters are normally contained in the audit working papers?   **(10–11)**

8. Why are doubts cast upon the usefulness of audit programmes?   **(12)**

9. Give the basic outline of an audit programme applicable in most businesses.   **(14–23)**

10. State the advantages and disadvantages of audit programmes.   **(24–25)**

11. Should audit staff be given any discretion as to the completion of the audit programme?   **(26)**

SPECIMEN QUESTIONS

1. You have been approached by the partners of Rowan and Co., who carry on a merchanting business, to audit the accounts of their business in place of Exewy & Co., Chartered Accountants, who, you are informed, have resigned.

You are required to state:

(a) The action you would take before accepting the appointment, giving your reasons; and

(b) On the assumption that you accept the appointment, the information which you would require before commencing the detailed audit work for the first year.   *C.A. (E.W.)*

2. The partners in Black & Co. inform you that their present

auditor, Mr. J White, an unqualified practitioner, will not be continuing as auditor as he is retiring from practice on December 31st, 1966. They ask you to undertake the audit of their firm's accounts as from January 1st, 1967.

You are required to state:

  (a) What action, if any, you would take (giving your reasons) before agreeing to undertake the audit.

  (b) Assuming you have accepted the appointment, what information you would require from Black & Co. to enable you to draft a suitable audit programme. *C.A.* (*E.W.*) (*Inter.*)

3. Discuss the advantages and disadvantages of a standard audit programme. *C.C.A.* (*Inter.*)

4. You have been appointed auditor to a partnership of three doctors. What steps would you take before accepting the appointment and what information would you require before commencing your detailed duties? *C.C.A.*

CHAPTER III

INTERNAL CONTROL

INTRODUCTION TO INTERNAL CONTROL

1. Purpose of internal control. Increasing attention has been paid to the methods of internal control in recent years. Not only the complexity of modern business techniques but also the increased size of business units have encouraged the adoption of methods which, whilst increasing the efficiency of the business, also act as safeguards against error or fraud. Furthermore, the regulation of business activities under an efficient system of internal control may obviate the necessity of protracted detailed work by external auditors with beneficial results to all parties concerned.

The Institute of Chartered Accountants' publication *Statements on Auditing* covering the subject of internal control provides a valuable guide to this matter, giving a basic outline of the techniques involved, and quotations given in this chapter are all from these statements.

2. Definition of internal control. Internal control is defined as "not only internal check and internal audit but the whole system of controls, financial and otherwise, established by the management in order to carry on the business of the company in an orderly manner, safeguard its assets and secure as far as possible the accuracy and reliability of its records."

The inclusive nature of internal control is immediately apparent as it embraces both internal check and the internal audit if there is a department or section engaged on this.

3. Internal check. This forms a valuable part of the internal control and consists of "the allocation of authority and work in such a manner as to afford checks on the routine transactions of day-to-day work by means of the work of one person being proved independently by another, or the work of a person being complementary to that of another," so affording a means whereby fraud is prevented, or its early detection is facilitated.

4. Internal audit. This is described as "a review of operations and records, sometimes continuous, undertaken within a business by specially assigned staff." Where there is an internal audit department, this may form a valuable part of the whole system of internal control, and according to its efficacy or otherwise, may influence considerably the conduct of the audit (*see* p. 35).

5. Internal control and the auditor. Where internal control is properly operated it may influence considerably the conduct of the audit. It will be necessary in the first instance for the auditor to satisfy himself as to its satisfactory working and in the case of a new audit this will take place on the first occasion. If he is not satisfied as to the efficacy of the internal control and its concomitant internal check he may be forced to do a greater amount of detailed work than would otherwise be the case.

On the other hand the overall system may be working satisfactorily but certain sections of the work may be inadequate, in which case he should inform the client in writing requesting the installation of certain methods whereby the weaknesses may be corrected. This would also apply if the system were unsatisfactory as a whole and he should be careful to point out the dangers of letting the prevailing state of affairs continue. Such notification should be of help to the client as well as safeguarding the auditor in the event of any errors or fraud arising. The letter itself is known as 'a letter of weaknesses'.

To quote the Institute of Chartered Accountants' recommendation, *General Principles of Auditing* U.1.

> "In exceptional cases, auditors may find that the records and the system of internal control are so seriously inadequate that no useful purpose could be served by embarking upon extensive detailed checking, because even the most exhaustive tests would not enable them to form an opinion on the balance sheet and profit and loss account. In that event their appropriate course will be to report to that effect to the shareholders and to inform the directors of the respects in which the records and system are deficient."

The auditor may still be able to curtail the detailed work where only certain weaknesses are revealed, but at the same time taking additional precautions in the sections where the system is not working satisfactorily.

Should the internal control system be adequate then the detailed work of the audit may be restricted and sectional auditing in depth may be applied.

6. Auditing in depth. In order that the auditor may test the efficient working of the internal control system it will be necessary to put into operation the system of auditing in depth. For this purpose the auditor will have to acquaint himself thoroughly with:

(a) The nature of the business and its activities.
(b) The system of book-keeping and accounting.
(c) The duties and responsibilities of the management and staff.
(d) The prevailing system of internal check.
(e) The internal audit, if such is in operation.

How the auditor may obtain the information he requires will no doubt differ from business to business. In some concerns he may be able to obtain net work analysis diagrams, flow charts, duties and responsibilities of staff set out in writing, but in other cases he may have to compile his own records from enquiries made. The Institute of Chartered Accountants has made the division of such work into three stages; that of *ascertainment*, *testing* and *assessment*, which summarises the work required and the order in which to carry it out.

7. Application of auditing in depth. Having become acquainted with regard to the matters mentioned above, auditing in depth may be applied, whereby examinations are made by probing into the system. Such an examination *in depth* "involves *tracing a transaction through its various stages from origin to conclusion*, examining at each stage to an appropriate extent the vouchers, records and authorities relating to that stage and observing the incidence of internal check and delegated authority. For example, verification of a payment to a creditor for goods supplied could be made by examination of a paid cheque which had been drawn in favour of the creditor and crossed 'Account payee only'.

Complete verification of this transaction 'in depth' might involve the examination of the transaction at all stages including the following documents or records:

(a) The invoice and statement from the supplier

(b) Evidence that the goods had been recorded in the stock records.

(c) The goods received note and inspection certificate.

(d) A copy of the original order and the authority therefor."

8. Difficulties in small companies. In the case of small companies certain difficulties may present themselves. The fact that the number of employees does not allow of such a division of work as will leave a sound internal control is the chief difficulty likely to be encountered. In these circumstances the supervision may have to be carried out to a large extent by the proprietor, manager, or other designated employee. This may be adequate in normal circumstances but may easily break down in periods of increased activity or illness on the part of the supervisor. Likewise where a business is expanding, work may be undertaken outside the recognised scheme of work, or the manager may be too preoccupied to attend to his supervisory duties.

The auditor should make himself aware of the weaknesses arising and inform those in authority concerned, as mentioned previously. Likewise he will have to use his discretion as to the amount of additional work he feels is necessary to maintain an adequate audit in view of the certificate he is to give. For example:

"... in the case of a small company the tests which the auditors make will normally cover a greater proportion of the transactions than is necessary for a larger company where a more comprehensive system of control can be and is operated. In selecting items for examination and deciding upon the extent of the work to be done the auditors should always consider to what extent the transactions under review are material in relation to the affairs of the company as a whole."

9. Internal control and management. By its designation it is implied that the responsibility for the application of internal control must rest with those in authority within the business itself. The auditor may help, advise and report, but has no power to demand that an adequate system of internal control should exist. The final responsibility remains with those in authority.

In any efficiently controlled organisation there must be clear lines of demarcation between the responsibilities and duties of the staff and these can only be operated in conjunction with properly compiled records of the various activities of the business and by the circulation of written information as to the duties of the staff.

10. Divisions of internal control. The three recognised divisions of the elements of the internal control are:

(a) The plan of organisation (with particular reference to the allocation of staff duties).
(b) Authorisation, recording and custody procedures (including internal check).
(c) Managerial supervision and reviews (including internal audit).

11. Plan of organisation. The necessity of an adequate plan of organisation has already been mentioned. Such a plan should cover the activities of both management and staff at all levels, stating clearly their duties, responsibilities and the power to authorise various activities of the business. This latter point is of importance since subordinate duties may on occasions have to be varied, which may leave the way open to abuse by those with authority over other members of staff who are not in a position to question directions they receive.

12. Authorisation, recording and custody procedures. Where authorisation, recording and custody procedures are concerned the financial and accounting controls should be such as to facilitate efficient working and at the same time obviate any chance of fraud or error arising.

Here the practical division of duties should be such as to ensure that the internal check system is operating at all stages. Internal check has already been defined as "the checks on day-to-day transactions which operate continuously as part of the routine system whereby the work of one person is proved independently or is complementary to the work of another, the object being the prevention or early detection of errors or fraud."

This internal check involves the need for the work of at least two persons to be conducted, as far as possible, independently. This in itself will involve the division of responsibility in the various procedures whereby transactions are authorised, performed and recorded, and on completion are verified and reconciled independently with pre-ascertained totals or by examination.

13. Managerial supervision and reviews.

By *managerial supervision and reviews* is implied the efficient working of management in constantly reviewing and giving consideration to the financial position and financial procedures within the organisation. This may include the use of an internal audit department, but not necessarily so. Budgeting control and standing costing systems greatly assist the working of internal control whereby variances are revealed and investigated. Special reviews of departmental systems may also take place from time to time apart from normal internal audit procedures.

14. Internal audit.

Internal audit, as stated above, has been termed "a review of operations and records, sometimes continuous, undertaken within a business by specially assigned staff" and where this is extant internal control is greatly facilitated, and may do much to ensure that the accounting systems are efficient and working in accordance with planned procedures.

Before turning to some practical aspects of internal control it is relevant to point out the danger of being so concerned with the system that the end product is overlooked. No two businesses are exactly the same, a set of procedures for one business may be quite unsuitable for another, it requires thought, skill and experience in actual working before suitable methods may be formulated, but in so doing the ultimate gain must be considered.

For example, one large group of departmental stores, having considered the losses which could arise on stocks, ceased to employ their internal auditors on routine stock checks as the expense involved in payment of salaries for such work considerably outweighed the possible stock losses which might arise.

This is an exceptional case, but it is useful in pointing out the necessity of making the internal control system suit the business rather than organising the business to suit the system.

We can do not better here than to follow closely, but rather more briefly, the procedures outlined by the Institute of Chartered Accountants in their notes on this subject of internal control.

PRACTICAL APPLICATION

15. Classification of sections. The sections involved in the operation of an internal control system can be classified as follows:

1. Overall financial control (*see* **16**).
2. Receipt and payment of cash, including balances held (*see* **17–22** below).
3. Remuneration of employees (*see* **23**).
4. Trading transactions (*see* **24** and **25**).
5. Stock control (*see* **26**).
6. Fixed assets and investments (*see* **27** and **28**).

16. Overall financial control. The proper allocation of work and responsibilities including internal check has been dealt with but for such to work effectively there must be:

(a) An efficient accounting system in operation.
(b) Adequate supervision with a clear and up-to-date supply of information to management. This would normally involve the preparation of interim statements with, if possible, a system of budgetary control whereby variances from standards are revealed, as well as reports being made from time to time on various sections of the system.
(c) Maintenance of adequate recording and duplicating systems.
(d) Efficient staff control with written directions as to responsibilities and duties of both management and staff.

In this respect care should be exercised to maintain the human touch. For staff control to degenerate into a machine-like system can do much harm in respect of harmonious and willing staff relationships, which can defeat the ultimate object for which the control system is installed.

17. Receipts and payment of cash, including balances held. The systems prevailing with regard to the receipt and payment of cash are covered in the relevant sections of chapter IV, but certain main precautions must be taken (*see* **18–22**).

18. Cash receipts.

(a) The internal check system once installed must be maintained. This may involve checks at irregular intervals by responsible members of the staff or the internal audit department if there is one. Likewise, arrangements must be made to meet exceptional circumstances, such as staff illness or holidays.

(b) The receipt of cash, including the opening of post, must be made under the supervision of a responsible official. An immediate recording of all cash receipts should be made for subsequent checking purposes at a later stage. All cheques, money orders and postal orders should be cancelled on receipt, this by means of a stamp with a crossing of "Not negotiable—account payee only."

(c) Specific instructions must be given with regard to receipt of cash by cashiers, travellers or otherwise, and the manner in which they are to be evidenced must be stated. For example, receipts to be issued for all cash (as opposed to cheques received) and sealed till-rolls to be in operation for cash sales.

19. Control of funds.

(a) Specific instructions must be given to members of staff for the handling of all cash receipts and payments as well as with regard to the recording and checking thereof.

(b) All moneys received must be recorded, crossed checked and banked frequently, preferably daily.

(c) Where cash registers or cash offices are used, definitive instructions must be laid down as to collection intervals and by whom.

(d) Duties as to preparation of bank paying-in slips and actual banking should be stated. Preferably this should be done by two different persons.

(e) Paying-in slips should not be prepared by those receiving and recording cash, and such slips should be checked regularly against the documents recording receipts of cash.

(f) Cash for disbursement purposes should never be deducted from cash received.

20. Balances held.

(a) Specific rulings must be made with regard to the number of cash floats to be held and their amount, including tills and cash desks, as well as petty cash balances for disbursement purposes.

(b) Persons to have access to balances as mentioned in (a) must be stated and limits imposed as to amount in respect of pety cash disbursements. Rules as to amount and duration of I.O.U.'s should be stated, as in certain cases the granting of sums on I.O.U.'s may be justified. All petty cash floats should be maintained on the imprest system.

(c) Rules should exist to ensure that cash floats are checked by responsible staff at frequent intervals, as well as to safe-keeping of moneys retained on the premises out of business hours.

(d) Stated procedures should exist for the handling of funds of employees, such as unclaimed wages, holiday funds, etc.

(e) Bank reconciliations should be required at stated intervals, if possible by a person whose work is independent of the receiving and disbursement of cash. If an internal audit department exists the regular checking of such reconciliations should be required. Whoever is deputed to check the reconciliations should be instructed to examine such exceptional matters as unpresented cheques outstanding for an undue length of time, or any stop-payment notices.

21. Cheque payments. The following are the main headings of points to receive attention:

(a) Safe keeping, control and supply of cheques.

(b) Who may prepare cheques and traders' credit lists.

(c) Supporting documents for cheque payments and safeguards, such as signatures for various stages of work, so ensuring no payment of same bill twice.

(d) Authorities to sign and limitations as to amount, and rules to obviate the signing of blank cheques in advance or in favour of persons signing.

(e) Cheques to be restrictively crossed.

(f) Rules to ensure cheques signed in time to obtain benefit of discounts receivable.

22. Division of duties. The size of staff employed may restrict the allocation of duties in such a manner as may be desirable for absolute safety, but as far as possible the following rules should apply:

(a) The cashier should not write-up accounts in respect of recepts and should not be responsible for the safe-keeping of securities or title deeds of the business.

(b) Staff preparing cheques or traders' credit lists should not be cheque signatories, or vice versa.

23. Remuneration of employees.

(a) *Allocation of duties.* The internal check system should be operative at all stages in employee remuneration. The work of making up wages sheets should be sub-divided to ensure that work is both checked and complementary to that of the previous stage. Such duties must be clearly defined and the following matters properly allocated:

   (i) Authority to engage and discharge employees and fix or change rates of pay.

  (ii) The recording of all notifications of the foregoing to be dealt with only on receipt in writing duly initialled.

 (iii) The method by which employee deductions are dealt with.

 (iv) Proper time recording (or work-recording in the case of piece work), the records of which should be counter-signed by the foreman.

  (v) The payment of holiday-pay or payments in advance; here, authorisation is important and designation of who shall deal with queries arising.

(b) *Payment of employees.*

   (i) Proper arrangements should be made for the drawing and encashment of the wages cheque.

  (ii) The staff making up wage packets should be different from those preparing the wages sheets, and the right amount of notes and change should be drawn in accordance with the wages sheet.

 (iii) The arrangements for payment of wages should include the supervision of a responsible official and payment should be made by a person other than any of those preparing the wages sheet and pay packets. Specific arrangements should be made for dealing with unclaimed wages.

 (iv) Special checks should be made at irregular intervals of balances held in wages departments, such as cash and National Insurance stamp floats.

  (v) In general, reconciliations should be made explaining the difference between total wages and deductions from one period to the next. Total columns and P.A.Y.E. deductions should be checked with the returns of the Inland Revenue as well as with the P.60 forms to be issued to employees.

24. Trading transactions: purchases. The factors to be covered are as follows:

(a) *Authorisation.* Procedures must be laid down to cover the requisition and authorisation of purchase orders. Certain firms should be listed with whom orders are to be placed, having been specified by those with authority to do so. Order forms should be kept in safe custody.

(b) *Receipt of goods.* The flow of goods received from their receipt, inspection, acceptation and transfer to departments, and authority of those concerned should be laid down. The checking of purchase orders against goods received must be arranged.

(c) *Accounting.* Proper allocation of duties must cover:

(i) Checking invoices received.

(ii) Maintaining a day book system (whether slip system or otherwise) regarding purchases and purchase-returns.

(iii) The writing up of the ledger accounts and checking of suppliers' statements.

(iv) Payment authorisation. Before this is given, the procedures stated (*see* p. 58) must be followed to ensure goods have been properly ordered, duly received and advantage taken of any discounts allowable.

25. Trading transactions: sales. The internal control should cover:

(a) *Authorisation and recording.*

(i) Arrangements to ensure that sales are made at correct prices and under agreed terms of discount or otherwise, and where part-exchanges are allowed correct allowance must be checked.

(ii) Authority to accept orders, grant credit terms, and to pass on orders for production or supply.

(iii) Proper allocation of duties and authority with regard to issue of invoices or credit notes, the completion of these as to quantities, prices and totals, and their retention, before use, in safe custody.

(iv) Procedure to be laid down regarding goods sent on approval, free, or on other terms.

(b) *Dispatch of goods.*

(i) Authority for dispatch of goods and evidence thereof to be fixed.

(ii) Arrangements to be made for examination and recording of goods dispatched by staff other than those concerned with stocks maintenance or invoicing duties.

(iii) Procedure laid down for the regular comparison of records of goods dispatched with original orders, dispatch notes and invoices.

(c) *Accounting.*

(i) If staff numbers make it possible, no sales ledger staff should be concerned with cash records or stock and should not be responsible for sales invoicing or sales staff duties.

(ii) If possible separate staff should be engaged on the duties of recording sales and sales returns, of maintenance of customers' accounts, and of preparation of statements to customers. Care should be taken that, when prepared, statements should not be subject to alteration before dispatch to customers.

(iii) Procedures to ensure that sales returns, price adjustments and special allowances are operated under an efficient system of internal check.

(iv) Where goods are dispatched in an accounting period but not invoiced then, adequate procedures should be in force to ensure that they are invoiced in the next period, and also that the goods held are not shown in stocks of the company if the sale is included in the earlier period.

(v) The proper allocation of authority with regard to arrangements for special terms and discounts (and how these shall be evidenced), the writing off of bad debts and who shall deal with customers' enquiries.

(vi) Procedure for the receipt of and dealing with overdue accounts.

(vii) The operation of control accounts on debtors' ledgers, including their regular preparation and review by an independent responsible official when completed.

26. Stock control. Stocks are not only particularly vulnerable to misappropriation, but have also been used as a cover for the payment away of sums of money other than on the stocks purported to be purchased. The procedures involved in internal check may in some cases be quite numerous, especially where various types of stock are held (whether of finished goods, work in progress or raw materials).

Each business will vary in its arrangements, and in installing these the use of internal control questionnaires can be most helpful. The following are some of the main items to be considered:

(a) *Receipt of goods.* The procedures to be followed in dealing with goods inward (including the receipt, checking, passing to departments and recording).

(b) *Allocation of responsibility.* The proper allocation of responsibility for the safeguarding and maintenance in good condition of stocks, including stock records authorisation for issues, and regular reconciliation of store records with those of the accounts department. To preserve internal check those engaged on stock-keeping should have no access to stock records in the accounts department.

(c) *Outside stocks.* Procedures with regard to stocks held outside the business and likewise goods held on behalf of others, as to authorisation and evidence required for issues to be made. Stock held at outside warehouses should be most strictly controlled and inspected as the notional holding of such stocks has been the source of serious irregularities.

(d) *Stocktaking procedures.* These are important with respect to independent checks, reconciliation of records, pricing of goods, the intervals at which stocks to be taken, including irregular checks from time to time. The "cut-off" procedures to be operated (*see* p. 148).

(c) *Writing off stocks.* The systems to be applied in valuation of stocks and the review of slow-moving or obsolete lines. The issue and receipt of returnable packages, the control of scrap and the authority required for writing off and disposal of old lines.

27. Fixed assets. The following are some of the main points to be dealt with:

(*a*) The designation of authority to sanction capital expenditure and in what way this should be evidenced.

(*b*) The designation of authority to sanction the sale, exchange or disposal of assets, how this is to be evidenced and the internal check regarding this, since this should not be under the authority of one person only.

(*c*) The maintenance of proper information of all fixed assets acquired by means of accounting records, plant registers, etc., and the arrangements for the physical inspection of such assets. Where assets are transferred to sites, branches, or within a group, the maintenance of adequate records and their checking from time to time independently to ensure that such records are up to date.

(*d*) The fixing of rates of depreciation or arrangement for revaluation, the authorisation of the staff concerned and the evidence to be supplied.

28. Investments. The internal control on these is important as they may afford the possibility of misappropriation, more especially by staff in higher paid grades.

Such arrangements should include:

(a) Authority to purchase or sell investments and the evidencing of such authorisation, preferably by staff working apart from cash or documents of title.

(b) The proper recording of all transactions, including the maintenance of records of investments held, the latter to be checked with the accounting records and the actual documents of title (or certificates where held outside), from time to time.

(c) Adequate arrangements to ensure that advantage is taken of rights issues, the due receipt of bonus issues and receipt of relevant share certificates and interest and dividends arising.

(d) The safeguarding of documents of title with not less than two persons evidencing the safe deposit of such documents, and authorising either access to them or their withdrawal.

RELATIONSHIP BETWEEN THE INDEPENDENT AND THE INTERNAL AUDITOR

29. Common interest. "On accounting matters the internal auditor and the independent auditor operate largely in the same field and they have a common interest in ascertaining that there is:

(a) An effective system of internal check to prevent or detect errors and fraud and that it is operating satisfactorily.

(b) An adequate accounting system to provide the information necessary for preparing true and fair financial statements."

30. Fundamental difference of work. "Although the two forms of audit have a common interest in the important matters mentioned in the preceding paragraph, there are some fundamental differences:

(a) *Scope.* The extent of the work undertaken by the internal auditor is determined by the management whereas that of the independent auditor arises from the responsibilities placed on him by statute.

(b) *Approach.* The internal auditor's approach is with a view to ensuring that the accounting system is efficient so that the accounting information presented to management throughout the period is accurate and discloses material facts. The independent auditor's approach, however, is governed by his duty to satisfy himself that the accounts to be presented to the shareholders show a true and fair view of the profit or loss for the financial period and of the state of the company's affairs at the end of that period.

(c) *Responsibility*. The internal auditor's responsibility is to the management whereas the independent auditor is responsible directly to the shareholders. It follows that the internal auditor, being a servant of the company, does not have the independence of status which the independent auditor possesses."

31. Similarity of method. "Notwithstanding these important differences, the work of both the internal auditor and the independent auditor, on accounting matters, is carried out largely by similar means, such as:

(a) Examination of the system of internal check, for both soundness in principle and effectiveness in operation.
(b) Examination and checking of accounting records and statements.
(c) Verification of assets and liabilities.
(d) Observation, inquiry, the making of statistical comparisons and such other measures as may be judged necessary."

The foregoing quotations from *Statements on Auditing, U4* (Appendix 2) serves to show that the work of the internal auditor and the statutory auditor may be beneficial in obviating unnecessary duplication of work.

32. Co-operation between statutory and internal auditors. The wide experience of the independent auditor may be of assistance to the internal auditor while on the other hand the latter's intimate acquaintance with the business concerned may be of help to the independent auditor.

Co-operation in planning of the respective audits may save unnecessary work, although the independent auditor must always satisfy himself as to the work carried out by the internal auditor.

33. Procedural co-operation. More specifically such co-operation may exist in such matters as:

(a) The independent auditor may be able to rely to a large extent on the internal auditor regarding the continuous operation of the internal check system and in the reliability he may place on the accounting records.

(b) Agreement as to various aspects of the work being carried out only by the internal auditor or together with the independent auditor such as cash counts and visits to branches.

(c) Where the internal auditor so co-operates the independent auditor may accept work done in respect of such matters as the confirmation of customers' accounts, the verification of assets and the audit working schedules prepared by the internal auditor.

Finally, to quote the *Statements on Auditing*:

> "The internal auditor's responsibility is to the management and he is in no sense a servant of the independent auditor. It follows therefore that the extent to which the internal auditor can so arrange his work as to be of specific assistance to the independent auditor will depend upon decisions of the management on the scope of the internal audit and the number of staff employed thereon. Consultation between the two auditors, and where necessary with the management, should however ensure that so far as is practicable the fullest possible assistance is available to the independent auditor."

PROGRESS TEST 3

1. Give a definition of internal control. (2)
2. Define internal check and internal audit. (3, 4)
3. Has the internal control system any influence on the conduct of the external audit? (5)
4. What should the auditor do if he is not satisfied with the efficiency of the internal control system? (5)
5. What is signified by the expression "auditing in depth?" (6)
6. With what must the auditor acquaint himself in order to test the efficient working of the internal control system? (7)
7. Give an illustration of how auditing in depth is carried out. (7)
8. Is it the auditor's responsibility to ensure that there is an efficient system of internal control? (7, 8)
9. State the main divisions of internal control. (10)
10. Classify the sections involved in the operation of an internal control system. (15)
11. State the matters which are necessary for efficient overall financial control. (16)
12. What are the essential features of the efficient control of funds? (19–21)

13. State the matters which comprise an efficient system of internal control regarding employee remuneration.   (23)

14. In dealing with purchases, what matters should be specified to preserve a proper system of internal check?   (24)

15. What are the main divisions of the internal control system affecting sales?   (25)

16. State the essential features of internal control regarding stocks held.   (26-28)

17. What matters are of common interest to the internal and external auditor?   (29)

18. What are the fundamental differences in the work of the internal and external auditor?   (30)

19.   In what ways may co-operation exist between internal and external auditors?   (32, 33)

SPECIMEN QUESTIONS

1. Outline the purposes and major characteristics of a sound system of internal control.

As auditor how would you determine the effectiveness of such a system?   *C.A.*

2. What is meant by internal auditing, internal check and internal control?   How may the internal auditor and the statutory auditor co-operate and what are the fundamental differences between them?   *C.C.A.*

3. Indicate the main considerations which determine the amount of detail checking to be carried out by the auditor of a limited company.   *C.A.* (*E.W.*) (*Inter.*)

4. On being appointed auditor of a firm for the first year, you find that there is no effective supervision of the cashier and that the cash receipts are not lodged in the bank in total, but are used to make cash payments for purchases and expenses.   What are the objections to such methods of dealing with cash and what recommendations would you make to the firm?   *C.C.A.* (*Inter.*)

5. Discuss the main principles of internal check and its advantages to the auditor.   Draw up a system of internal check for the sales side of a wholesale supplier.   *C.C.A.* (*Inter.*)

6. Indicate ways in which the work on the audit of a substantial limited company can be facilitated by the company's own internal organisation and the help of the company's officers.   *C.A.* (*E.W.*)

7. In addition to the audit required by statute, many large companies have in internal audit carried out by staff appointed for this purpose.

Discuss, briefly, the fundamental differences between the two forms of audit and the extent to which the statutory and internal auditors can co-operate to their mutual benefit.   *C.C.A*

8. What is meant by internal audit and what are the fundamental differences between it and the statutory audit? *C.C.A.*

9. Lapwills Ltd., of which you are the auditor, has decided to
dispense with the use of personal ledgers in its accounting system
for purchases.

Indicate the matters to which you would direct particular
attention in relation to internal control. *C.A.* (*E.W.*)

10. In addition to the audit required by statute, many large
companies have an internal audit carried out by staff appointed
for this purpose.

Discuss, briefly, the fundamental differences between the two
forms of audit and the extent to which the statuory and internal
auditors can co-operate to their mutual benefit. *C.A.* (*E.W.*)

CHAPTER IV

DETAILED WORK PROCEDURES

In dealing with the detailed work procedures to be carried out by the auditor, it should be mentioned first that *in all cases* he should satisfy himself as to the *satisfactory operation or otherwise of the system of internal control, including the internal check system and internal audit (if the latter exists)*. These have been dealt with in the previous chapter and will only be mentioned here in passing, but their importance as to the amount of work and methods of procedure will be of significant influence in all matters affecting the detailed work carried out.

In order to afford a simple guide as to the amount of work likely to be undertaken, the following classification is often used in respect of each type of audit.

"A" class. Organisation with efficient system of internal control, qualified staff and internal audit department.

"B" class. Efficiently run organisation but with no internal audit department and not so many qualified staff as in "A" above.

"C" class. Large, or more often, a medium sized company with an internal control system, not of same standard as in the previous classes and subject to certain weaknesses.

"D" class. Medium and small companies with little internal control and ineffective allocation of authority.

"E" class. Small companies with no internal control and authority mostly residing in one person.

We commence with the audit of the monetary transactions of a business.

CASH RECEIPTS

1. Auditing difficulties and internal check.

(a) *Indirect evidence.* In vouching cash receipts, the auditor is faced with peculiar difficulties in ascertaining the true position, if certain transactions are kept out of the double entry system entirely, it is difficult for the auditor to detect this and often evidence can only be obtained of an indirect nature.

It is essential, therefore, that the auditor should first ascertain that a system of internal check is operating efficiently and he should be careful to obtain a list of books maintained with regard to all transactions.

(b) *Rough cash book.* In the previous chapter, the maintenance of a rough cash book in respect of daily cash receipts was mentioned. Such a book should be checked exhaustively by the auditor with the main cash book kept by the cashier, ensuring that each day's takings agree with the daily receipts shown in the main cash book, as, in the event of teeming and lading (*see* **3** (b)), or if the cashier is misappropriating funds, these two books would not agree on one or more occasions. Likewise, the paying-in book should be checked to the main cash book to ensure that cash entered as received is duly banked.

2. Cash sales.

(a) *Necessity of internal check.* The auditor should satisfy himself as to the system of internal check in operation, as cash sales afford easy opportunity for misappropriation of funds.

Where cash registers are used, the daily till rolls should be checked with the total day's takings shown in the cash book.

(b) *Checking receipt counterfoils.* Where receipts are hand written in conjunction with the use of tills, the counterfoils should be checked with the daily summaries of sales staff, and these daily summaries should be checked with the cash takings shown in the cashier's analysis thereof. The daily totals of the receiving cashier's cash books should be cross-checked with the main cash book, agreement being reached in conjunction with credit sales bankings of the amounts banked according to the paying-in book counterfoils.

3. Credit sales.

(a) *Non-use of receipts.* As under the *Cheques Act, 1957*, receipts are not usually issued in respect of cheque payments, the auditor cannot normally verify the receipt of cheques in respect of credit sales, although by consulting the sales ledger accounts he may obtain information of assistance in this respect. Furthermore, it is possible to detect any misappropriation of funds where teeming and lading takes place by examination of the "rough" cash book maintained on postal opening in conjunction with the main cash book.

(b) *Teeming and lading* is the term used to express the method of misappropriation of cash received by falsifying records of subsequent transactions. (In Scotland, the expression, "carry over frauds," is used.)

If, for example, a cheque for £100 is received in full settlement of a debt by A, this may be misappropriated. A's debt, therefore, is still shown as outstanding. At a later date, a cheque for £100 is received from X. In order to not leave A's account in debit for too long a period, which might cause the other staff concerned to send a reminder to A, the more recent cheque from X is entered as received from A and is posted to A's account. X's account is now shown as unpaid, and the foregoing procedure may be repeated. The most simple method has been illustrated in order to make clear the procedure. It may be complicated by the splitting of amounts over various accounts, and more than one misappropriation may be in the course of being covered at the same time.

(c) *Prevention of teeming and lading.* To ensure that such fraud is not practised, the following procedures should be carried out:

(i) Examine the make-up of the sales ledger balances making special inquiry into accounts which appear to be falling into arrear, particular attention being given to accounts where credits have been entered for payments on account where previously the debtor has settled his accounts regularly.

(ii) Obtain the original paying-in slips from the bank and compare the details thereon with the entries in the cash book, to see if any remittances have been split, part having been credited to one account and part to another.

(iii) If receipts for remittances are issued, check the counterfoils with the entries in the cash book, noting differences in the amounts and dates of entry.

(iv) Send statements of account, prepared under the supervision of the auditor's staff, to all debtors, asking for confirmation of the amounts shown to be outstanding to be sent direct to the auditor.

4. Vouching receipts.

(a) *Checking receipt counterfoils.* In some businesses or organisations, such as charities, receipts are still issued for moneys received, whether by cheque or otherwise. In this case the auditor should vouch a number of these with the main cash book. It is realised that it is not difficult for a receipt to be issued for an amount and a different amount to be entered through a carbon on to the receipt counterfoil, nevertheless, should the copy differ from the amount in the cash book, the auditor might be considered to have failed in his duty had he not checked any such counterfoil receipts. The dates as well as amounts should be checked and the top copy of all cancelled receipts should be required to be attached to the counterfoils.

(b) *Collection of moneys by travellers.* Where travellers have authority to collect payments, their counterfoil receipts should be checked with the counterfoil paying-in books, where they bank away from the main office, as well as with the subsequent entries in the main cash book. Their returns should be checked with the main cash book where moneys are handed in at the main office.

(c) *Discounts allowable.* Where discount is allowed, the possibility of entering discount against debtors' accounts instead of cash received must be considered. Therefore, the internal check regarding this should be ascertained as to who agrees these with debtors, and a list of such discounts allowable should be obtained where there is no one overall policy regarding such discount. The rates of allowance should be tested with a number of accounts. The total of discounts allowed should be checked to the relevant account after casting the columns in the cash book.

5. Rents receivable. Briefly, the auditor should:

(a) Inspect agreements and counterparts of leases, note terms as to rents receivable and repairs to be carried out.

(b) Ascertain that all rents have been received, carefully checking all deductions from amounts receivable.

(c) Vouch rent books. A number of tenants' rent books should be vouched and tests made of total collections made with amounts handed in by collectors on particular dates.

(d) Investigate all payments in arrears for any undue length of time and enquire into un-let properties to ensure whether amounts are being paid but are not being paid into the business.

(e) Where agents collect rents, examine their accounts and vouch with amounts received.

6. Investment income. Separate accounts should be kept for each investment held, with particulars as to dates on which regular income is due. The auditor should:

(a) Note that all dividends and interest due are received.

(b) In respect of fixed interest or dividend stocks, check the amount received with the nominal value of the stock and the rate receivable.

(c) Where no fixed rate is receivable, examine counterfoil dividend warrants.

(d) Note that when stocks are sold *ex div*, the dividends are duly received, and likewise, where stocks are purchased *cum div*.

7. Sales of investments. The brokers' sold notes should be vouched with the amounts received.

(I.C.Q. and S.A.P. for investments and income (p. 106).)

8. Interest received.

(a) *Interest on bank deposits.* Where interest is received on bank deposits:

(i) Vouch with bank statement.

(ii) Check the amount in accordance with the agreement, although fluctuating rates may complicate this.

(b) *Interest on loans:*

(i) Where the loan is *unsecured*, the agreement should be inspected and the amount receivable calculated.

(ii) In the case of a loan *secured by a mortgage*, the deed should be inspected for particulars of amounts receivable.

INTERNAL CONTROL QUESTIONNAIRE

CHEQUES AND CASH RECEIPTS

1. Is mail opened by at least two persons under the supervision of a responsible official?

2. Are cheques, postal orders, and money orders crossed when mail is opened?

3. Can unopened letters, other than private mail, go direct to any member of staff?

4. Is a list of receipts prepared when the mail is opened?
5. Is this list checked by someone other than the cashier?
6. Is a reconciliation prepared daily between the total cheques and cash received and total credited to debtors?
7. Are receipt books used by the cashier for all cash received in the form of notes and coin?
8. Are such receipts numbered?
9. Is a record kept of serial numbers of such receipts?
10. Are unused books kept securely and recorded on issue?
11. Can receipts be issued by the cashier for special purposes?
12. Is there a control to prevent fictitious discounts being allowed to customers?
13. Are all cash and cheques received banked daily?
14. Are there proper safeguards with regard to taking monies to and from the bank?
15. Are the paying-in slips prepared by the cashier? If not, by whom?
16. Are duplicate paying-in slips received stamped by the bank?
17. Are bank debit advices notified to anyone other than the cashier?
18. Are bank reconciliations prepared regularly?
19. Has the cashier any connection with debtors' control or writing-off bad debts?
20. Has the cashier any connection with the keeping of the nominal ledger?
21. Has the cashier any connection with the purchases day-book or creditors' ledger?
22. Does the cashier make journal entries or originate any entries otherwise than through his own book?
23. Are rent, dividends, interest received, etc., controlled so that if not received on due dates it would be observed?
24. Does the cashier count and balance his cash daily?
25. Are the staff permitted to cash personal cheques?
26. If so, are the cheques made payable to "Cash"?

STANDARD AUDIT PROGRAMME

CASH RECEIPTS

(A) *Cash received via post*

1. Ascertain that procedures are laid down for post opening and are complied with.
2. Check items in "rough cash book" to main cash book and ascertain that staff have initialled on their having compared these.
3. Verify with remittance advices, etc., so as to ensure correct amounts entered.

4. Check entries with counterfoil receipts where issued, ensuring counterfoils are complete numerically, with spoiled or cancelled receipts attached.
5. Check copy paying-in slips are stamped and initialled by bank with the cash books, identifying a number of individual items in the rough cash book and the paying-in slips. Investigate thoroughly any alteration in the paying-in slips.

(B) *Cash sales*
6. Check items from original sources, *e.g.*, till rolls, cash desks, into cash book (recent periods), noting that reconciliations are prepared daily.
7. Test a number of copy cash receipts with summaries.
8. Verify that copy cash receipts are numerically complete and that any spoiled or cancelled receipts are attached to copies.
9. Ascertain that receipts are controlled on issue and that those used in the period have been currently supplied.
10. Check that staff have initialled on comparison of till roll and cash sales summaries with cash book and paying-in slips.

(C) *Miscellaneous income.* Cash received by travellers and salesmen.
11. Note serial continuity numbers on copy receipts and agree these with receipts books issued.
12. Test-check casts on travellers' receipt books of amounts paid in.
13. Check items from original cash received documents prepared by travellers to cash book.
14. Rents received, etc., check income with original documents as to amount receivable and when due.
15. Investment income. (This is dealt with under Investments, p. 107.)
16. Check postings to nominal ledger.

CASH PAYMENTS

9. Main cash.

(a) *Cheques Act, 1957.* Since the *Cheques Act, 1957*, has been in force, it is not usually the practice of businesses to give receipts in respect of amounts received. The auditor has often, therefore, to rely on a returned cancelled cheque as evidence of payment, for (in accordance with the Act) paid unendorsed cheques may be accepted as evidence that the payee named therein has received the amount stated on the cheque. Two points to notice are:

(i) The cheque must be unendorsed, *i.e.*, a cheque payable to A must not be endorsed over or transferred to B by A.

(ii) It is not regarded as evidence of payment in respect of any particular matter, *i.e.*, it only states the sum shown has been paid over and not the consideration for which it was given.

(b) *Returned cheques as evidence of payment.* If cheque payments are made with the crossing "account payee only", they cannot be endorsed to third parties, and the auditor can accept them as evidence of payment to the party concerned, and where further evidence is available as to why the payment, is made, such as he will obtain in vouching the bought day book and in dealing with the bought ledger accounts, then the returned cheques are sufficient for his purposes. Where, however, cheques are not restrictively crossed, "account payee only", then the auditor may request the production of an actual receipt where he considers this necessary, *e.g.*, in the acquisition of assets. When accepting unendorsed paid cheques, these should be checked with names and dates shown in the cash book (*see also* p. 80).

(c) *Omission of bought ledger.* Numerous businesses, to obviate the work in writing up bought ledger accounts, now retain invoices received during each month until a specified date and then make out cheques in settlement of all invoices received. In such cases the auditor should request that the returned cheques should be attached to the invoices and statements concerned, in this way he may obtain:

(i) *Evidence of the payment.*

(ii) *Evidence of the consideration* for which payment is made.

In respect of trading purchases, the auditor will, in vouching the day book, ascertain the consideration for which such payments are made, the same will also apply with regard to the system mentioned above, but where payments of a different nature are made, such as in respect of assets acquired, the auditor must satisfy himself that the consideration was in

respect of the requirements of the business, with proper
authorisation and initialling by those responsible.

INTERNAL CONTROL QUESTIONNAIRE

CHEQUES

(A) Issue

1. Who has the authority to sign cheques and are there any
   limits to their authority?
2. Are all cheques drawn "to order" and marked "a/c payee
   only—not negotiable"?
3. Is a mechanical cheque signer used, if so, what system
   prevails to prevent its unauthorised use?
4. Are cheques and traders' credit lists prepared on production of authorised vouchers or cheque requisitions,
   and are these vouchers produced to the signatories?
5. Who carries out the checking process, and are all such
   vouchers cancelled?
6. Are all cheques drawn, despatched immediately?   If not,
   who has control over these and how are they dealt with?
7. Is there a fixed date in each month when payments are
   made?
8. Are payments on account made, and if so, who authorises
   these?
9. What control is maintained over the issue of cheques?
10. How are cancelled cheques controlled?
11. Are subsidiary bank accounts fed only from the main
    account and not by miscellaneous items?

(B) Recording

12. Who keeps cash payments records?
13. Who has authority to open bank accounts?
14. On whose authority can bank loans or overdrafts be
    arranged?
15. How are transfers between banks controlled?
16. Has the paying-cashier any control over sales, purchases,
    or nominal ledgers, sales invoices or credit notes, or other
    funds?
17. What system is in operation to ensure that full advantage
    is taken of interest receivable?
18. How frequently are bank reconciliations prepared?
19. Who prepares the reconciliations?
20. Do receiving and paying cashiers have access to bank
    statements?
21. Are the bank reconciliations checked and initialled, and
    if so, by whom?

STANDARD AUDIT PROGRAMME
CHEQUE PAYMENTS

(A) Generally

1. Verify items—including those in payment of purchases invoices selected for testing the internal control system— a number covering the most recent period.
2. Note properly authorised signatories on cheques tested.

(B) Payments for goods and services

3. Obtain invoices and bills rendered and ascertain that these have been properly checked and authorised, ensuring that all such documents have been properly cancelled.
4. In respect of traders' credits, trace items selected for testing to copies of lists of suppliers stamped by bank, and verify amounts of cheques made in settlement of totals on lists.
5. Verify all discounts have been taken advantage of.
6. Examine suppliers' statements with bought ledger accounts.
7. Verify all payments in respect of wages, salaries, petty cash with their relative records, such as wages sheets, etc.
8. Ascertain that cheque numbers agree with control records of books issued. Enquire as to any missing numbers, ensuring that spoilt or cancelled cheques are properly cancelled.
9. Check transfers to petty cash or other books maintained.
10. Test check additions and test check balances brought forward.
11. Check postings to nominal ledger, including control accounts.

(C) Bank reconciliation

12. Check all payments and receipts with bank pass sheets near end of period and for selected periods covered by reconciliations during the period under review.
13. Ascertain that all items in the reconciliation of the previous period are cleared in accordance with the reconciliation.
14. Verify all contra items in both cash book and pass sheets.
15. If possible, check through items in reconciliation through to next period.
16. Verify that reconciliations are made at regular intervals throughout the period.
17. Obtain bank certificate direct from bank (clients' permission necessary for this) requesting bank to give details of all accounts held by them.

10. Employees' remuneration.

(a) *Internal check*. The internal check system is vital regarding employee remuneration. (*see* p. 30).

(b) *Auditor's duties*. The procedures with regard to auditor's duties are as follows:

   (i) Ascertain that the wages sheets have been initialled by those compiling them and by comptometer operators for checking of additions. The whole to be signed by a responsible official.

  (ii) Test-check rates of pay of new staff and alterations in rates with the written authorisations.

 (iii) Check items with the P.A.Y.E. cards and the auditor should ensure that National Insurance cards are held for all employees.

 (iv) Check deductions with records applicable to individual employees, *e.g.*, holiday funds, savings fund, etc.

  (v) Test-check additions on wages sheets and check the totals to the relevant accounts and the total with the control account, if kept. The total amount should be checked with the amount drawn from the bank.

 (vi) Check the method of dealing with uncollected wages, whether immediate recording is made of them, and examine the records maintained in respect of these.

(vii) The auditor should also attend the actual payment of workmen from time to time.

11. Time-rate workers. The auditor's duties are to make the following queries:

(*a*) The clock cards of a selected number of employees should be called for and checked.

(*b*) The rates of pay should be checked and, in conjunction with the hours worked, the gross wages should be agreed. (Overtime working should also be checked.)

12. Piece-work employees.

(a) *Production tickets*. These should be examined in respect of a selected number of workers, noting that any deductions in respect of defective working are made.

(b) *Piece-work rates*. These should be obtained and in conjunction with the production tickets, the gross pay should be checked, subject to any minimum rates of pay which may supersede the piece-work earnings.

INTERNAL CONTROL QUESTIONNAIRE

WAGES AND SALARIES

(A) *Generally*

1. Who has authority
   (a) to engage,
   (b) to dismiss employees?
2. Are history cards maintained of all employees, containing the employee's signature?
3. Who authorises (a) overtime, and (b) general and individual increases in pay?
4. Is such authority always evidenced in writing.
5. Is the person with such authority separate from the salaries personnel?

(B) *Recording*

6. What records are maintained in respect of
   (a) time work,
   (b) piece work?
7. How are piece work quantities checked and how is partly finished work dealt with at the end of each week?
8. If job cards or piece-work cards are produced, who authenticates these?
9. Are those authenticating records on the shop floor independent of the wages department?

(C) *Payroll*

10. Who prepares the payroll?
11. Is the work so allocated that no one aspect of the compilation of the payroll is carried out completely by one member of staff?
12. Is the payroll checked periodically with the history records as to names and details of payment?
13. Is this carried out by a person independent of those preparing the payroll?
14. Are all calculations and additions checked independently?
15. Are all sections of the work duly initialled by those carrying them out?
16. Is the payroll authorised by a responsible official when completed and before the cheque is drawn?

(D) *Payment of wages*

17. Is the cheque drawn for the gross or net amount of the wages?
18. If the gross wages are drawn, how is the cash in respect of deductions dealt with?
19. Is the exact amount of notes and coin drawn from the bank?

20. Are those who distribute wages independent of those who prepare the payroll?
21. Is authority in writing required before a representative of an employee is paid?
22. What arrangements are in force to deal with any disagreement as to the amount paid over?

(E) Unclaimed wages
23. When are unclaimed wages recorded?
24. Who retains unclaimed wages?
25. How long are they retained before being paid into the bank?
26. Who authorises the payment of unclaimed wages?
27. Is written authority required before payment to a representative of an employee (*see* 21 above)?
28. Do both payer and payee sign before payment is made?

(F) Graduated P.A.Y.E. and Pension Scheme payments
29. Are Inland Revenue standard cards completed, or is another system operated authorised by the Inland Revenue?
30. Is a control operated in respect of gross earnings, income tax, and pension funds in conjunction with employees' P.45 forms?
31. How often are payments made in respect of P.A.Y.E. and graduated pension funds?

(G) National Insurance and Pension Funds
32. Are national insurance contributions dealt with by
     (*a*) purchase of stamps,
     (*b*) franking machine,
     (*c*) direct payment?
33. Are the national insurance cards stamped or franked at regular intervals, and is a record kept of machine quantities?
34. Are payments made in respect of
     (*a*) National insurance stamps,
     (*b*) direct payments,
     (*c*) franking machine usage agreed with the payroll?
35. Are national insurance cards checked regularly against the payroll and checked that they are up to date?
36. Is this checking carried out by a member of staff independent of those keeping the cards or franking machine, or making the direct payments?

(H) Pensions
37. Are all pensions approved by the board?
38. By what methods are payments made and are receipts obtained?

39. Are any written authorisations in use in respect of receipt of pensions for others. If so, what action is taken to ensure the existence of the pensioner?

STANDARD AUDIT PROGRAMME

WAGES AND SALARIES

(A) *Generally.* Test a selected number of employees from both wages and salaries sections as to:

1. Engagement and termination of employment, verifying that written authorities in both cases have been countersigned.
2. Verify salaries and wages are according to agreements and any changes have been properly authorised.
3. Where wages paid on time basis, check with clock cards or time sheets.
4. Where wages paid on production, check with piece-work or job slips and note work properly countersigned.
5. Verify that overtime working is properly authorised.
6. Verify authorities for deductions completed by employees and check deductions with summarising records.
7. Check gross wages on to P.A.Y.E. cards. In certain cases these may be dispensed with—only final figures being supplied to the Inland Revenue from salary sheets—in this case check on to the sheets.
8. Check wages and salary sheets as to calculations, additions and cross casts to net pay.
9. Verify that salary sheets initialled by those dealing with the various stages of preparation and checking and that the whole is signed by a designated responsible official.
10. Check totals to control accounts.

(B) *Unclaimed wages*

11. Test the entries in the unclaimed wages book with entries on the wages sheets.
12. Test a number of items to ensure that payments have been authorised and receipts obtained from employees, or if paid to representatives of employees, that proper authority was given to receive payment.
13. Ensure that both payer and payee sign the book.
14. Examine a number of signatures for receipt of payment with original signatures on commencement of employment and enquire into any names appearing frequently on the records.
15. Ascertain that balances of unclaimed wages are banked regularly in accordance with the directive.

c

(C) Salary and wage deductions

16. Ascertain that such deductions are paid over to the funds concerned and that P.A.Y.E. payments are paid over to the Inland Revenue. (This check is greatly facilitated if the gross wages and employers national insurance and the deductions are recorded on a control account basis.)

17. National insurance cards should be inspected and tested with the wages records. Where any weeks are blank on cards, the fact of illness should be verified with the wages records.

18. Ascertain that agreement is made from time to time between gross wages and deductions for income tax and national insurance with employees records.

PETTY CASH

13. Importance of petty cash. The term *petty cash* suggests that it is of minor importance viewed from the point of view of the complete audit. Such an idea, however, is quite erroneous. Often quite large balances are maintained, especially where the petty cash system may be used for the purpose of paying out weekly wages in cash for certain departments in a business.

14. Internal check and petty cash.

(a) *System involved.* Before proceeding to the actual audit of the petty cash book and its relative balance of cash on hand, the auditor should ascertain that an adequate system of internal check is in operation covering such matters as:

(i) The duties of the petty cashier being both properly designated and defined.

(ii) Ensuring that the person in control should, if at all possible, be someone other than the main cashier and that he should be a responsible person. The latter point signifying that the responsibility of dealing with loose cash should not be allocated to someone in such a position that it is likely to constitute a temptation. Being considered of an unimportant nature, petty cash duties are sometimes allocated to young members of staff who, not always due to dishonesty but sometimes owing to lack of experience, are inclined to become confused in their task and the temptation then arises to put through fictitious entries to make the figures agree.

(iii) The only receipts entered into the petty cash book should be in respect of cheques cashed for petty cash purposes.

(iv) The method applied should be that of the imprest system with the amount of the float being specified.

(v) Sums should be paid out only on production of a petty cash voucher duly initialled and limits up to which certain members of staff may obtain payment without further authorisation should be laid down.

(vi) Where the granting of sums on I.O.U.'s is allowed, rules governing this should be specific and also the length of time for which such I.O.U.'s may be left outstanding should be fixed. I.O.U.'s should only be granted in respect of advances for expenses to be incurred on the firm's business.

(vii) A responsible official should be required to check and inital the petty cash book and vouchers at irregular intervals, the length of time within which such checks should be made being stated.

(b) *Adequacy of system.* Before proceeding to the audit of the petty cash book, the efficacy of the prevailing internal check system should be investigated. If this appears to be satisfactory, then much detailed checking work may be avoided. If, however, the auditor is not satisfied with the system being operated, then it may be necessary to vouch a large number of items (although discretion would still be exercised as to trifling amounts). In such circumstances the auditor should report the position to his client, making recommendations as he thinks necessary and pointing out his inability to assess the true position due to the unsatisfactory state of affairs.

Where the internal check system is sound it should only be necessary to check items at random or to *block vouch* certain specified months throughout the year.

(c) *Vouching.* When vouching, it will be necessary to examine supporting vouchers where required, *e.g.*, receipts for office purchases of any material amount, and also to note that identifiable initials are appended as required. Vouchers should be examined up to the date of the checking of the petty cash in hand.

Where transfers are made to further subsidiary books, such as additional petty cash books or postage books, these should all be checked and the books examined and balances counted as necessary. Balances of stamps in hand should not be overlooked as in same types of business these may be quite large.

15. Petty cash control account. In some cases a petty cash control account is maintained in the impersonal ledger, the details of the petty cash book being posted therefrom to the various accounts, otherwise the totals of analysis columns are posted from the petty cash book direct to the various accounts. After casting the petty cash book, total columns and checking cross-casts, the various postings should be checked into the relative accounts. The amount shown as the petty cash balance in hand in the book should be agreed with the amount shown in the impersonal ledger control account where such an account is maintained, as well as with the figure shown on the trial balance.

The verification of the balances of petty cash and the bank balances are dealt with in Chapter VII.

INTERNAL CONTROL QUESTIONNAIRE
PETTY CASH AND POSTAGE

A list should be prepared in the first instance in respect of all floats stating:

    (a) petty cashier,
    (b) amount of float,
    (c) purpose for its maintenance,
    (d) method of reimbursement.

1. Does petty cashier control other funds, in particular, receipt of cash?
2. Has the petty cashier sole access?
3. Are vouchers issued on all payments and signed by recipient?
4. Is a limit fixed on the amount of disbursements, if so, what is the limit?
5. What system is operated in respect of I.O.U.'s?
6. What limits as to amount and duration of time is fixed on I.O.U.'s?
7. Are employees allowed to cash cheques, and if so, is any limit imposed?
8. Is the petty cash book regularly examined by a responsible official and initialled? Is such an examination carried out on the event of each reimbursement?
9. If such examinations take place, by whom are these done?
10. Is the float reasonable bearing in mind the purposes for which it is maintained?
11. Is a proper double entry system operated with an imprest amount as the balance?

12. Is the float reasonable in view of the use involved? (In the case of airmail and parcel post the float may be comparatively large.)
13. Is the postage book examined and the balance checked periodically by an independent member of staff?
14. Who authorised the reimbursement of the float?
15. What system of control is in operation regarding the franking machine?

STANDARD AUDIT PROGRAMME

I. PETTY CASH AND POSTAGE

1. Vouch the petty cash expenditure including items of recent date (i.e., after end of period), ensuring that external payments are supported wherever possible by external receipts.
2. Ensure that all petty cash payments have been properly authorised, and cancelled, and are within the prescribed limits.
3. Ensure that the books have been properly initialled in respect of periodic examination and balance checks.
4. Check transfers to any subsidiary petty cash books and to postage book, ensuring that balances held are reasonable having regard to the purpose for which they are held.
5. Examine postage books to see amounts of expenditure are of reasonable amounts.
6. Check casts and balances carried down of petty cash book.
7. Check postings to nominal ledger.

II. CASH AND PETTY CASH COUNTS

1. Make surprise counts in respect of cash and petty cash and postage balances held. Such balances may include luncheon vouchers and balances on staff funds. Where more than one balance is held, all should be produced at the same time.
2. Ascertain that all cheques held have been crossed in favour of the client "a/c payee only—not negotiable."
3. Check totals of cash counted with balances on books— which should be properly written up-to-date. The "Cash" cheques drawn for petty cash or other funds should be checked through to date (i.e., after the period under audit).
4. Ascertain that cheques held and counted are subsequently met.
5. Note I.O.U.'s and enquire where any appear excessive or outstanding an undue period of time.

6. Verify stock of unused receipts, check with control records and printers' invoices.
(National insurance stamps are dealt with under Wages and Salaries.)

PURCHASES

16. Purchases.

(a) *Slip system and bought day books.* It has been mentioned when dealing with cheque payments that bought day books are frequently dispensed with, settlement being made direct from invoices and suppliers' statements received. Nevertheless, the information for which the day books are maintained is still necessary, namely, the total purchases made, and where necessary, their proper analysis.

Where the original form of day book is maintained, the total column should be cast and individual sub-totals checked to the main total for the period under review. Similarly, cross-casts of analysis columns should be checked.

If slip systems are in operation, then the required information as to total purchases should be checked in the main cash book which will be necessarily analysed as to payments in respect of trading transactions. In this case the invoices will be vouched in conjunction with the cash book records.

(b) *The settlement of invoices.* This usually takes place after the month end, so care should be taken to ensure that all invoices awaiting payment are included in the outstanding liabilities. A list of such unsettled invoices should be requested by the auditor. The goods received books or copy goods inwards notes for the period prior to the end of the financial period should be checked to ensure invoices have been received and are properly included in the list of unsettled items, if not already paid.

(c) *Vouching invoices.* By vouching invoices is signified their checking in order to establish their authenticity for inclusion in the records of the business. This involves checking:

(i) That it was properly addressed to the client.
(ii) The date of the invoice.
(iii) That it was in respect of goods normally dealt in by the client—if this is not so, then special attention must be paid as to its authenticity.

(iv) The accuracy of the document as to extensions and total.

(v) That those responsible for the work of checking the invoice in its various aspects and passing it for payment have duly appended their initials.

(vi) That the goods or services have actually been received by the business.

(vii) That the order was properly placed in the first instance.

viii) That items in respect of capital expenditure or expense items are properly segregated from trading purchases.

(d) *Goods received book.* The goods received book is an important link enabling the auditor to ensure that goods have been received for which invoices have been rendered and a number of items should be checked into the goods received book. In some cases copy goods received notes may be attached to the invoices, so facilitating checking.

(i) *Inclusion of invoices.* It is of the utmost importance to ensure that goods included in stock figures at the end of the financial period should be shown as having been purchased, since the inclusion of such goods would inflate stock values so erroneously creating a greater profit, or reducing a loss. Care should be exercised, therefore, to ascertain that goods shown as received in the goods inward book towards the end of the period are checked with the purchases day book. Invoices received after the closing date should also be examined as these may reveal a delivery date prior to the close of the period. If a sound system is not in operation in respect of goods received, suppliers' delivery notes should be examined or stock records as to date of inclusion in stock.

(ii) *Unsatisfactory records.* The additional work involved for the auditor may still not lead to an entirely satisfactory conclusion and his dissatisfaction with the state of affairs should be pointed out to the client, stating his non-acceptance of responsibility with respect to the stock figures concerned.

(e) *Forward purchases.* In some cases businesses may enter into contracts for the purchase of goods at a later date at a fixed price. Such deals are termed "forward purchases." If the contracts are abnormally large and it is anticipated that a loss may arise which would materially affect the company's position after the balance sheet date, then provision should be made against such losses. If this is not done, then the auditor should qualify his report accordingly.

17. Purchases returns.

(a) *Ensure credit received.* Where goods purchased may be returned to suppliers, it is essential that a proper system should be in force for ensuring that due credit is received. Without such a system the credit receivable may afford an easy source for misappropriation of funds.

(b) *The internal check system.* Such a system should cover such matters as notification by the returning section to the accounts department in duplicate, the second copy being returned to the department of origin duly initialled. If the original invoice for the goods has not been settled, the returns outwards note should be attached and the amount deducted. If the invoice has been settled, then a credit note is obtained from the supplier to which the returns outwards note referenced, while the credit note should be entered in the purchases returns book and attached to the invoices awaiting settlement to ensure deduction from the subsequent amount due.

(c) *Audit procedure.* The auditor should check the returns outwards book maintained by the dispatch department with the purchases returns book, and the credit notes should be vouched with the purchases returns book and those attached to the invoices awaiting settlement to ensure deduction from the subsequent settlement.

18. The bought ledger.
Before dealing with the final aspect of the purchasing side of the business, it is reiterated that a considerable amount of work may be obviated if the system of internal check regarding the compilation of the bought ledger is sound.

(a) *Postings.* They may be checked into the ledger from the purchases and purchases returns day books, but this should only be necessary on a test basis, and provided the internal check system is considered satisfactory, it may be omitted, assuming that a control account is maintained. Opening balances should be checked in from the list compiled in the previous period and casts within the ledger may be checked, but in any case the balances should be examined and the total creditors' figure checked with the control account.

(b) *Suppliers' statements.* These should also be examined in conjunction with suppliers' statements received after date as well as cash payments made after date. The checking of the suppliers' statements constitutes a further safeguard with regard to the proper inclusion of invoices for goods received and shown as stock, as mentioned previously. If debit balances are shown on any accounts, these should be enquired into as they may signify payments in respect of invoices withheld for the same reason.

(c) *Transfers.* If these are from the bought ledger to the sales ledger, or vice versa, where amounts are set off, they should be carefully examined and the documents arising regarding them should be vouched.

INTERNAL CONTROL QUESTIONNAIRES

I. PURCHASES AND PURCHASES RETURNS

(A) *Ordering*

1. Is there a separate buying department?
2. Are all purchases orders executed in writing?
3. Who authorises requisitions to the purchasing department?
4. Are official orders issued and copies
    (a) sent to goods inwards bay,
    (b) retained in accounts department?
5. Are such orders serially numbered and are there safeguards against misuse?
6. Is an agreed list of suppliers with discount details retained?
7. Who authorises orders and what are their authority limits?

(B) *Receipt of goods*

8. On receipt of goods:
    (a) Are arrangements made for inspection?
    (b) Is a goods inwards book made up from goods inwards notes properly referred to purchase order?
    (c) Is a copy of goods inwards note sent to
        (i) Buying Department,
        (ii) Accounts Department?

(C) *Return of goods*

9. What documents are prepared on return of goods?
10. What arrangements are made to ensure
    (a) Accounts and Buying Departments are notified?
    (b) Credit notes are received?
    (c) Whose duty is it to ensure that due credit is received?

(D) *Passing invoices for payment*

11. On receipt are invoices compared with
    (a) original orders,

(b) copies of goods inwards notes?

12. Are invoices properly authorised for payment as to
    (a) price,
    (b) quantity,
    (c) extensions and total?

13. Who finally authorised payment?

14. Are arrangements made for copy invoices to be stamped "Copy" on receipt?

15. Are invoices passed for payment duly stamped to prevent double payment?

II. PURCHASES LEDGER

1. What system is maintained, e.g.,
    (a) handwritten,
    (b) mechanised,
    (c) slip system?

2. How is it ensured that employees' purchases are charged to them?

3. What system is in operation as to inter-branch or inter-company purchases?

4. Is a purchases ledger control account maintained?

5. How often is the control account prepared?

6. Are suppliers' statements compared with accounts, and how frequently is this done?

7. Is the ledger independently examined by someone other than the ledger clerk from time to time?

STANDARD AUDIT PROGRAMME

I. PURCHASES AND PURCHASES RETURNS

1. Verify that invoices are supported by copy requisitions, copy orders and copy goods received notes.

2. Test to ensure that authorities for requisitions, orders, and passing for payment, are within agreed limits.

3. Verify that credit notes have proper supporting documents, e.g., copy goods returned notes.

4. Check extensions and additions of invoices.

5. Ascertain that purchases other than for resale are properly allocated to nominal accounts.

6. Test the numerical sequence of goods received and returned, and enquire as to missing numbers.

7. Inspect goods received or returned notes not matched to invoices or credit notes and enquire as to any outstanding for an undue length of time.

8. Check casts and cross-casts of purchases day book, and ensure that pre-lists are prepared for control accounts prior

to passing to ledger clerks or cashiers department for payment.
9. Check postings to nominal ledger.
10. Check control accounts.

II. TRADE CREDITORS

1. Select a number of accounts and check these on the list of creditors, ensuring that all *comparatively* large accounts are checked, ensure that balances are composed of identifiable amounts, and if not so, compare with suppliers' statements.
2. Test check a number of the accounts with suppliers' statements.
3. Test additions of the accounts and check out balances to list.
4. Check addition of list of balances and total with control account, ensuring that control accounts are regularly maintained.

III. ACCRUALS

1. Obtain list of amounts due and payable and check this with nominal ledger. Each account in the ledger should be scrutinized and any items not shown on the list which should be brought into account should be inquired into.
2. Where necessary, invoices, statements, or other documentation should be examined as to amounts due and not settled.
3. Invoices and payments received and made after date should be examined to ensure all liabilities are brought into the correct period.
4. Compare list of outstanding liabilities with list on previous year's audit file, enquiring into any relevant differences.

SALES

19. Cash sales. For the method employed in dealing with cash sales, *see* p. 41).

20. Credit sales.

(a) *Vouch invoices.* Where sales day books are maintained, a number of copy sales invoices should be checked with the entries and the casts of the book may be tested, the total of the sales being checked to the sales account. The usefulness of checking a large number of copy invoices is doubtful since carbon copies are in any case not completely reliable evidence of the original.

(b) *Slip systems*.   Often, as in the case of bought day books, a slip system may be used whereby copy sales invoices are filed in numerical order and machine lists are prepared. Here again, a number of copy invoices may be checked with the lists and the totals should be checked to the sales account.

(c) *Audit in depth*.   Various systems may prevail, the auditor should therefore test the system from its origin, the original order received, to its conclusion, the dispatch of the sales invoice to the customer. Normally a number of copies are made of the invoice and distributed to the various departments concerned, *e.g.*, the store, the despatch department (two copies, one for retention, one to be used as a delivery note) and the accounts department.

(d) *Omission of sales ledger*.   Where the type of business transacted allows, the copy invoices may be filed in separate folders for customers.   When payment is received the invoices are removed and filed.   Likewise, where credit notes are issued these are put into the customer's folder.   Such a system obviates the use of a sales ledger but is only practical where customers pay regularly and mostly in full.   In such a case the auditor must ascertain that an efficient control account system is in operation as there is the obvious possibility of the removal or loss of copy invoices.   (The control accounts are made up from the total of sales invoices and credit notes and of the cash received, the remaining total balance representing the total of the unsettled accounts still in the folders.)

(e) *Sales control account*.   The method to be employed by the auditor will vary according to the system, but in all cases he should pay particular attention to the control accounts maintained—if by any chance they are not kept, he would be wise to compile his own. Where sales ledgers are maintained, he should check a number of day book postings to the ledger, in addition to the work outlined above.

(f) *Purchase tax*.   Where purchase tax is charged, this should be segregated in order to credit the amount to an account maintained in respect thereof which is payable over to Customs and Excise Departments.

(g) *"Abnormal" sales*.   If sales other than those of a normal trading nature are made, such as sales of plant, etc., these should be checked to ensure that they are not included in the sales figures but are dealt with through the relative asset accounts.

(h) *Auditing procedures.* To ensure that the *cut off* procedures are properly operated at the end of the period a number of invoices should be checked with the goods outwards book to ensure that the goods shown as sales have actually been despatched. If they have not been sent out then they may still be regarded as sales, but it must be ascertained that they are not included in the stock held at the end of the period, so inflating any profit figure. This matter is also dealt with in Chapter X regarding stock.

21. Exclusion of goods not actually sold. It is essential to ensure that goods shown as sales in accounts do actually fulfil that designation, for although the relative purchases may be shown against them, the gross profit will automatically be included in the accounts. The inclusion of items in respect of sales transactions not finally completed should, therefore, be avoided. Such transactions frequently fall under the following headings:

(a) *Goods on sale or return.* Where separate records are maintained in respect of goods sent out on the understanding that they may be returned if not wanted, no difficulty should arise regarding their being excluded from normal sales, but if such goods are debited in the ledger accounts of prospective purchasers and are credited on return, it will be necessary to check the records of goods dispatched and returned with individual accounts.

It will also be necessary to request that details of goods held by customers be compiled, which should be reconcilable with the records mentioned above. The sum involved must then be excluded from the sales account and trade debtors' figures and the goods concerned valued at cost or as otherwise advisable.

(b) *Goods on consignment.*

  (i) *Change of location only.* Where goods are sent on consignment for sale, the transaction only constitutes their transfer from one place to another, no sale being concluded until the agent has disposed of them.

    Such goods should therefore be included as stock and not sales, properly valued, but with the addition in this case of the expenses involved in despatching them to the agent, and with any expenses incurred by the agent.

(ii) *Elimination from accounts.* If such goods on consignment are debited to the agent concerned, whether at cost or otherwise, then it should be ascertained that a corresponding entry is made to eliminate the debit and that no figure is included with that of the normal sales. If a consignment account is kept and the goods at cost shown as a deduction from the normal purchases, then the figure on the consignment account plus charges involved in the transaction may be shown as a stock of goods on consignment figure.

(iii) *Goods received for sale.* Where such goods are received by the client, as consignee, for sale, then these should not appear within the double entry system, any charges incurred in respect thereof being debited to the consignor's account.

22. Hire purchase sales. There are various methods of dealing with hire purchase sales which are covered in the accountancy textbooks. The main concern of the auditor should be to ensure that only profit on that part of the contract already carried out should be included in current profits.

(a) *Provision against unrealised profit.* If full credit is taken in the year of sale for the cash price of the contract, the auditor should ascertain that a provision against unrealised profit is created in respect of profit taken on instalments not due. Where cash received during the period is brought into the accounts, the outstanding amount in respect of the contract should be reduced by the profit element in order to supply the figure for the value of the stock out on hire to be brought into the accounts. In any case, only such interest as refers to the period being dealt with should be taken as profit earned.

(b) *Examination of controls with accounts.* A number of the hire purchase contracts should be checked with the details shown on the hire purchasers' accounts in the ledger. The balances on the accounts should be examined and a note taken of those in arrear, care being taken to ensure that any in arrear, where goods have been repossessed are taken out of the schedule of hire purchase debtors and transferred out as bad debts, after crediting the value of the amount received or receivable on disposal of the goods.

23. Forward sales. In certain trades, contracts are entered into for delivery of goods at a future date at an agreed price. Although a valid contract exists, nevertheless it is advisable for the auditor to ensure that no profit is taken into account before the delivery date, especially in view of the fact that often large sums are involved in such forward commitments. Where part of such goods have already been delivered, however, a proportionate sum may be brought in.

24. Returnable packages. The method prevailing with regard to returnable packages should be examined. Various systems are operated but whichever is used it should be sufficiently effective to reveal the stocks held both by the company and in the customers' hands. Where a lesser figure is allowed on return than originally charged, there can be no objection to taking the difference as a profit when containers are despatched. Care must be taken to see that the full amount allowable on return for containers in customers' hands is provided against where the full amount has been debited to the debtors accounts.

25. The sales ledger. As with the bought ledger mentioned above, the work of the auditor will be influenced considerably by the effectiveness of the internal check system prevailing.

(a) *Verification of balances.* After checking in the opening balance from the previous period, it should not be necessary to check many postings from the day books and cash book to the ledger, but the casts should be tested and very particularly the make-up of the balances outstanding should be examined, note being taken of increasing balances where amounts are paid at intervals on account. Likewise, the age of the balances should be noted. Each balance should be ticked down to the new period and checked with the list of debtors to be agreed with the control account. Notes against accounts may be made regarding any queries as to length of time outstanding and any balances which may be considered to be bad debts or against which a provision should be made. (*See also* p. 145 as to Verification.)

(b) *Journal postings.* Any special posting from the journal should be checked, likewise any transfers between the bought and sales ledgers and the documents arising in respect thereof should be vouched.

INTERNAL CONTROL QUESTIONNAIRES
I. SALES AND SALES DEBTORS

(*A*) *Goods despatched*

1. At what stage does accounting control first arise? (Normally this would be on receipt of order but this may vary according to the business concerned.)

2. What record is compiled on receipt of order?
3. Are all orders approved before being passed for execution by a person independent of the sales department?
4. Are records compiled under 2. above duly referenced on completion of order and are checks made regularly to ensure completion of orders, and are any outstanding orders investigated after a certain period of time?
5. Are there a number of despatch centres and are procedures similar in all cases?
6. What records are compiled in respect of goods despatched? Are the records numerically controlled?
7. Are despatch staff entirely independent of sales department staff?
8. How are despatch notes referenced to relevant sales invoices and who is responsible for this? Are such documents initialled by the person responsible?
9. What procedure is in operation to ensure that all despatch notes are duly covered by sales invoices?

(B) *Sales returns*

1. What records are compiled on return of goods from customers or claims in respect of short delivery or incorrectly priced goods?
2. Are records as in 1. above prepared by persons independent of the sales ledger and cashiers' departments?
3. Are such records filed consecutively, and are such documents matched with credit notes?
4. Is the person responsible for carrying this out independent as in 2. above, and also of the despatch and control of goods?
5. Is investigation made as to any numbered documents unmatched?

II. SALES INVOICES AND CREDIT NOTES

(A) *Invoices—generally*

1. How are sales prices
   (a) ascertained,
   (b) authorised?
2. Who authorises trade discounts and what are their limits of authority?
3. How is such authority evidenced?
4. From what sources is information supplied for the preparation of sales invoices?
5. Are those preparing sales invoices independent of staff dealing with
   (a) acceptance of orders,

(b) despatch of goods,
(c) cash receipts?
6. Are all invoices pre-numbered and controlled?
7. How many copies of sales invoices are prepared and to whom are they distributed?
8. Is the use of copy invoices for original sales obviated by the use of suitably marked copies?
9. How are invoices cancelled, altered, or marked "NO CHARGE," dealt with? Who authorises these?
10. In the case of cancelled invoices what action is taken to ensure that the goods are retained in the business.
11. Are sales invoices referenced to sales orders or estimates and the goods despatched book?
12. Are sales invoices checked as to
    (a) price,
    (b) calculations and additions,
    by someone other than those preparing them?
13. Are reconciliations made between sales invoices and issues from stock, and if so, how often, and by who are these made?
14. Is any statistical data in respect of sales checked with actual sales? Whose duty is it to do this?

(B) *Invoices—sales of a special nature*
1. What system prevails in respect of goods sent on consignment?
2. What system is in operation in respect of inter-company sales (if any)? Who authorises the rates of uplift on such sales?
3. What systems are in operation in respect of
    (a) staff sales,
    (b) sales of scrap?
4. If purchase tax is charged on sales, is this properly segregated, and are adequate records maintained?

(C) *Credit notes*
1. What sources supply the information for the preparation of the credit notes?
2. Are credit notes prepared by someone other than staff engaged on
    (a) receipt of cash,
    (b) maintaining the sales ledger,
    (c) maintaining goods returned records?
3. Are all credit notes referenced with goods returned records?
4. Are extensions and totals checked, and are all credit notes authorised—both these functions to be carried out

by a person independent of those preparing the credit notes and goods returned records.

5. Is authorisation carried out by a responsible official, and is the official independent of such work as
   (a) sales ledger preparation,
   (b) receipt of cash?

6. What system prevails to ensure adjustment of any sales commission disallowed on return of goods?

III. SALES LEDGERS

1. Are sales ledger staff independent of those recording the receipt of cash?

2. Does the system provide for an independent preparation of information, *e.g.*, pre-listing, before information is passed to sales ledger personnel for processing.

3. Are control accounts maintained in respect of each sales ledger, and how often are such control accounts prepared?

4. Are the control accounts prepared by personnel independent of those maintaining the ledgers?

5. How often are statements sent to customers? Are these sent to all customers including those with credit or nil balances?

6. Are such statements prepared by staff other than those maintaining the ledgers?

7. Who authorises terms of trade and discount allowance, and how is this evidenced?

8. At what intervals are ledger balances examined for action to be taken regarding balances outstanding longer than the normal period?

9. Is special attention paid to accounts where amounts are paid on account? (*See* p. 42.)

10. Is such an examination carried out by staff other than those engaged on
    (a) maintaining the sales ledger,
    (b) receipt of cash?

11. What procedure is operated for the collection of outstanding debts?

12. Are queries relating to outstanding accounts dealt with by staff other than those maintaining the ledgers?

13. What rules apply to the removal of ledger sheets?

IV. BAD DEBTS

1. What evidence is supplied to justify the writing off of bad debts?

2. Is the approval of a responsible official required before any debt may be written off?

3. Is the responsible official independent of those maintaining the ledgers and those dealing with the receipt of cash?
4. What system is in operation to ensure that any subsequent payments received are properly received by the business?
5. How is any bad debts provision compiled?

STANDARD AUDIT PROGRAMMES

I. SALES AND SALES RETURNS

(A) *Sales*

1. Test a number of recent transactions relating to sales shown on records completing sales, such as copy goods despatched notes or completion orders.
2. In conjunction with the transactions investigated, verify these with originating documents, such as customers' orders, contracts or correspondence, ensuring that orders are approved.
3. Continuing with the transactions investigated, obtain the relevant copy sales invoices and check prices charged with independent evidence, such as price lists, tenders, etc.
4. Test-check calculations and additions on copy sales invoices. (This is in the nature of a safeguard for the auditor as such copies may be falsified.)
5. Test a number of items with stock records to ensure deduction from stock, particularly items near end of period.
6. Check sales analysis.
7. Test check postings to sales ledger.

(B) *Sales returns*

1. Verify a selected number of items with evidence giving rise to their issue.
2. Check with goods despatched records and ensure full numerical sequence maintained.
3. Verify that all credit notes have been properly authorised by an official engaged other than in maintaining sales ledger or dealing with cash receipts.
4. Check extensions, additions, and prices. In the latter case with original invoices, enquiring into any difference. Check analysis of credit notes.
5. Where goods have been returned, check these with stock records.
6. Check postings to sales ledger.

II. TRADE DEBTORS

1. Examine a number of accounts chosen from various sections of the ledger, in consecutive order, and check these on to list of debtors.

2. Examine evidence of any inter-ledger accounts or inter-sales and purchase ledger transfers.

3. Note age of accounts and check these with analysis of age of accounts if kept, and ascertain the likelihood of settlement in cases of doubt.

4. Note any accounts showing payments on account and investigate these as to any teeming and lading or as to credit worthiness of the debtor. (This will necessitate tracing back to original paying-in slips. *See* p. 42.)

5. Examine discounts and allowances and enquire into any items which appear exceptional or excessive.

6. Obtain list of bad debts written off and scrutinise a number of these, also examine payments in respect of credit balances. Ensure that all have been properly authorised.

7. Ensure that the system is adequate and functioning properly in respect of sending monthly statements and pursuing overdue accounts.

8. Compare the debtors to credit sales ratio with previous periods and enquire as to reason for any material difference.

9. Test check additions in the sales ledger and check down balances and on to list of debtors.

10. Check totals of balances (debit and credit) to control account. Ascertain that control accounts are regularly maintained.

11. Obtain confirmation of debtors' balances. (*See* p. 99.)

26. The journal. There is a tendency to obviate the use of a journal containing details of extraneous items and no objection can be raised to this where the documents arising in respect of various adjustments are referenced to the various ledgers concerned.

For certain matters however the auditor should request that a journal, or its equivalent, with supporting vouchers should be used, transfers direct between various accounts being deprecated as transfers may easily be made as between revenue and capital accounts. Adjustments on accounts should be dealt with via the journal, and in particular regarding allowances made. Such allowances granted to customers or others must be examined carefully by the auditor since if a sum of money should be misappropriated, the matter might easily be concealed by the credit to the account of an allowance or discount.

Any allowances, therefore, shown in accounts should be properly dealt with through the journal or other book kept for the purpose, supported by records properly authenticated.

27. The nominal ledger.

(a) *Sub-division.* The nominal ledger may be further sub-divided by the keeping of a private ledger where accounts may be maintained of a nature not to be made readily available to members of staff.

(b) *Examination of accounts.* The items comprising the postings to this ledger will have been vouched at their origin, but in certain cases the information contained within accounts will necessitate further investigation. For example, the postings in respect of directors' salaries will have been vouched in the cash book, but whether the amounts paid are in accordance with directors' agreements will necessitate authentication by consulting the audit notebook, where details of such agreements should be shown.

In addition to checking the postings and casting the various accounts, the auditor should examine their contents. Any transfers between accounts here should be journalised with authenticating documents.

(c) *Prepayments and accruals.* When examining the accounts, adjustments required due to prepayments and accruals will be apparent, and it will be necessary to check these. This aspect of the work is dealt with in Chapter VII concerning the verification of balance sheet items. (S.A.P. *see* p. 63.)

PROGRESS TEST 4

1. When dealing with detailed aspects of the audit, what is the first matter to which the auditor should pay attention? **(1)**

2. Why is there unusual difficulty in the auditing of cash receipts? **(1)**

3. Why is it essential that a rough cash book should be maintained? **(1)**

4. Is there any usefulness in checking counterfoils of receipts issued? **(2)**

5. What is implied by the expression "teeming and lading?" **(3)**

6. How may teeming and lading be prevented? **(3)**

7. Why is discount allowed of particular interest to the auditor? (4)

8. State the audit procedures involved in rents receivable and investment income. (5, 6)

9. Of what importance is the *Cheques Act, 1957*, to the auditor? (9)

10. In what way is the auditor's work influenced by the omission of bought ledgers? (9)

11. Enumerate the procedures required in auditing the work involved in employee remuneration. (10–12)

12. What specific points should the auditor pay attention to when auditing the wages paid to (a) time rate workers (b) piece work employees? (11, 12)

13. What matters of internal check should operate regarding petty cash? (14)

14. "Petty cash is not of great importance and therefore little attention should be paid to it when auditing." Criticise this statement. (15)

15. In what ways is the auditor's work influenced by the use of slip systems instead of bought day books? (16)

16. To what points should the auditor pay attention when vouching invoices? (16)

17. Why is the goods received book of particular importance to the auditor? (16)

18. Why should the auditor be particularly concerned with purchases returns? (17)

19. When sales day books are omitted, in what way does this influence the work of the auditor? (20)

20. What are "cut-off" procedures? (20)

21. Why are "cut-off" procedures of vital concern to the auditor? (20)

22. What goods should the auditor pay special attention to, so as to ensure that they are excluded from stock? (21)

23. What should the auditor insist upon with regard to inter-account transfers? (25)

SPECIMEN QUESTIONS

1. Explain what is meant by a "carry over" fraud.

How would you, as auditor, endeavour to detect such a fraud?

What internal check procedures would you advocate in order to minimise the risk of this type of fraud?   *C.A.*

2. (a) Summarise briefly the provisions of the *Cheques Act, 1957*.

   (b) Indicate the extent to which routine auditing procedure was affected by this legislation. *C.C.A.*

3. How would you verify the following items appearing in the cash book of a limited company:

(a) Agents' and travellers' commissions.
(b) Customs duties paid.
(c) Directors' expense allowances.
(d) Rent received? C.A. (E.W.)

4. Detail the points which you consider would render a voucher inadequate for the purposes of the audit of a limited company's accounts.   Give two examples of inadequate vouchers and detail the procedure you would adopt to verify the items in the accounts to which these vouchers relate. C.C.A. (Inter.)

5. State the advantages and disadvantages of "test-checking" and describe what factors must be taken into consideration by an auditor when deciding upon the extent of the "test-check" to be made. C.C.A. (Inter.)

6. Having been appointed auditor of East Coast Engineers Ltd., a company employing large numbers of men both on time rates and on piece-work, state the procedure you would adopt in test-checking the calculation and payment of wages.   It may be presumed that an adequate system of internal check is in force. C.A.

7. You are auditor of a company employing some fifty employees.   State the points to which you would direct particular attention when examining employees' national insurance cards. C.A. (E.W.)

8. A manufacturing company, of which you are the auditor, employs some 250 persons.   The factory workers are paid weekly. About 40 are paid on an hourly basis and the remainder at piece-work rates.   Management and office staffs are paid monthly.

State the steps you would take to check the payroll and the wages records. C.A. (E.W.)

9. You wish to provide your audit staff with practical guidance as to the matters that they should include in their enquiry into, and observations of, the arrangements made by clients with regard to the safe custody, control and recording of cash received.

Draw up a form of questionnaire suitable for this purpose. C.A. (E.W.)

10. In the course of your audit of the accounts of a limited company you find that:

(a) Forward contracts are made for the supply of particular materials.
(b) The purchases ledger contains a number of debit balances.
State concisely what inquiries you would make in each case. C.A. (E.W.)

CHAPTER V

MECHANISED ACCOUNTING

MECHANISED ACCOUNTING

Although mechanised systems have basically similar methods of use, nevertheless there are slight variations in their operation and design, it is essential, therefore, for the auditor to acquaint himself personally with the system which he is to audit.

1. Installation of system. If he is consulted on the installation of the system at the outset, valuable co-operation may exist between the auditor and client whereby the system may be applied not only for the efficient running of the business but also to assist the auditor in carrying out his duties, so eliminating work in unnecessary checking. For example, often an additional carbon copy can be taken of various aspects of the work, such as pre-lists of ledger postings, which may be used for audit purposes.

2. Vital need of internal check. The danger in the installation of mechanised systems is to be so concerned with its efficient and economical working that the matter of an internal check is overlooked. The auditor should therefore pay particular attention to this aspect of the internal control system, and if satisfied in this respect, and with regard to the arithmetical accuracy of the records (which may be proved by means of control records), then he may concern himself more particularly with vouching from prime documents direct to ledgers.

Control systems must constitute a form of internal check and not merely rely upon a control account proving the mechanical accuracy of the machine. Work should be suitably sub-divided amongst staff, the most common illustration being that of the pre-listing and totalling of invoices by one operator and the posting of these by another.

3. All-purpose machines. Using an all-purpose machine for illustrative purposes, the pre-listing and totalling of sales invoices should be carried out by one operator, possibly on a separate adding-listing machine, these then being passed to the machine operator who in one operation prepares the ledger account and statement at the same time as compiling the figures for the control account. A method of *double pick-up* is operated whereby the recording of the opening balance is checked, affording a safeguard against the bringing forward of an incorrect balance and by throwing out a nil figure at the end if correct. The figure for the total amount of postings, which is stored in the machine, should agree with the original pre-list, the total figures being used for inclusion in the sales account in the normal ledger.

From such it may be seen that the arithmetical accuracy of the figures should not be in doubt. The auditor should therefore be more closely concerned with items making up the pre-lists. Similar processes apply with regard to the posting of purchases invoices and the recording of cash items.

4. Sub-division of work. A particular type of error likely to arise is that of the mis-posting of items. Due to the use of code numbers this is more likely to arise than under the use of manual methods, and from the auditor's point of view, is more difficult to detect, for despite the seriousness of the error, the details may be put through the whole system, whilst at the same time relevant control accounts would still agree. The sub-division of work should do much to obviate this, whilst it serves to emphasise the attention the auditor should pay to original records.

5. Variations in the system. Should the system be varied in any way, the alteration should be fully examined by the auditor. The method employed in the correction of errors should be ascertained. Where operators are allowed to do this, there is considerable danger of *defalcation*, and the auditor should request that an adjustment journal be maintained, but if this is not kept he should ascertain whether every adjustment is verified at the time of the adjustment by a responsible official. Furthermore, the work entailed in maintaining an adjustment journal could be kept to a minimum by the filing of relevant documents or slips in respect of adjustments made.

6. The danger of fraudulent manipulation. It is felt that fraud may be facilitated by the use of mechanised systems. This is not considered to be the case provided suitable safeguards are instituted. Some of these have been mentioned, others arise from the nature of system itself, *e.g.*:

(a) The rigid application of internal control and check systems. Where "general purpose" machines are used by one operator, an internal check system must be laid down at the commencement and strictly maintained.

(b) The difficulty of alterations of records. To alter records may mean the reproduction of complete sheets, but on the other hand some machines can be manipulated regarding total figures.

(c) The necessity of collusion where a sound system of internal check prevails. This type of fraud would necessitate the manipulation of such an area of the whole system that access would be difficult to obtain.

(d) Likewise, where systems are properly installed and audited, it would require considerable knowledge in the manipulation by those likely to perpetrate such fraud whilst not engaged on the actual work. But where such systems have been in operation for some time, it is possible to gain such a knowledge.

SPECIFIC AUDIT DIFFICULTIES

In the Institute of Chartered Accountants' publication, *Mechanised Accounting and the Auditor*, a section is devoted to "Specific audit difficulties," wherein the following matters dealt with briefly here are explained more fully.

7. The elimination of books of prime entry. Slip systems have been mentioned earlier (*see* p. 58). Original documents are utilised whereby day books are obviated.

If documents are numbered serially, the number may be used for cross-referencing purposes with ledger accounts and otherwise. If these are suitably pre-listed and totalled and the resulting batches of documents are again serially numbered, the tracing back of items should be facilitated. Likewise, the totalling of such batches for the purpose of sectional balancing is advantageous.

It follows that the operation of efficient filing systems are essential for the subsequent checking of records.

8. The use of code numbers. These may be used extensively under machine accounting systems and clients' staff may not experience difficulty in identifying these due to their constant use of them. The auditor on the other hand may find his work made difficult due to the lack of narrative, particularly in the checking of nominal accounts.

Whilst there is no easy remedy to this, the auditor's work may be facilitated as follows:

(a) On the commencement of his work he should acquaint himself with the system under which the code references are applied. Code numbers are usually allocated on a specified basis and broken down under various sections.

(b) He should be supplied with clearly referenced lists for his use on the audit.

(c) In particular instances he should request that the narrations should be appended to entries such as those in certain nominal ledger accounts. The advantage to the client should be pointed out as to these narrations in accounts. Some more obvious entries, such as those in the sales account need not be in narrative form.

(d) Specially designed stationery carrying headings as to the nature of the details given on them should be advocated.

9. The composition of ledger balances. From the auditor's standpoint, the composition of ledger account columns is most important. Where mechanised systems are used, there may not exist an easily identifiable method of applying debits against credits. This may cause serious difficulty in analysis of the make-up of balances when the auditor is concerned with:

(a) Bad and doubtful debts.

(b) The veracity of the amount shown as outstanding.

(c) The constitution of nominal ledger accounts where transfers are put through from one account to another.

The auditor has the advantage here when requesting the undermentioned matters of being able to point out to his client the danger inherent in leaving balances in an inexplicable state. He should request therefore that the items should be cross-referenced by code symbol to the items on the other side of the account. It should be part of the normal accounting procedure to identify the composition of balances at relevant dates.

The Institute's recommendation covers the employment of

query or *credit control* staff to be employed on this where the amount of the work involved warrants it.

10. Absence of normal ledger accounts. For the method of employing systems where payment is made direct against documents (*see* p. 58).

It is obvious that for this sytem to prove satisfactory from not only the auditor's point of view but also in the interest of effective working, it is essential that there should be efficient filing, the maintenance of control accounts, and where "the complexity and value of the transactions are considerable," the maintenance of normal ledger accounts.

11. Misuse of accounting terms. Where control accounts are maintained, it should be ascertained that they constitute control accounts in the accounting sense, and not merely prove mechanical accuracy. This has been mentioned above (*see* p.76).

Due to the method of operation of machines covering positive and negative, the terms *credit* and *debit*, are sometimes used in ways likely to lead to misunderstanding. It really rests with the auditor here to make himself so thoroughly acquainted with the system tht he may make recommendations regarding the operation of the system which will obviate any misunderstandings likely to arise.

PUNCHED CARD ACCOUNTING

12. Difference from all-purpose machines. Punched-card accounting systems differ fundamentally from the all-purpose type of accounting machine, for in the latter case the machine is similar to a typewriter in its effect of printing the information at once on to the final records, whereas punched-card accounting machines, whilst finally printing the information fed into the machine in the first instance, only produces holes at intervals on a card.

13. Punching-on information. The holes punched may be read from the card since the cards are pre-printed and subdivided under various headings. This would only be used for examination purposes, however, since it can only be done slowly, and the punching may be checked much more quickly and efficiently by means of a verifier.

14. Verifying the punching. As the whole system is mechanised from the first punching of the information on the cards, it is essential that the original information shall be punched correctly. To check this, the only human activity, the cards, after their first punching pass to a second operator. who, from the original documents, re-punches the cards, Any difference in the punching is revealed by two round holes being punched over the original oval hole. It is not necessary, however, to examine the cards visually, as, when put through the sorter a coloured card will automatically be inserted where any difference arises. In some cases the verifier when punched differently will automatically lock, so revealing the difference.

15. Automatic sorting and printing. Once the holes have been punched on to the cards they may be sorted into any order required for statistical as well as accounting purposes.

The actual printing of invoices, statements, etc., is carried out automatically by the tabulator when the cards are put through the machine.

16. Auditor's duties. From the foregoing it is apparent that, being automatic, whatever is put into the machine in the first place will go right through the system, *e.g.*, printing the sales invoice to the monthly statement and to the total sales for posting to the sales account and for the sales control account. The auditor should, therefore:

(a) Verify the soundness of the internal check system, ensuring that the *original* documents are dealt with by the machine operators.

(b) Ensure that the lists of documents are pre-listed and added *e.g.*, on a simple adding listing machine.

(c) Ascertain that all original punching is checked from the original documents on the verifier.

(d) Select a number of cards and request the operator to put them through the machine, thereby testing the punching with the information revealed on the original documents.

(e) Test all sections of the work as in (d) above. The auditor should concern himself particularly with the purchases and sales control accounts, the balances shown on the control accounts being compared with the list of balances.

(f) Check the nominal ledger accounts in detail.

PROGRESS TEST 5

1. What is the particular danger likely to arise on the installation of a mechanised system of accounting? (2)

2. Illustrate briefly the work carried out on an *all purpose* accounting machine. (3)

3. When machine accounting systems are varied, what should the auditor do? (5)

4. Is there greater chance of fraudulent manipulation by the use of machines than by normal accounting methods? (6)

5. In what ways may the danger of fraud be obviated in the use of mechanical systems? (6)

6. Mention specific audit difficulties encountered in the use of machine accounting. (7)

7. How may the difficulties mentioned in *6* above be overcome? (7–9)

8. In what ways does punched-card accounting differ from the other types of machine accounting? (12)

9. Explain briefly the methods employed in punched-card accounting. (13–15)

10. What are the auditor's duties regarding punched-card accounting? (16)

SPECIMEN QUESTIONS

1. In auditing the accounts of a company having a fully mechanised accounting system (but not utilising punched cards) what are:

(a) The main difficulties peculiar to such a system.

(b) The safeguards available to overcome these difficulties.

(c) The special points to which attention should be directed?
C.A.

2. The accountant of a company has asked you, as auditor, to examine his draft instructions for the operation of a system of mechanised accounting (not punched cards) which is being installed in the sales ledger section.

Set out the matters which would have your particular attention both as regards internal control and the conduct of the audit.
C.A. (E.W.)

3. Peanuts Ltd., of which company you are the auditor, has converted its sales ledgers from manual to machine methods, employing code numbers in place of names and descriptions.

You are required:

(a) To indicate the difficulties you would expect to meet as the result of the change.

(b) To state how the difficulties might be overcome.

C.A. (E.W.)

4. A limited company of which you are the auditor has recently introduced keyboard accounting machines for the sales ledgers.

State the main points to which you would direct attention when examining the system of internal control. *C.A.* (*E.W.*)

5. Describe in detail the procedure you would adopt in the audit of the purchase day book and bought ledger of a company employing a mechanised system of accounts. *C.C.A.* (*Inter.*)

6. It is not infrequently stated that the institution of a system of mechanised accounts increases the possibility of fraud. State the arguments for and against the validity of this statement. *C.C.A.*

7. You are auditor of a company which carries out a large volume of small transactions and, at present, has a staff of six book-keepers who keep a manual set of books. Your client asks you whether their system should be mechanised and you are required to draft a report stating the factors to be borne in mind when making a decision. *C.C.A.*

8. Discuss:

(*a*) Modern trends in auditing practice.

(*b*) The contention that the installation of a mechanical accounting system will increase the possibility of fraud. *C.C.A.*

9. Discuss briefly the special features which arise in the audit of accounts kept by a punched card system. *C.A.* (*E.W.*)

10. Explain the special problems with which an auditor is confronted when dealing with punched-card accounting records and indicate the steps he should take to meet them. *C.C.A.*

CHAPTER VI

ELECTRONIC DATA PROCESSING

1. Co-operation with Management. The increasing use of computers necessitates a knowledge on the part of auditors of the procedures employed in auditing their output and investigating their control. In this chapter some acquaintance with computer techniques is assumed. The methods outlined are of general application, in practise it would be necessary for the auditor to acquaint himself with the facets of the particular installation concerned.

Wherever possible the auditor should be in close consultation with the management from the installation of the machine. In this way he may request the incorporation of various checks which, if put in later, may be expensive to install. Experience may necessitate certain alterations at a later stage, but such can be minimised by early co-operation with management.

In the first instance the auditor should seek to gain an overall picture of the system either operating, or to be operated, and to do this he should request the client to supply him with:

(a) Any data outlining the system such as may be presented by the company installing the system on its installation, or such as may be given to new staff.

(b) Flow charts—if these have not been prepared by the client the auditor may find it most useful to compile his own.

(c) Designations and names of all staff engaged on the various phases of the work.

(d) The instruction manual given to staff engaged on the various stages.

PROCEDURAL CONTROLS

A computer will, subject to breakdown, give the answer required of it, the likelihood of error or fraud will arise from

(a) the feed-in of incorrect information,

(b) incorrect programming.

2. The auditor and internal control. Commencing with procedural controls the auditor will be concerned with generally, internal control and, in particular, internal check.

The auditor should ascertain the efficient operation of the internal control by ensuring that the system provides for:

(a) The control of all input by a section devoted to this (if at all possible).

(b) The control section to be responsible for ensuring that the designated flow of work is complied with and with the authenticity of input.

(c) Operators do not have access to computer files and pro-grammes. Test runs should be the duty of operators and not programmers.

(d) Proper authorisation by a responsible official of all pro-gramme alterations.

(e) Input data is not altered by operators, any queries arising being referred back to the control.

(f) Operators' duties should, if possible, be interchanged subject to safeguards as to work passed from one operator to the next.

3. Control section and log book. The control section should, if possible, be separate from staff engaged on the working of the computer. If such a section exists, the auditor's work may be greatly facilitated subject to his satisfying himself as to the effectiveness of the operation of the section. It should be the duty of the staff to reconcile output with information supplied and also to maintain the computer records. This includes the maintenance of a log book. The information contained in the log book should reveal that:

(a) Correct programmes are used with relevant files.

(b) No unauthorised alterations are made to programmes.

(c) Reconciliations are made with manual totals prepared prior to input.

The auditor should examine the log book, which may be kept in a printed control form, and ensure that it is properly maintained.

4. Original input data control. As computers will only supply accurate information according to that which is fed

D

in, the strictest control should be observed to ensure the correct submission of input data. Such control will involve the use of mechanised devices as mentioned in the previous chapter; this will include the use of a verifier punch in the case of punched cards or duplicate verified tape where paper tape is used. Comparison of pre-list totals with those on processing runs should be made. The computer itself may be made to operate other controls by means of editing (*see* 10 post).

5. Processing controls. The efficient operation of a system of internal check should lead to the operator dealing with the setting up of runs and controlling these whether by console typewriter or by the manual control of switches and dealing with any errors or exceptional items. It is possible for the operator to influence the system. It is, therefore, essential for the auditor to satisfy himself as to the internal check being both clearly defined in writing and properly maintained.

The matters involved include:

(a) Proper recording of work executed referenced to programmes and master files and the maintenance of a computer log.
(b) The recording of action taken on errors or exception reports.
(c) Definite instructions as to the examination and certification by a responsible official at regular intervals of the computer log book.
(d) Strictly enforced rules whereby only computer processing staff may have access to the computer room and whereby only authorised staff may withdraw files from the library.

6. Master file control. Retaining as they do, standing data (*see* 11 (iii) (*a*)), such files have nevertheless to be frequently up-dated, for example, changes in staff will require up-dating in the wages programme. Whilst first ensuring the operation of a sound internal check system operating, the auditor will be particularly concerned to see that the following safeguards are operated to ensure that:

(a) Only authorised staff may incorporate changes.
(b) Detailed print-outs are made for amendments to be checked by the control section.
(c) Amendments are only made on receipt of forms specially printed and serially numbered for the purpose.

(d) Cross checks are made of output with information contained in other departments, such as control accounts compiled from pre-input lists.

(e) Verification of output is made by examination of information produced with identifiable items, *e.g.*, in the case of debtors, balances with monthly statements.

(f) The clear and unambiguous labelling of spools, containers, etc.

(g) Comparison being made of output with information maintained in user departments, for example, print-outs being compared with records maintained of employees in the wages department.

7. Output control. The internal control of interest to the auditor would cover such matters as:

(a) Efficient overall supervision by the control section.

(b) Comparison of output with originating data, *e.g.*, pre-list totals.

(c) Checking that queries have been dealt with properly, and, where errors have been found, that these have been dealt with.

(d) The proper distribution of output to departments and checking with department information as deemed necessary.

8. Stand-by procedures. The auditor will be concerned to ensure the efficient maintenance of internal control, and although it is not so much his concern as to the actual running of the computer, nevertheless, he will be interested to see that a proper standby system is prepared for the event of the break-down by the computer, as records might suffer without a proper system being ready for use on such occasions.

Often, it is of advantage to postpone various operations rather than obtain the use of another computer. Other processes might be carried out manually on an approximate basis, e.g., the payment of set sums for wages, correction being made at a later date.

9. Service bureaux. If the client uses the services available on an "outside" computer, the same controls mentioned above should still be operated in respect of the input and output of data. The procedural controls may be assumed to be effective, subject to the auditor being satisfied that no collusion is possible between the client's staff and those of the bureau. If there is the slightest possibility of this, the auditor will have to investigate the internal check thoroughly.

COMPUTER SYSTEM CONTROLS

Having dealt with the controls to be exercised over the processing operations, we consider those matters of importance to the auditor regarding controls over the actual computer. These include such matters as:

(a) Programme checks within the system.
(b) Adequacy and frequency of print-outs.
(c) Error correcting procedures.

10. Programme checks. Computers may be programmed to incorporate checks of an "editing" nature, and wherever possible, the auditor should request their inclusion from the commencement. These may include:

(a) Limit checks—limits may be set whereby no item may fall outside the limit, *e.g.*, 60 hours working in week.
(b) Validity checks—where punched cards or paper tape are used any malfunctioning due to an operating error, (or breakdown in the machine), is revealed.
(c) Priority checks—these guard against the rendering of incorrect information due, for example, to tape damage.
(d) Reference checks—these may be sub-divided as to:

  (i) Cross referencing. Print-outs may be obtained of each programme as it is brought into use ensuring not only that authorised programmes are used, but also the continuous activity of the machine.
  (ii) Serial numbering of forms. This applies to invoices, cheques, or similar documents. The computer can be made to match the numbers on the pre-numbered forms, so ensuring that no numbers are inserted or withdrawn.
  (iii) New items counts. Where master files are transferred, the number of items on the new file can be counted, so facilitating agreement with old master file and the adjustments made on up-dating.
  (iv) Compiling a log. Where there is an automatic typewriter on the operator's console, any item fed into the machine from the console will be automatically typed, so compiling a log serving as a double check in conjunction with the operator's manual log. The possibility of cutting out the typing exists, but internal check by supervision should obviate this.

11. Print-outs

(a) *Computer output.* These print-outs constitute the end products for which the computer is used, for example:

- (i) Documents of a financial nature, *e.g.*, invoices, orders, accounts, etc.
- (ii) Management control reports. These include statistical, accounting, and other data, as well as "exception" reports, covering overdue accounts, excess stock usage, etc.
- (iii) Print-out of data from master files for computer control.

It may be mentioned that data contained on files may be either

- (i) Standing data—this may be used for repeated operations and includes a certain number of related items, *e.g.*, stock price lists, or
- (ii) Data referring to a particular transaction, *e.g.*, number of hours worked.

(b) *Auditor's examination of print-outs.* It will be necessary for the auditor to ensure that the information contained on the files is kept up-to-date and regularly printed out and verified with the items to which it refers, for example, comparison of stock figures with balances held. This will involve his examination both of the print-outs and the internal control operated.

Provided the overall internal control is efficiently operated the auditor need only make some checks on the most important matters, but he must see that such information is *available* for examination.

As master files are of particular interest to the auditor he may reasonably ask the client to have special print-outs made of matters which are his particular concern, such as lists of debtors' or creditors' ledger accounts for the purpose of examining the make-up of certain accounts. He may also request certain tests be made to ascertain whether master files have been properly brought up-to-date.

(c) *Test packs.* Print-outs may be obtained by the use of test packs which are used for the purpose of testing programme controls. These consist of punched cards, paper tape, or whatever input media is used. They are expensive to prepare, requiring as they do a detailed knowledge of the procedures and considerable time in their preparation; furthermore, the information they produce may involve considerable work in translating for audit purposes.

The actual method of testing involves the introduction of specified transactions into the operations involved and checking the results with previously prepared information. If they are available the auditor may use them to good advantage, but for the auditor to insist on the production of these would seem unjustifiable in normal circumstances in view of the difficulties mentioned above, especially as other methods of testing the operation of the procedures are available.

(d) *Random tests.* Having made exhaustive enquiries and various tests on taking up the audit, thereafter the auditor may confine his testing rather more to items of special importance carried out on a random sampling basis. For example, the retention of a payroll print-out for a selected week may be retained and compared with a selected week later on, investigation being made as to the differences which have arisen within the period.

The computer itself may be usefully applied to select certain items at mathematically formulated intervals with the elimination of less important items. For example, with regard to debtors' ledger balances, the balances below a certain amount may be omitted, with a selection being made of the remainder, while at the same time for control account purposes the total of all the balances, both selected and omitted, may be obtained.

(e) *Stopping and re-starting the computer.* To ensure that no unauthorised change is made between stopping and re-starting the computer, the auditor should request that print-outs be made on stopping and on re-starting the computer. In order to ascertain that none of the required print-outs are omitted, he should examine the log book to see that all such operations are accounted for.

12. **Error correcting procedures.** Where the computer reveals the fact of errors arising, it is usual to have it reject these. The process of correction, however, may prove expensive if the system is interrupted; it is usual, therefore, to deal with such errors manually. For example, if a mistake is made in an employee's wage, this is prepared manually to correct the error, but it is necessary to feed-in the correct information to bring the record up-to-date, care being taken to obviate the payment being made twice.

If errors are discovered prior to feed-in, it may be sent back for correction and re-presentation. If, however, incorrect information has been fed in it may be allowed to continue through the system, being marked for examination prior to despatch to the relevant department.

The auditor will be concerned to see that the internal control operating is efficiently maintained to ensure that the records are properly recorded, checked and cleared by the control section.

PROGRESS TEST 6

1. By what means should the auditor seek to gain an overall picture on first commencing an audit involving a computer? (1)

2. For what matters should an efficient system of internal control provide? (2)

3. What information of interest to the auditor would be normally found in a computer log book? (3)

4. Specify the main aspects of internal check covering processing controls. (5)

5. What procedures should be operated with regard to the safeguarding of master files? (6)

6. Are there any controls which may be exercised over output? (7)

7. Are stand-by procedures of any interest to the auditor? (8)

8. Enumerate the controls which may be incorporated in the computer of an "editing" nature. (10)

9. In what ways are print-outs of interest to the auditor? (11(b))

10. It has been advocated that auditors should make extensive use of test-packs. Do you agree with this statement? (11(c))

11. To what information may the auditor apply random tests? (11(d))

12. By what means may correction of errors be carried out? (12)

See Appendix I for Developments of Auditing Techniques and Specimen Questions.

CHAPTER VII

VERIFICATION OF BALANCE SHEET ITEMS

INITIAL PROCEDURE

1. Verification of existence of assets. After having vouched the entries in the books the auditor may be satisfied as to the authenticity of the transactions by which assets may have been acquired or liabilities incurred, but his examination thus far will not have proved the existence of the actual items, nor, in the case of assets, of their being held by the body concerned.

An audit, consisting as it does mainly of the examination of the books, accounts and vouchers of an establishment, it is easy for the auditor to lose sight of the more practical aspect of the work, but to omit to verify the existence of assets or liabilities is to run the risk of being liable to damages for negligence in the execution of his work, as was held in the case of *London Oil Storage Co. Ltd.* v. *Seear, Hasluck & Co.* (1904) (*see* p. 227).

In a number of instances it will be possible for the auditor to inspect the assets personally, but where documents are held by those likely to hold them in the normal course of business, such as solicitors or banks, a relevant certificate may be obtained.

2. Precautionary measures. Certain general precautions have to be taken in order to ascertain that there is no manipulation of assets whereby the absence of certain items may be covered. For example, where a number of petty cash floats are maintained, the auditor should insist on the production of all the balances held at one time. Likewise, where verification takes place after the balance sheet date and various items, such as current assets, have changed since the closing date, then the transactions resulting in the change will have to be vouched back in order to verify the item at the original date.

3. Disposal of assets. Where assets are disposed of, the auditor should vouch the authority in writing authorising the sale and he should ascertain that the amount received on disposal is adequate and is likewise approved. Great care should be exercised here as there is a possibility for those having authority in any department to dispose of assets, before their condition warrants, to outsiders, with whom agreement may be reached for the payment of a commision or of the private payment of part of the price.

VERIFICATION OF ASSETS

4. Goodwill. Goodwill may arise on the purchase of a business, and where this is so, the original agreement on acquisition of the liabilities and assets concerned should be available. On the other hand, goodwill may be created on the retirement of a partner in a firm, again, the relevant agreement affecting the transactions should be inspected.

Goodwill may be written off and where this has been done and it is proposed to restore goodwill or to increase its value as shown on the balance sheet by an amount already written off, no objection can be raised to this, *e.g.*, *Stapley* v. *Read Bros. Ltd.* (1924) (*see* p. 175).

5. Patents. Patents may be taken out only by individuals and in most cases have a life of sixteen years. Where corporate bodies are concerned, patents may be acquired by assignment only and when examining actual patents, the auditor should also ascertain that it has been properly transferred by means of a registered assignment.

In certain companies a comparatively large number of patents may be held, in which case the auditor should request that a list giving details of the patents, including their expiry dates, is compiled. If such a schedule is kept up to date, much of the auditor's time may be saved.

Renewal certificates should be examined, as failure to renew will allow the patent to lapse, and where any have lapsed the auditor should ascertain that this has been agreed by those responsible.

6. Trade marks. Certificates are issued in respect of trade marks by the Patent Office if registered direct; where obtained by transfer it should be properly assigned, the auditor should therefore examine the document applicable. The costs incurred in obtaining the trade mark may be capitalised as an asset and the expenses, whether on assignment or in designing and registering, should be checked.

7. Copyrights. Under the *Copyrights Act, 1956*, a copyright subsists until the end of fifty years after the year in which the author dies, or in the case of films, recordings or works other than those of a literary nature, until fifty years after the year in which the publication first took place.

Where the client is the author there should be a signed copy of the contract available for inspection. If he has assigned the copyright he will normally retain a copy of the contract giving details of the terms on which the copyright has been assigned. The auditor should then vouch any documents received when royalties are paid by the publisher.

If a copyright has been purchased, then the assignment should be examined and compliance with the terms as to payment of royalties, etc., checked.

8. Land and buildings. The responsibilities of the auditor here are as follows:

(a) *Freehold property.*

    (i) *Examination of title deeds.* Where freehold property is owned, the title deeds should be inspected. The auditor need only be satisfied that they appear to be in order, since it is for the legal advisers of the organisation concerned to deal with the actual validity of title. However, there are obvious facts with which the auditor should be conversant, such as, that the sequence of deeds is complete and that the last conveyance duly passes the title to his client.

    If the title deeds have been deposited with a bank or a solicitor for safe custody, he should obtain a certificate to this effect, requesting that he should be notified if they are held under any charge or lien. Where property has been mortgaged, then the title deeds will be held by the mortgagee or his representative from whom a certificate should be obtained.

    If there are a number of deeds covering various titles, rather than inspect them on every audit, much time may be saved if they are carefully inspected and immediately thereafter are sealed in the auditor's presence. Subsequently, they may be inspected *en bloc* by examination of the unbroken seals.

(ii) *Registered land.* Increasingly, land is being registered under the *Land Registration Acts*, and where this is so, the *Land Registry Certificate* should be inspected, noting any incumbrances thereon as well as examining the details mentioned above with regard to deeds of title. The certificate is dated and may be returned to the Registry for the purpose of bringing up to date. Therefore if the auditor feels it is necessary to investigate further, he may request that the certificate be sent back for this purpose.

If a certain part of the freehold is leased, a so-called *freehold ground rent* is receivable. The auditor should examine the counterpart of the lease, taking note of its expiration date as well as the amount receivable from the lessee, at the same time the due receipt of the freehold ground rent on the relevant dates should be checked.

(iii) *Depreciation.* Due to the increase in property value, (*see* VIII) it is not usual nowadays to provide for depreciation of properties. This may in some instances take place, but is not legally necessary.

(b) *Leasehold property.*

(i) *Leases granted.* The title deeds should be inspected and thereafter the counterpart of the lease should be examined, noting the details of the ground rent receivable.

(ii) *Leases acquired.* Leases may be acquired direct from the owner of the freehold or by assignment, the auditor should examine the lease, and if so acquired, the assignment thereof, noting the terms of the lease and its expiry date. Compliance by the client with the terms of the lease, such as the agreed rent on the due date, should be ascertained, for noncompliance may involve forfeiture.

(c) *Sub-tenants.* If property has been sub-let, whether in respect of a freehold or a leasehold property, the agreement should be examined and note taken of the rent receivable, due receipt of which should be checked.

9. Plant and machinery.

(a) *Vouching and inspection.* The original invoices from the suppliers should be vouched where possible. If on taking up a new audit these cannot be produced, the auditor will have to check back from the records available. Furthermore, in the case of a new audit, it has proved most useful in practice to actually inspect the assets held, for it has been discovered that even income tax allowances have been claimed on assets no longer held. Such inspection should be carried out at intervals deemed necessary by the auditor, and in any case of doubt.

Where plant registers are maintained the verification of the assets is greatly facilitated, as well as the checking of the depreciation written off, and if the number of machines or plant held is of any justifiable total, then the auditor should strongly recommend that such a register be kept if this is not done.

(b) *Retention of own records.* The auditor should retain a list in his working papers of the plant and machinery owned and this should be kept up to date. It should give brief particulars of the number of the machine, date of purchase and depreciation rate. Selected items should then be checked by inspection, and although the auditor may not be expected to value the machines, nevertheless by comparison with the purchase date and the depreciation rate, he may obtain some idea of the expected life of the machine and when verifying the existence of the asset may form his opinion as to the adequacy or otherwise of the depreciation rate.

(c) *Checking accounting entries.* The accounting entries with regard to the plant and machinery account and the depreciation account should be checked with the details as maintained in the plant register and any discrepancies queried.

The cross-checking of the assets actually held with the taxation records has already been touched on above and the list maintained in the audit records should facilitate this. Likewise the insurance cover may prove a useful check, not only for valuation, but also for verification purposes.

10. Loose tools. Stock should be checked each year and the auditor should examine the original stock sheets. Where a proper system of requisitioning is in operation, the auditor should test check a number of items ascertaining that loose tools are returned to stock if it is possible to re-use them. The consumption of loose tools will no doubt vary from year to year, but any abnormal consumption should be accounted for by such matters as increased production or a change in production methods.

11. Furniture, fittings and office equipment. In verifying the existence of the furniture and fittings of a business no great difficulty may arise in the case of a small business, but in larger organisations the auditor should request the maintenance of adequate records. These need not be so detailed as in the case of plant and machinery, and furthermore, as the acquisition and disposal is not so frequent, the maintenance of up-to-date records should not be an onerous task.

With regard to office machinery, records similar to that of a plant register are justified, care being taken to ensure that the numbers of all machines are shown. The expense involved on certain types of machines will justify actual inspection of selected items from time to time.

The remarks with regard to plant and machinery are applicable here as to ascertaining that due authority for purchase and sale of items is obtained in writing, although the risk of any collusion with outside purchasers is less likely in these cases.

12. Motor vehicles. Where the number of vehicles held justifies it, records similar to those of a plant register should be maintained. If this is not kept, full details of make, year, registration numbers, etc., should be shown in the ledger accounts, subdivided as to transport vehicles, travellers' cars, directors' cars, etc.

The auditor should vouch the registration books, noting particularly that the vehicles are registered under the name of the client; where this is not the case, the auditor must be sure to vouch a written statement from the person shown as owner that he has no charge over the vehicle which he confirms is the property of the client.

Acquisition and disposal authorities should be vouched, care being exercised to ensure that no collusion with outside agents exists. It may be mentioned that this type of asset is most vulnerable to such collusion, and the auditor would be wise to ensure that he examines and notes the written authorities and that he queries all cases where he has doubts as to receipts on disposal or as to prices of any second-hand vehicles purchased.

The checking of the assets held with the taxation records is again of relevance.

INTERNAL CONTROL QUESTIONNAIRE

FIXED ASSETS

(A) Acquisitions and disposals

1. Are all applications for capital expenditure required in writing in a specified manner stating, cost, reasons, any items to be replaced, and possible return on capital?
2. List officials who authorise capital expenditure and their authority limits.
3. Is any comparison made with actual and authorised expenditure, and, if so, who is responsible for this?
4. What is the procedure if the authority limit is exceeded?
5. Who authorises work of a capital nature to be carried out by the company's employees?
6. What records are maintained in respect of such work?
7. Who authorises work of repair to capital items, and what is his authority limit?
8. Who authorises the disposal of assets; is any independent check made thereof?
9. Are any inter-company or branch sales made of fixed assets and is any inter-company or branch profit eliminated from the group accounts?
10. Is any reconciliation made between company records and those on the returns to the Inland Revenue in respect of fixed assets?

(B) Depreciation and appreciation

11. Are registers kept in respect of
    (a) plant and machinery,
    (b) motor vehicles,
    (c) other fixed assets? (state which).
12. Who fixes rates in respect of the foregoing for depreciation, or revalues them? (list).

(C) Verification

13. Where are the documents of title retained in respect of
    (a) freehold and leasehold properties,
    (b) motor vehicles?
14. Which officials have access to the foregoing?
15. Is a period inspection made or certification received in respect of these?
16. How often is a physical check made with the records as to fixed assets held, and is this shown on the records concerned?

STANDARD AUDIT PROGRAMME
FIXED ASSETS

(A) *General*

1. Prepare or obtain full details of all fixed assets as to cost, aggregate depreciation and net value, reconcile with figures on previous year's balance sheet.
2. Verify all items of a material sum, and test others, with completion statements, suppliers' invoices, architects' certificates, and costing or other records as to expenditure on works orders, etc.
3. Any additions during year test with authorisations, investigating any marked differences.
4. Investigate the whole procedure with respect to any disposals of material sums, checking authorisation for disposal and the reasonableness of any amounts received.
5. Where inter-company or branch acquisitions have been made, ascertain whether any uplift, and ensure that it is eliminated from the group accounts.
6. Inspect title deeds in respect of freehold and leasehold properties, or inspect seals where inspected previously and sealed, or obtain bankers' certificates with statement as to freedom from lien or charge.
7. Inspect as many fixed assets as deemed necessary and in consideration of their nature, especially any new capital projects, ensuring in the last case the correct allocation between buildings and plant and machinery.
8. In respect of motor vehicles:
   (a) Verify that the registration books are held.
   (b) If any vehicles held in names of employees or others, obtain certificate as to ownership by client.
   (c) Prepare reconciliation of vehicles at opening and closing dates.

(B) *Depreciation*

9. Obtain a list giving details of rates applied to the various classes of assets for permanent file. This list should be checked annually as to suitability of rates in view of prevailing circumstances.
10. Check that all such rates have been properly authorised.
11. Where any change in the basis of calculation of depreciation is made, investigate as to reasonableness and also as to whether this will have to be specially disclosed in the accounts.

13. Debtors. The amounts due from debtors should be verified in the course of the normal audit procedure. The agreement of debtors' schedules with control accounts should be ascertained.

The verification of debtors' balances is considered of such importance as to justify the issue of Recommendation U7 from which the following extracts are taken.

> The auditor will use his individual judgement as to the tests he makes but "in the absence of any similar properly controlled procedure carried out by the company itself, the auditors should consider direct communication with debtors as one of the means by which they can form an opinion as to the adequacy of the system of internal control over sales and its operation in practice. It may also be useful as a check on the accuracy of the cut-off procedures . . . and the test will be useful in ascertaining whether the balances are genuine, accurately stated and not in dispute.
>
> The decision to request the client to carry out a test circularisation of debtors should not be construed as an assumption by the auditors of the directors' duties. Circularisation is essentially an act of the client, who alone can authorise third parties to divulge information to the auditors.
>
> When circularisation is undertaken the method of requesting information from the debtor may be either positive or negative. Under the positive method the debtor is requested to confirm the accuracy of the balance shown or state in what respect he is in disagreement. Under the negative method the debtor is requested to reply if the amount stated is disputed. In either case the debtor is requested to reply direct to the auditor. Both methods may be used in conjunction.
>
> Weak internal control, the suspicion of irregularities or that amounts may be in dispute, or the existence of numerous bookkeeping errors are circumstances which indicate that the positive method is preferable as it is designed to encourage definite replies from those circularised.
>
> Good internal control, with a large number of small accounts, would suggest the negative method as likely to be appropriate. However, in some circumstances, e.g., where there is a small number of large accounts and a large number of small accounts, a combination of both methods, as noted above, may be appropriate.
>
> It is seldom desirable to circularise all debtors and it is therefore necessary to establish an adequate sample, . . . based upon a complete list of all debtor accounts.
>
> The request sent to debtors may be either a specially prepared form of letter or an attachment to the client's normal statement giving a copy of the debtor's ledger account for an appropriate

period and, in the case of a "positive" request, being accompanied by a pre-paid reply form.

14. Loans.

(a) *Ascertaining security.* Where loans are granted, it is usual to require some security to ensure their repayment. Therefore, the auditor, when verifying the loan, should ascertain whether any security has been given, in which case it will also be necessary to verify this, ensuring at the same time that it constitutes an adequate safeguard, being of sufficient value to cover the amount of the loan.

On his first attendance after the loan has been granted the auditor should inspect the documents which have arisen, such as an application for the loan and a receipt for it when it is paid over. A proper authority for granting the loan must be inspected, which in the case of a company should take the form of a resolution passed at a director's meeting, or in the case of a partnership, it should be authorised by all the partners. It should also be ascertained that the terms of the loan have been properly recorded and agreed by both parties.

(b) *Receipt of interest.* Due recepts of interest and repayments should be checked, care being taken to note any deviation from the agreement which might lead to forfeiture of the loan and the right to utilise the security.

Where it is part of the normal course of business to make loans, then the auditor should operate the procedure mentioned above with regard to sales ledger balances, and send requests direct to the borrowers for confirmation of the outstanding debts due.

15. Loans to directors. *The Companies Act, 1948, Section 190* forbids a company from making a loan to any person who is a director or a director of its holding company, or to enter into a guarantee or provide security in connection with a loan. The exceptions are briefly:

(a) Anything done by a subsidiary where the director is a holding company.
(b) Advances to meet expenses for fulfilment of duties.
(c) Where the ordinary business of the company is the lending of money or the giving of guarantees.

There is a proviso with regard to the foregoing, namely, that the loan or guarantee may be given provided:

(a) Prior approval is given at a general meeting where the purposes and amount are disclosed.

(b) If approval is not given at or before the next annual general meeting, the loan or guarantee shall be discharged within six months from the conclusion of the meeting.

The auditor should pay careful attention therefore to any loan to a director to ascertain that the foregoing requirements are complied with.

16. Loans to subsidiary companies. Where it is necessary for the auditor of the holding company to audit this item, no difficulty will arise if he is also auditor of the subsidiary. If he is not, however, he should request certification from the auditors of the other company. As to its soundness, he should use his own judgment on examination of the latest audited accounts of the subsidiary which he should examine when auditing the accounts of the group.

17. Loans on mortgage. The mortgage deed should be inspected and the following matters ascertained:

(a) The mortgagee's name, which should be either that of the client or his nominee. In the latter case the nominee should be requested to confirm that he has no beneficial interest in the mortgage.

(b) The nature of the property mortgaged, which should accord with that of the title deeds accompanying the mortgage.

(c) The details of the loan, as to amount, interest rate and date from which payable.

(d) In the case of a loan made to an employee, there should be an agreement in writing for deduction from salary, if such applies, and a certificate should be obtained as to the agreement of the amount still due at the end of the financial period.

NOTE.

(i) If notes of the foregoing are inserted in the audit notebook and the deeds are deposited for safe custody, a covering certificate will be sufficient for future audits.

(ii) If the registration of title has taken place, particulars of the charge will be shown on the Land Registry Certificate on the relevant charges section.

(iii) The auditor should ascertain that the value of the property is sufficient cover for the loan, and with rising prices in respect of land and property, this should not require re-checking in the case of freehold properties, but he should request that the fire insurance receipt be made available for inspection. In the case of a leasehold property, he should ascertain that the adequacy of the cover is maintained and that the last receipt for the payment of ground rent is available for inspection.

(iv) Where a second mortgage is given as security, the deed should state the prior charge, the title deeds being in possession of the first mortgagee. The auditor should request certificates as to the holding of the deeds from the first mortgagee and also as to his knowledge of the second charge.

18. Loans on security of investments. The procedure for the verification of the investments concerned will follow that described above (*see* **14**).

Valuation of the investments is necessary to ensure that the cover for the loan is adequate.

19. Loans on security of life policies. The auditor should inspect the life policy and the receipt in respect of the latest premium due. Where the policy has not been assigned, confirmation should be requested from the insurance company as to their knowledge of the deposit for the loan. The surrender value should be ascertained which should be sufficient to cover the loan.

20. Loans on guarantees from third parties. Such guarantees in respect of loans must be in writing and the auditor should inspect this and also satisfy himself as to the standing of the third party. It is essential that some provision should be made in order to be able to ensure the guarantor's continuing ability to meet any loss arising, such as the supplying of a bank reference from time to time.

Compliance with the terms of the guarantee should be checked in order to make certain that no provision has been broken which would invalidate the guarantee.

21. Checking investments.

(a) *Adequate recording.* Where holdings of investments are considerable, a proper system of recording of holdings and their acquisition and disposal should be in operation and verification will be facilitated if carried out with reference to these. In any case, the auditor should request that a list be supplied of all holdings with cost and market values shown.

(b) *Retention of documents of title.* Frequently the investments will be held by banks or other recognised institutions from whom certificates should be obtained direct, requesting that the presence of any charges on the documents be stated.

Where the documents are held by the client, the auditor should ensure that he is able to examine all the investments at the one and the same time to obviate any substitution for missing documents, and where any investments are not shown to be held in the name of the client, as in the case of nominee holdings, he should require that a deed of trust be produced.

22. Types of investment. The following are the most common types of investment held:

(a) *Inscribed stocks.* These stocks have now been superceded by registration and the issue of certificates. Any reference to them in students' reference books may be ignored.

(b) *Registered stocks and shares.*

(i) *Verification of title.* Registered stocks and shares imply that the title of the owner has been entered on the register of the company. A certificate under the seal of the company is granted giving details as to the numbers of the shares held and the owner's name. The auditor should examine this.

Where stock has been sold before the close of the financial period but delivery has not been completed, the auditor should examine the certificate still held and the broker's sold note. If delivery has been effected, then the receipt of the proceeds should be ascertained, although this may be shown in the following financial period.

If part of the holding has been sold and the certificate has been handed over but no new certificate has been received, the auditor should request the stockbroker who handled the matter that a new certificate be issued for the balance

On the other hand, when shares have been purchased but no certificate has been received, the auditor should likewise request the stockbroker to issue a certificate for the shares

(ii) *Bonus- and rights-issues.* Where investments are held in companies, bonus issues are sometimes made. It may be difficult for the auditor to know of such matters, but enquiries must be made in order to ensure that any such issues have been duly brought into the books. This will also apply with respect to *rights* issues. Shareholders may be given the right to take up shares at a lower rate than that prevailing on the market.

(iii) *Sale of rights.* Renounceable allotment letters are often forwarded with the notification since if the shareholder does not wish to take up the rights he may renounce the allotment and sell the rights on the market by transfer of the allotment letter duly renounced.

The difficulties arising in such transactions as these from the auditor's point of view must be apparent, since rights could be received and sold without any entries in the books to reveal the transaction. It will be necessary for the auditor to acquaint himself with securities when any movements are likely to take place, and also to make full enquiries with the clients or other stockbrokers.

(c) *Bearer securities.* These must, under the *Exchange Control Act, 1947,* be lodged with an "authorised depository" which normally would be a bank, although they may be deposited with solicitors or insurance companies, stock exchanges, or others. This is required as bearer securities are transferable on delivery and are subject to easy misappropriation.

The auditor should obtain a certificate from the bank, or otherwise, on which is shown the details of the securities concerned and stating that the coupons are attached which it is required shall be surrendered for the purpose of receiving the interest or dividend payable.

In the case of bonds only recently acquired, where the actual certificate or bond has not been received, the auditor should vouch allotment letters and receipts for calls paid to date.

(d) *Tax reserve certificates.* Where these are held by the client they should be examined to see that they are held in the client's name and are not out of date. If they have been deposited with a bank, a certificate should be obtained to that effect.

If the certificates have been surrendered for settlement of tax prior to the attendance of the auditor, the receipt issued by the Inland Revenue should be vouched, the interest credit being checked as to the amount. As the interest is not paid over to the client but is used in reduction of the tax payable, care should be taken to ensure that the sum is duly entered in the taxation account and credited to the profit and loss account as interest received.

(e) *Treasury bills.* As these bills are payable to bearer they are normally deposited with a bank and where this is the case the auditor should obtain a certificate to that effect from the bank, requesting that their value and date be stated and that they are free from any charge.

If they are in the client's possession they should be examined, care being taken to ensure that they are not out of date. Where the bills have matured prior to his attendance, the receipt of the proceeds should be vouched with the bank statement and the bank's notification.

(f) *Investments in building societies.* Where shares or deposits are made in building societies a pass book is issued. The auditor should examine this noting due receipts of interest, but as with bank pass sheets, the deposit book should not be accepted as final evidence but a certificate to be forwarded direct to the auditor should be requested from the building society.

(g) *Loans to local authorities.* The relevant documents stating the terms of the loan should be inspected. A receipt for the loan should be vouched and a certificate should be applied for from the local authority concerned confirming the amount on loan.

INTERNAL CONTROL QUESTIONNAIRE

INVESTMENTS AND INVESTMENT INCOME

(A) Control of investments

1. Are securities held
    (a) as investments,
    (b) on customers' behalf,
    (c) as collatoral for bonus or otherwise?
2. Where are securities held?
3. Are adequate records kept differentiating between own securities and otherwise?

4. Are not less than two responsible officials required to have access at any one time? Name these.
5. Who has control of keys or is otherwise empowered to gain access to the securities?
6. Are requests in writing required before withdrawal of securities is permitted?
7. What procedure ensures that all withdrawals of securities are properly recorded?

(B) *Verification of investments*

8. Are verifications, as to holdings, made regularly by staff?
9. What procedures are operated on verification?
10. Are securities verified compared with securities records?
11. Are verifications made by persons other than those maintaining the securities records, or cash transactions?

(C) *Investment income*

12. Is a record maintained showing the dates on which income is receivable?
13. Are the receipts checked and marked with these records?
14. Is this checking carried out by a person independent of cash receipts duties and security control?
15. By what means is it ensured that notification of rights or bonus issues is received and acted upon?
16. Do the records ensure that dividends are received when sales ex div. or purchases cum div. take place?
17. If securities are sold cum div. and due to non-registration before books are closed the dividends are subsequently received, what procedure operates to ensure such dividends are forwarded to the holder?
18. What procedure is laid down as to receiving income from bearer securities?

STANDARD AUDIT PROGRAMME

INVESTMENTS AND INVESTMENT INCOME

(A) *Investment holdings*

1. Request list of present holding of investments, distinguishing between quoted and unquoted, and reconciling present book value with that on last balance sheet. Request also market value at end date be shown.
2. Verify purchase or sale of investments during year with documentary evidence, *e.g.*, contract notes or agreements.
3. Examine minute book for proper authorisation of purchase or sales.
4. Check list as to market values shown with stock exchange list where quoted. If unquoted, inspect companies' accounts.

5. Enquire as to any material falls in value since end date.
6. Inspect certificates or bonds, ensuring that transfers and declarations of trust are attached in the case of nominee holdings. If deposited with bank, obtain certificate stating in whose name they are registered and whether they are free from lien.

(*B*) *Investment income*. To ensure that all income due is actually received:

1. Where interest fixed, scrutinise to ensure amount due is received.
2. Verify a proportion of the equity holdings as to income received, especially in respect of those purchased or sold during the period. This may be done in conjunction with stock exchange lists or company accounts in respect of unquoted investments. At the same time information should be obtained as to bonus and rights issues during year and where these apply to the companies holding the due receipt of bonus issues or action taken as to rights issues should be investigated.

23. Cash and bank balances.

(a) *Petty cash*. In verifying the amount of petty cash in hand, where more than one balance is maintained it is essential that all of them should be produced simultaneously. If this is not done one balance may be used to make up a missing or deficient balance on another account.

It is not necessary for the auditor to attend on the last day of the financial period, but he may request that any such balances be banked on that date. However, this should not be necessary for he may check through the vouchers for payments since made and verify the balances still in hand on the day of his attendance. Where I.O.U.'s are shown amongst the vouchers he should have these certified by a responsible official. If any of these I.O.U.'s have been outstanding for any length of time he should pay particular attention to them, querying whether they should not rather be regarded as loans and so shown in the accounts.

When verifying petty cash balances through to the date of the audit, the amounts paid over from the main to the petty cash book should be checked.

(b) *Bank balances*. The balances shown on the bank pass-sheets are not sufficient evidence as to the balance at the bank on the final date. Such sheets have been altered and others have been forged from time to time. Although the pass sheets should be checked with the cash book receipts and payments, the auditor should write direct to the bank requesting certification of all balances shown on the books of the bank in the name of the company.

To request the bank to certify all such balances rather than to specify particular accounts is preferable as accounts not shown in the books may be revealed thereby. The auditor should ensure that he receives notification direct from the bank.

(c) *Foreign balances*. In the case of balances held abroad, a certificate should be obtained from the agent concerned.

S.A.P. for Bank reconciliation, *see* p. 48.

24. Deposits including customs duty.

(a) *Exclusion from revenue*. Deposits may be required in a number of instances where a service is supplied, for example, in respect of electricity or telephone charges. Such deposits may easily be overlooked and charged with the amount transferred to the revenue account for the year. Where this is done the business may lose the benefit of a refund on removal or otherise.

The auditor should ensure that the sum is properly segregated on the original bill and is carried forward as a balance, details of the deposit being given on the heading of the account.

(b) *Customs duty*. Deposits in respect of customs duty may represent a considerable amount, and where these are made the auditor should pay careful attention to this matter, especially in view of the fact that the customs authorities do not normally issue receipts for the actual deposits.

The system prevails where goods are subject to duty, they may be left in bonded warehouses from which they are released on payment of the necessary duty. To obviate numerous separate payments and the work involved, a deposit may be made against which the duty is set on release of the goods by the authorities.

(c) *Internal check on customs duty*. The auditor should first ascertain that the internal system with regard to the recording of deposits and subsequent releases is adequtae. He should also obtain a certificate from the authorities with respect to each deposit balance as the authorities are prepared to certify the balance remaining at any date.

Where payment is made in respect of transactions, the customs authorities are prepared to acknowledge the payment and the auditor should request that such acknowledgments be obtained and retained for future examination.

PROPRIETORS' FUNDS AND LIABILITIES

The items included in the balance sheet which require verification in respect of proprietors' funds or amounts due to creditors include the following:

(a) Share capital.
(b) Capital and revenue reserves.
(c) Loan capital.
(d) Liabilities and provisions.

25. Share capital.

(a) *Verification.* The authorised and issued share capital of a business must be shown on the balance sheet as required by the *Companies Act 1948.* The authorised share capital is stated in the Memorandum of the company. Its division into shares of a certain amount and into various classes may be stated in either the *Memorandum* or the *Articles.*

On the occasion of the first audit a note may be made of these particulars in the audit notebook and thereafter any changes may be checked as they arise.

It is not considered necessary for the balances on the share registers to be checked on every audit with the amounts on the share capital and provided the auditor examines the lists of balances maintained by the staff of the business and notes that these total the amount of shares issued, this should be sufficient. But if movements of shares warrant it, a share transfer audit may be undertaken. (*see* p. 190.)

If during the period under review some major capital changes take place, then it will be necessary to check these.

(b) *New issues.* In the case of a new issue the receipt of application and allotment moneys should be vouched and the entries into the relevant accounts checked. If a bonus issue takes place, he should check the entries in the accounts and ensure that the share register balances agree with them.

The minutes in respect of such capital issues should be examined and likewise if any forfeiture of shares takes place, the minutes as well as the adjustments required in the accounts should be checked. If any shares are issued for consideration other than cash, the relevant minutes and the copy of the contract should be examined, ascertaining that the contract has been filed with the Registrar of Companies.

(c) *Redeemable preference shares.* The special treatment to be accorded to this type of capital may be conveniently dealt with in the section concerned with the capital redemption reserve fund (*see* **30**). The matter of dividends payable on such shares is dealt with. (*see* p. 176.)

(d) *Shares issued at a discount.* It is unlikely that the auditor will have much to do with such shares since there are more effective ways of issuing shares than by offering them at a discount, since this in itself would militate against the success of the issue. Nevertheless he should be aware of the clauses contained in the *Companies Act, Section 57*, which specifies that a company may issue such shares provided:

   (i) They are of a class already issued.
  (ii) It has passed a resolution in general meeting to that effect, and obtained the sanction of the court.
 (iii) The resolution specifies the maximum rate of discount.
 (iv) The issue is made more than one year after the company was entitled to commence business.
  (v) The issue is made within one month (or extended time) of the date of the court sanction.

Every prospectus of the issue must show particulars of the discount or as much as has not been written off at the date of the prospectus.

The amount of the discount not written off must be shown in every balance sheet of the company.

26. Capital and revenue reserves. When verifying the various items shown on the balance sheet, the auditor will not be so much concerned with the amounts set aside to reserves from the point of view of prudent policy or otherwise, he will be concerned, however, to see that such items reflect a true and fair view as to what has taken place, and also that, where applicable, certain requirements of the *Companies Act 1967* are complied with.

27. Classification of reserves. Before dealing more specific-ally with various types of reserve, the following extract from the Institute of Chartered Accountants' publication, *Terms used in the Published Accounts of Limited Companies* is apposite:

(a) The descriptions CAPITAL RESERVE(S) and REVENUE RESERVE are normally appropriate as headings to groups of reserves or as descriptions of single items.

(b) The expression CAPITAL RESERVE is appropriate for a reserve which for statutory reasons or because of the provisions of the memorandum or articles of association of a company or for other legal reasons is not free for distribution through the profit and loss account.

(c) The expression CAPITAL RESERVE may also be applied to any other reserve which although legally distributable is regarded by the directors as not available for distributon through the profit and loss account at the date of the balance sheet.

(d) Subject to any provision in the articles of association prescribing another name, it will normally be appropriate to describe a reserve as GENERAL to distinguish it from another reserve specifically described, or in the case of a revenue reserve to distinguish it from the profit and loss account balance.

(e) The description RESERVE FUND is not appropriate unless the reserve is represented by specifically earmarked investments (or other assets) realisable as and when required at not less than the amount of the "reserve fund." Exceptions arise from the statutory requirement to describe a "capital redemption reserve fund" as such and from any provision of the memorandum or articles of association, or other instrument constituting or regulating a company, requiring a reserve to be described as a "fund."

28. Distinction between capital and revenue reserves. The distinction made between Capital and Revenue Reserves is not required under the *Companies Act, 1967*, but the aggregate amounts of reserves and provisions must be shown and any material movements thereon. Although amounts may be set aside to capital reserves for reasons such as in accordance with the articles of a company, it is possible, however, to transfer amounts so set aside back to a revenue reserve for subsequent distribution.

Concerning the various types of reserve which may be created, the following matters are of particular interest to the auditor. He should ascertain either that the legal requirements have been observed or that the reserves comply with the articles of the company.

29. Share premium account. When shares are issued at a premium, it is a requirement of *Section 56* of the *Companies Act 1948* that the amount received in respect of the premium shall be placed to the credit of a share premium account and shown as a separate item on the balance sheet. The same section specifies that the share premium account may only be used for the following purposes:

(a) In paying up unissued shares of the company to be issued to the members as fully paid bonus shares.

(b) In writing off preliminary expenses.

(c) In writing off the expenses of, or the commission paid or discount allowed on, any issue of shares or debentures.

(d) In providing for the premium payable on redemption of any redeemable preference shares or debentures.

30. Capital redemption reserve fund (and redeemable preference shares). A capital redemption reserve fund may arise on the redemption of redeemable preference shares. Such shares may be issued by a company if so authorised by its Articles, provided that

(a) No such shares shall be redeemed except out of profits available for dividend, or out of the proceeds of a fresh issue of shares made for the purpose.

(b) At the date of redemption the shares must be fully paid.

(c) Where any such shares are redeemed otherwise than out of the proceeds of a fresh issue, there shall, out of profits which would otherwise have been available for dividend, be transferred to a reserve fund, to be called the *capital redemption reserve fund*, a sum equal to the nominal amount of the shares redeemed, and the provisions of this Act relating to the reduction of the share capital of a company shall, except as provided in this section, apply as if the capital redemption reserve fund were paid up share capital.

(d) Any premium payable on redemption must have been provided, before the redemption, out of profits, or out of the company's share premium account.

If so desired, the capital redemption reserve fund may be used for the purpose of paying up unissued shares of the company to be issued as fully paid bonus shares to the members

If new shares are issued for the purposes of redemption of the old shares, no *ad valorum* stamp duty will be payable provided the old shares are redeemed within one month of the issue of the new shares: *Section 58, Companies Act 1948.*

The *Companies Act, 1967*, Schedule 2, requires disclosure of

"any part of the issued capital that consists of redeemable preference shares, the earliest and latest dates on which the company has power to redeem those shares, whether those shares must be redeemed in any event or are liable to be redeemed at the option of the company, and whether any (and if so, what) premium is payable on redemption."

31. Reserve funds. In the quotation from the Institute of Chartered Accounts' publication given above, it will be observed that the description reserve fund should normally be applied only to such reserves where the profits which they represent have been applied in the purchase of investments earmarked specially for the purpose.

The auditor is particularly concerned with such reserve funds since, although there is no statutory requirement as to the specific investment of funds set aside out of profits for a particular purpose, often such conditions are required under a deed or in accordance with a provision in the memorandum or articles of a company. The most common of these being the *debenture redemption reserve fund.*

32. Debenture redemption reserve fund.

(a) *Funds available for redemption.* This type of reserve is frequently met, for where debentures are redeemable, in certain circumstances, as specified in the debenture deed, or more particularly on a specified date, it is a matter of expediency to ensure that the necessary funds are available as required. This being stated in the deed the auditor should make himself conversant with the terms of the deed and should satisfy himself that its requirements are carried out. If the sums set aside are to be invested in specially earmarked securities, the auditor should ascertain that this is being done. He should also be satisfied that the sums set aside are adequate having regard to the redemption date.

Such matters as the amounts to be invested and the rate of yield to be received are calculated prior to issue of the debentures to ensure that with interest received on the investments the necessary sum due on redemption will be forthcoming.

(b) *Redemption*. Where debentures are redeemed during their life-time and investments are realised for the purpose, the auditor should ascertain that any profits or losses arising on realisation or on the redemption of the debentures is carried to the reserve fund and are not to the general profit and loss account.

On redemption of the debentures, the nominal value of the debentures redeemed, or if on final redemption, the balance shown on the reserve fund account should be transferred to a general reserve as the profits the fund represent will have been absorbed into the general assets of the business.

33. Company taxation. The institution of corporation tax has simplified the presentation of the liability to taxation of companies. Normally, it may be expected that a company where liable will show a figure under its current liabilities, although if not agreed with the Inland Revenue, it should more correctly be shown as a provision. To prevent undue fluctuations a reserve for the equalisation of taxation charges may be created, and this is mentioned as to its presentation in the *2nd Schedule*, para. 7A of the *Companies Act, 1967*, shown below.

The auditor will need to ascertain that the amounts provided for taxation are adequate which will involve checking the draft computations, and if received, their agreement by the Inland Revenue. The checking of the claims in respect of writing down allowances can sometimes be revealing as compared with the records maintained in respect of fixed assets (*see* p. 96).

The Institute of Chartered Accountants in their recommendation "Treatment of Taxation in Accounts of Companies" (N.19) have stated, *inter alia*:

(a) A deferred taxation account should be established and maintained at current rates of taxation whenever there exist material taxation liabilities which may crystallise at some future date on profits and surpluses already brought into account.

(b) A credit balance on the deferred taxation account should not be treated in the balance sheet as a reserve or grouped with reserves. It should be separately stated, but may be grouped with any liabilities or provisions which fall outside the heading of "current liabilities" (para. 33).

The foregoing paragraph is now covered by the *Companies Act, 1967, 2nd Schedule,* 27 (1) *b,* which states,

"The expression reserve shall not . . . include any sum set aside for the purpose of its being used to prevent undue fluctuations in charges for taxation."

and, para. 7A,

"If an amount is set aside for the purpose of its being used to prevent undue fluctuations in charges for taxation, it shall be stated."

The other relevant statements under the *Companies Act, 1967,* are (Para. 11(8A)):

"If a sum set aside for the purpose of its being used to prevent undue fluctuations in charges for taxation has been used during the financial year for another purpose, the amount thereof and the fact that it has been so used . . . shall be stated."

Para. 12 (1) (*c*):

". . . the amount of the charge to revenue for U.K. corporation tax and, if that amount would have been greater but for relief from double taxation, the amount which it would have been but for such relief, the amount of the charge for U.K. income tax and the amount of the charge for taxation imposed outside the U.K. of profits, income and (so far as charged to revenue) capital gains."

34. Dividend equalisation reserve. A dividend equalisation reserve is formed by the setting aside of profits to enable the payment of dividends in a year when profits do not warrant the payment out of current funds, or to maintain a regular distribution of dividends from year to year when profits earned are of a fluctuating nature.

Since share prices are largely governed by dividend payments it is prudent policy to maintain regular dividends and to obviate undue variations. This reserve may be especially applicable in the following circumstances:

(*a*) Where companies are operating in businesses subject to sudden changes in income, *e.g.,* those dealing in agricultural crops; or are dependent on overseas harvests. '

(b) Where raw materials forming a large proportion of prime cost of manufacture are subject to wide price fluctuations.

(c) Where sales are subject to fluctuations due to changes of fashion or taste.

(d) Where the business is of a hazardous nature, such as financing new business undertakings.

Where such reserves are created it is always advisable to ensure that they are represented by investments outside the business. These should be easily realisable and as income on them is not the main consideration, they should be in the nature of gilt-edged securities.

35. Loan capital: debentures.

(a) *Definition.* A debenture is a written acknowledgment under seal of a debt due by a company undertaking to pay the debt in certain circumstances or on a specified date and to pay a specified rate of interest in the meantime.

Such debentures may be *simple* or *naked* debentures, giving no security for the loan; or, more usually, they may give security either as a *fixed* or *floating* charge over the assets of the company—a fixed charge being in respect of certain assets and a floating charge being over the whole assets of the company at the date on which the charge crystallises, *i.e.*, when the debenture holders, on the occurrence of a certain event, enforce their security, *e.g.*, on the non-payment of interest or principal.

(b) *Issue of debentures.* If an issue of debentures takes place during the period under audit, the auditor should ascertain that the issue is in accordance with any clauses contained in the articles of the company. If no such clauses exist, then a trading company has implied power to borrow money and to give security therefor.

(c) *Issue at a discount.* The receipt of the cash should be vouched, and if the debentures are issued at a discount, the transfer to the debenture discount account should be checked, so ensuring that the debenture will be shown at the full value of indebtedness both in the account and on the balance sheet.

The discount should also be shown on the balance sheet until written off. In compliance with the *Companies Act*, the auditor should ascertain that such debentures are duly registered with the Registrar of Companies, and that they are entered in the Register of Charges.

E

(d) *Issue at a premium.* If the debentures are issued at a premium, there is no restriction on the use of the premium, but being in the nature of a capital profit, it would be preferably used for some capital purpose, such as the writing off of any ficticious assets or otherwise used for the purpose of augmenting a debenture redemption reserve fund (*see* **32**).

The auditor should take notes of the terms of the debentures for inclusion in the audit notebook as well as confirming such matters as the rate of interest payable and the redemption date and any premium payable on redemption.

36. Loan capital: convertible loan notes. These may, or may not, give a charge on the assets of the company. The terms of their issue should be ascertained, noting the interest rate and the conversion date. There may be a prospectus in respect of their issue where they are offered by a quoted company to the public, but in the first instance the shareholders must be given the right to take them up. This right may be waived by the company in general meeting, however.

If they give a charge over the assets, the auditor should ascertain that this is duly registered with the Registrar of Joint Stock Companies.

37. Liabilities and provisions.

(a) *Liabilities.*

  (i) *Trade creditors.* The method of ensuring that all liabilities in respect of goods purchased has been dealt with (*see* p. 59).

  (ii) *Taxation.* The liability in respect of taxation is a matter of importance to the auditor.

  The amount set aside in respect for liability to tax can materially affect profits available for distribution; it is essential, therefore, that the auditor should check the computation of the amount set aside for taxation purposes. If the sum has been agreed it should be shown as a liability, otherwise it should be considered a provision.

  (iii) *Accruals.* These will include the amounts due on the various nominal accounts, such as rent, rates, lighting, heating, loan interest, etc. These should be checked when examining the accounts in the nominal ledger, and by their nature should reveal amounts due. The calculations involved should be checked and vouched with relevant documents as necessary. Changes in recurring charges, such as rent, should be watched for, and enquiries made to ensure that any new or non-recurring items have been accounted for, especially if invoices in respect of these have not been received.

Wages and salaries are not always paid up to the balance sheet date, and any liability in respect thereof should be obtained.

(b) *Provisions*. These are dealt with (*see* p. 166), where certain legal decisions affecting them are quoted.

PROGRESS TEST 7

1. What precautionary measures should the auditor take when verifying assets? (2, 3)

2. In what way may goodwill be verified? (4)

3. How may costs on acquisition of trade marks be dealt with? (6)

4. How should freehold properties be verified? (8)

5. What is signified by the term *registered land*? (8)

6. With regard to freehold properties, what should the auditor particularly concern himself with to ensure complete ownership? (8)

7. How may plant and machinery be verified? Is it expedient in any case to personally inspect such assets? (9)

8. How may ownership of motor vehicles be verified? (12)

9. How may debtor balances be verified? (13)

10. State the requirements of the *Companies Act, 1948*, with regard to loans made to directors. (15)

11. What are the most common types of loans made on security? (17–20)

12. When inspecting a mortgage deed, what matters should receive particular attention? (17)

13. What is an essential part of audit procedure when inspecting investments actually held by the client? (21)

14. What special difficulty arises in auditing *rights issues*? (22)

15. How is interest received on tax reserve certificates? (22)

16. Where various petty cash balances are held, what procedures should the auditor observe? Should he attend on the last day of the financial period? (23)

17. Are bank pass sheets sufficient evidence of balances held at the bank? (23)

18. State the procedures to be observed in the case of a new share issue. (25)

19. Give a definition of a capital reserve. What is a reserve fund? (26, 27)

20. In what ways may a share premium account be used? (29)

21. For what reason is it important to invest the funds set aside to debenture redemption reserve funds outside the business? (32)

22. In what circumstances may dividend equalisation funds be set up? (34)

23. What is a debenture? Are there different kinds of debentures? (35)

24. In what way should accruals be verified? (37)

SPECIMEN QUESTIONS

1. Write brief notes on the points to be observed in the verification of the following assets of a limited company:

(a) Freehold properties.
(b) Motor vehicles.
(c) Plant.
(d) Trade debtors. *C.A. (E.W.)*

2. As auditor of a limited company, you ascertain that, during the year under review, the company had purchased:

(a) A plot of freehold land adjacent to the factory.
(b) £25,000 of Uptown Corporation 5% Stock 1968–73.
(c) Tax reserve certificates.
(d) A fork lift truck for use in the works.

State how you would vouch these purchases and verify the assets. *C.A. (E.W.)*

3. In the course of your audit of the accounts of a limited company you ask for the title deeds to a freehold building purchased during the year under review.
State:

(a) Four points appearing in the conveyance to your client which you would require to note.
(b) How you would vouch the payments for the acquisition of the property including the incidental costs.

C.A. (E.W.) (Inter.)

4. How would you verify the following items included in the balance sheet of a limited company:

(a) Machinery being acquired on hire purchase.
(b) Loans to employees (not officers of the company).
(c) Leasehold premises? *C.A. (E.W.)*

5. State what steps you would take to verify the amounts shown in the annual accounts, for:

(a) Plant and machinery.
(b) Additions and alterations to factory premises carried out by own employees.
(c) Motor vehicles.
(d) Loose tools. *C.A. (E.W.)*

6. A limited company, whose accounts you are auditing, has made a loan to a director.

You are required to tabulate the provisions of the Companies Act, 1948, relating to such a loan. *C.A. (E.W.)*

7. You are auditor of a limited company. State how you would verify the existence of the following assets and liabilities, and ensure that they appear at a proper value in the accounts:

(a) A motor vehicle purchased seven years ago.
(b) The balance due at the end of the financial year to a finance company in respect of a machine bought on hire purchase.
(c) The amount of the telephone account which is accrued at the balancing date.
(d) The petty cash float held at the company's store twenty miles away.
(e) A life policy on the life of the managing director assigned to the company. *C.C.A. (Inter.)*

8. (a) How would you verify the valuation of loose tools manufactured by a company for its own use and what steps would you take to verify the quantity on hand at the balancing date?

(b) What steps would you take to verify the existence of and all the information required by the Companies Act relating to investments made by a company in shares of a quoted company?

(c) Give your views on a proposal by the directors of a contracting company to establish a dividend equalisation reserve. *C.C.A.*

9. Beesee Ltd., a trading company whose accounting year ends on 31st December, purchased 10,000 £1 shares in Ellem Ltd. at 30/- each on 1st February, 1961; 4,000 of these were sold on 30th November, 1961, at 35/- each ex a dividend payable on 20th December, 1961, of 20% less income tax. The shares in Ellem Ltd. are quoted on the London Stock Exchange.

As auditor of Beesee Ltd., state the evidence you would require to verify the above transactions and to ensure that all benefits arising therefrom had been properly accounted for. *C.A. (E.W.)*

10. State the particular points to which you would direct your attention in carrying out the audit of an issue of debentures to the public by a limited company. *C.A.*

11. How would you verify the amount appearing in the balance sheet of a limited company for current taxation? *C.A. (E.W.)*

12. As auditor of Parent Ltd., a holding company, you are examining the consolidation schedules with the accounts of the individual companies in the group in order to make your report to the members of the holding company on the consolidated accounts relating to the year ended 31st December, 1961.

During 1961 Parent Ltd. acquired for cash, three new wholly owned subsidiaries; the accounting year of each ends on 31st December.

You are required to state how you would expect the following matters relating to the three new subsidiaries to have been dealt with in the consolidated accounts, viz.:

(a) The amounts paid for the shares of those companies.

(b) The dividends paid or proposed to be paid by them since acquisition.

(c) The revenue reserves, including the balance on profit and loss account, appearing in their balance sheets on 31st December, 1961. *C.A. (E.W.)*

13. When verifying debtors' balances:

(a) In what circumstances might an auditor consider adopting the procedure of confirmation by direct communication?

(b) What factors will influence his choice between the negative and the positive request methods?

(c) What considerations should he take into account when selecting a sample of the debtors' accounts for test circularisation?

(d) Draft a suitable form of letter to be sent to the debtors selected. *C.A. (E.W.)*

CHAPTER VIII

DEPRECIATION AND APPRECIATION OF ASSETS

DEPRECIATION

Before proceeding to the subject of valuation of the items included on a balance sheet, it is apposite to consider the factor which so vitally affects the ultimate valuation of assets, namely, depreciation.

1. Definition. Depreciation may be defined briefly as the diminution in the value of an asset over a period. No one particular cause is reckoned to reduce the value of an asset by depreciation, rather, a combination of factors, internally, those inherent in the asset itself, such as wear and tear, or externally, such as intervening obsolesence. In itself, therefore, depreciation might be considered to cause no great difficulty from the auditing point of view. There are, however, various aspects which require careful attention.

2. No actual expenditure involved. As opposed to other charges made against the revenue of a business or other undertaking, the charge made for depreciation, whilst reducing the profit, does not entail any actual expenditure on the sum currently set against profits. The initial capital outlay having been made, no further amount is actually expended, nevertheless the business is suffering a real loss in the diminution of the value of the asset being retained for the purpose of earning profits.

3. Auditor's responsibility. Since the figure set against the profits will affect the resultant excess or deficiency, it is the auditor's responsibility to ascertain that this sum is adequate, being neither too small nor too great. Should the figure be understated, then profits may be shown as distributable, which if paid out would cause the value of the business to decrease, and at the same time cause an inadequate sum to be set aside for the future replacement of the asset or assets concerned.

It may be argued that even if an adequate sum should be shown in the accounts it does not follow that the profits which would otherwise have been shown as available for distribution will be set aside specifically for the replacement of the assets, as the amount of profit made available may be expended on some other item, and be lost in the general assets of the business. This is true, but nevertheless the amount set against profits will ensure that the amount is retained within the business in whatever form. The argument does reveal, however, the importance of setting aside the amount of depreciation shown in the accounts by the maintenance of a sinking fund with the investment of the funds in a manner which will make them readily available when the replacement date falls due.

4. Replacement reserves. The additional complication now arises as to the actual sum to be made available for the replacement of assets. With the operation of inflationary tendencies, an annual amount set aside for the diminution of asset values, even if invested, may on the date for replacement only ensure that the original cost figure is available. For this reason it is now considered prudent policy to invest additional sums, so building up an asset replacement reserve. In compliance with the *Companies Act, 1967*, such sums set aside are properly shown under a reserve as any amount in excess of the depreciation provision is rightly considered an appropriation of profits rather than a charge against them. In this respect, the auditor will need to have some particular information as to the nature of the assets being dealt with, for it is possible to transfer a more than adequate amount to replacement reserves, though this would not be of such moment as the contrary policy of under-providing depreciation on assets.

APPRECIATION

5. Adjustment of balance sheet values. We have been concerned thus far with the problems arising when it is necessary to replace assets after a period of inflation, but as some assets, such as freehold land and properties, are often held over considerable periods, inflationary and other economic effects have to be dealt with during the period over which such assets are retained.   Though, as in the case of freehold properties, some assets may suffer loss in value due to normal wear and tear, owing to economic factors, their intrinsic value may quite rapidly increase.

Accountants, however, are rightly hesitant to bring into consideration profits of an estimated nature and which have not actually been realised, and which may make such profits appear available for distribution, or expendable purposes. Nevertheless, although unrealised, the increase in value of an asset, which if disposed of could bring in a considerable profit, cannot be ignored.   This has led to the writing up of assets on balance sheets with the creation of corresponding reserves. Furthermore, pressure due to such matters as take-over bids, and share valuation, have forced some companies to re-value their assets, putting the resulting increase to reserves, thereby showing the assets at their current value, and so improving the "appearance" of the balance sheet, whereby the full value of the company as a whole is shown.

6. Capital nature of reserves.   Still wishing to preserve an attitude of prudence with respect to such reserves, accountants have generally considered it advisable to designate the amounts created on revaluation as capital reserves.   By this designation it is hoped to mitigate the desire to appropriate unrealised profits by way of revenue distributions while at the same time encouraging the capitalisation of distributions to shareholders by means of bonus issues if distribution is desired.   Legally, however, there are only two capital reserves which it is not possible to appropriate for revenue purposes, namely, the share premium account and a capital redemption reserve fund.   Therefore, from the auditor's point of view, provided the revaluation is to his satisfaction, he can only offer advice as to that which is considered prudent policy, but thereafter his duty would extend only to compliance with the requirements of the *Companies Acts*.   This subject is also dealt with in Chapter XI.

METHODS OF DEPRECIATION

Turning to the accounting aspect of the auditor's duties

regarding depreciation, the most common methods by which this may be provided may be summarised as follows:

7. The straight line or fixed instalment system. As its designation signifies under this system, a fixed amount is written off the asset annually. This is simple to operate and is recommended by the Institute of Chartered Accountants as being considered most suitable in the majority of cases. (*See* **13**).

8. The reducing instalment system. The amount set off against the asset steadily reduces as the same is allocated according to a fixed percentage of the balance remaining after the deduction of all prior depreciation.

It has been advocated that as an asset decreases in value, the charges for repairs and renewals increases, therefore depreciation should be shown more heavily in the early years and less when the repairs and renewals charges increase, so, it is claimed, maintaining an even charge against profits

The argument is, however, considered to confuse the two separate and distinct matters of depreciation and repairs. Furthermore, to maintain a charge of a rate comparable with that under a straight line system, a very heavy percentage has to be written off in the earlier years.

9. Revaluation system. This system may be applied to various types of asset which are not retained over a lengthy life and which do not render themselves easily to an estimated even sum over the period of their retention. This might be used in such instances as loose tools or stocks of expensive packing cases.

10. Depletion unit or machine hour rate systems. These may be included under one heading due to their similarity of operation.

Where a mine or similar exhaustable asset is being used up, an estimate of the total value of deposit available is made, and the amount of tonnage or otherwise taken out during the period is written off at a rate in proportion to the whole.

Likewise, the workable machine hours are estimated in the case of a machine, and according to the number worked during the period so a proportionate fraction of the total value of the machine is written off.

All the foregoing mention the charge to be made against profits, but as stated earlier, for replacement purposes it is advisable to invest funds covered by the depreciation charge by some method which would make them available on the extinction of the life of the asset. This may be done by the application of the methods detailed below. (*See* **11, 12**).

11. Depreciation fund system. By the use of compound interest tables, a fixed sum is calculated which, when invested outside the business in a fixed interest bearing security makes possible the replacement of the asset at its original cost. The charge for depreciation is made as under the foregoing methods, but the assurance that the required sum will be available is no doubt an advantage. The influence of inflationary factors on the replacement price, however, have been mentioned previously.

12. The insurance policy system. An insurance policy maturing at the end of the estimated life of an asset and in accordance with its replacement price may be taken out. This is another form of investment outside the business and is again affected by the operation of inflationary movements. Difficulties may arise as to the amount to provide as compared with the depreciation charge and the reduction to surrender value of the annuity held. However, in the case of the last two systems the outstanding advantage of ensuring adequate funds may be made available from outside the business has much to commend it.

13. Amortisation. The foregoing constitute a brief summary of the methods of depreciation which may be applied, but before proceeding, the amortisation method should also be explained.

The term *amortisation* is applied in the case of leases where the life of the asset is *dying* by the mere passing of time. The effect for accounting purposes is the same as that of depreciation.

The following extracts from Recommendation N.9. are of importance regarding depreciation.

Fixed assets, whatever be their nature or the type of business in which they are employed, have the fundamental characteristic that they are held with the object of earning revenue and not for the purpose of sale, in the ordinary course of business. The amount at which they are shown in the balance sheet does not purport to be their realisable value or their replacement value, but is normally an historical record of their cost less amounts provided in respect of depreciation, amortisation or depletion.

Depreciation represents that part of the cost of a fixed asset to its owner which is not recoverable when the asset is finally put out of use by him. Provision against this loss of capital is an integral cost of conducting the business during the effective commercial life of the asset and is not dependent upon the amount of profit earned.

The assessment of depreciation involves the consideration of three factors: the cost of the asset, which is known, the probable value realisable on ultimate disposal, which can generally be estimated only within fairly wide limits, and the length of time during which the asset will be commercially useful to the undertaking. In most cases, this last factor is not susceptible of precise calculation. Provisions for depreciation are therefore in most cases matters of estimation, based upon the available experience and knowledge, rather than of accurate determination. They require adjustments from time to time in the light of changes in experience and knowledge, including prolongation of useful life due to exceptional maintenance expenditure, curtailment due to excessive use, or obsolescence not allowed for in the original estimate of the commercially useful life of the asset. This method does not accord with a strict view of depreciation and may distort the annual charges to revenue.

The different natures of assets involve consideration in deciding on the method of depreciation appropriate in each case. Unless the methods adopted are applied consistently the usefulness of periodic accounts for the purpose of comparison of one period with another may be vitiated.

Whatever be the method adopted, the periodical revision of depreciation rates and the ascertainment of the residue of cost which has not been covered by depreciation provisions made up to any given date are greatly facilitated by, and often impracticable without, the maintenance of fixed asset registers showing the cost of each asset, the provisions for depreciation made thereon and the basis on which these have been calculated.

It is therefore recommended that:

1. Provisions for depreciation, amortisation and depletion of fixed assets should be applied on consistent bases from one period to another. If additional provisions prove to be necessary, they should be stated separately in the profit and loss account. Where practicable, fixed assets *in existence at the balance sheet date* should normally be shown in the balance

sheet at cost and the aggregate of the provisions for depreciation, amortisation and depletion should appear as deductions therefrom. The extent to which these provisions are being kept liquid will then be ascertainable from the balance sheet as a whole.

2. Such provisions should be computed on the basis mentioned below as being appropriate to the particular class of asset concerned:

(a) *Goodwill and freehold land.*

Depreciation does not arise through use in the business, except in the case of freehold land acquired for purposes such as are referred to in (*d*) below. Amounts set aside to provide for diminution in value do not constitute a normal charge against revenue and should be shown separately in the profit and loss account.

(b) *Freehold buildings, plant and machinery, tools and equipment, ships, transport vehicles and similar assets which are subject to depreciation by reason of their employment in the business.*

Provision for depreciation should, in general, be computed on the straight-line method. Assets of very short effective life, such as loose tools, jigs and patterns, may, however, frequently be dealt with more satisfactorily by other methods such as re-valuation, which in no case should exceed cost.

(c) *Leaseholds, patents and other assets which become exhausted by the effluxion of time.*

Provision for amortisation should be made on the straight-line basis, including, in the case of leaseholds, allowance for the estimated cost of dilapidations at the end of the lease or useful life of the asset if shorter. If a leasehold redemption policy is effected with an insurance company, the charge of the annual premiums to profit and loss account provides a satisfactory method of amortisation if supplemented in respect of dilapidations.

(d) *Mines, oil wells, quarries and similar assets of a wasting character which are consumed in the form of basic raw material or where the output is sold as such.*

Provision for depreciation and depletion should be made according to the estimated exhaustion of the asset concerned. In the case of an undertaking formed for the purpose of exploiting this particular class of asset, if the practice is to make no provision this should be made clear in the accounts so that shareholders may realise that dividends are, in part, a return of capital.

3. Where a method different from that recommended has

hitherto been followed and it is not considered practicable or desirable to make a change in the case of assets already in use, it is suggested that the methods recommended should be followed in cases of assets subsequently acquired.

4. Details of all fixed assets should be kept (preferably in registers specially maintained) to show the cost of each asset, the provisions made for its depreciation and the basis of the provisions made.

5. Amounts set aside out of profits for obsolescence which cannot be foreseen, or for a possible increase in the cost of replacement are matters of financial prudence. Neither can be estimated with any degree of accuracy. They are in the nature of reserves and should be treated as such in the accounts.

LEGAL ASPECTS OF DEPRECIATION

Certain specific assets have been mentioned in the foregoing extract which are dealt with (see IX), dealing with particular types of assets.

The legal aspect of depreciation is closely bound up with the consideration of profits and the amount which may be properly used for distribution purposes, but whilst the following cases are of importance to the auditor from the latter point of view, they are also relevant as to the charge which should, or should not, be included for depreciation purposes.

14. Verner v. General and Commercial Investment Trus. Ltd., 1894. In this case, the capital value of some of the company's investments had fallen considerably, and the company proposed to pay a dividend without providing for the obvious depreciation of its main assets. The aid of the court was sought to restrain the company from carrying out its proposal. The injunction was refused, as it was held that the company was solvent and acting within its articles.

An important statement from the auditor's point of view was made during the course of the judgment, namely:

> Fixed capital may be sunk and lost, and yet the excess of current receipts over current payments may be divided; but floating or circulating capital must be kept up, as otherwise it will enter into and form part of such excess, in which case to divide such excess without deducting the capital which forms part of it will be contrary to law.

15. Lee v. Neuchatel Asphalte Co. Ltd., 1889. Here, the company's main asset consisted of a concession to mine a bituminous substance in Switzerland.

The company had been formed specifically to acquire and work the asset and a clause had been inserted in the articles stating that no provision for depreciation or wastage of fixed assets need be made before payment of dividends. An ordinary shareholder sought the aid of the court to restrain the payment of a dividend on the preference shares.

It was held that a company may, by its articles, provide for the distribution of profits before making good the depreciation of fixed assets.

During the course of the judgment it was stated that:

> If a company is formed to acquire or work property of a wasting nature, e.g., a mine, quarry or patent, the capital expended in acquiring the property may be regarded as sunk and gone, and . . . any excess of money obtained by working the mine over the cost of working it may be divided among the shareholders; and this is true, although some portion of the property itself is sold and in one sense the capital is thereby diminished.

The principle applied in the foregoing cases is adequately clear in that it is not necessary to provide for depreciation of fixed assets before declaring a dividend out of current profits. The following cases are alo relevant, but it will be observed they are all still concerned with the aspect of depreciation on *fixed* assets.

16. Bolton v. Natal Land and Colonisation Co. Ltd., 1892. Ten years earlier, in 1882, the company had suffered a heavy bad debt of £70,000 but had avoided showing a loss for the year by writing up the value of the lands to approximately the same amount. In 1885, current profits were made and a dividend was then paid out of these profits

It was held that, despite the fact of there having been no justification for the writing up of the land, and that it was excessively valued in the accounts, following the decision in *Lee v. Neuchatel Asphalte Co. Ltd.*, it was not illegal to distribute the current profits without making any adjustment for the loss of the capital.

17. Wilmer _v._ McNamara and Co. Ltd., 1895. The principle that a company may distribute dividends out of current profits without providing for depreciation of fixed assets, was maintained in this case. Having been formed to acquire an existing business including its goodwill, amounts were written off the assets taken over. On revaluation, however, it was discovered that there was a deficiency of £43,000 in the value of the assets as against capital of £120,000. It was proposed to declare a dividend on the preference shares which would entail the distribution of the current year's profits.

Although the sufficiency of the depreciation charge for the year was questioned, it was held that this had little relevance with regard to the proposed payment of the dividend since the principle as applied to the _Lee_ v. _Neuchatel_ case applied here.

18. Brown _v._ Gaumont British Picture Corporation Ltd., 1937. Where a company has holdings in subsidiary companies and these have depreciated, it is not necessary to provide against this before payment of dividends on cumulative preference shares. Whilst the balance sheet of the holding company showed a large reserve mostly in the form of a share premium account, the consolidated balance sheet of the group showed that heavy losses had been made by the subsidiary companies. Here again the _Lee_ v. _Neuchatel_ principle was maintained.

BUSINESS POLICY AND DEPRECIATION

19. The Accountant's view-point. The foregoing constitute sound legal decisions, but from the accounting point of view do not constitute prudent business policy. If the desire is to maintain a continuing business where assets are depreciating, they must at some stage be renewed. Therefore, to run down the fixed assets and to make no provision for their replacement is to invite disaster. The courts are not so much concerned with prudent business policy as are accountants, and as the money expended on fixed assets has to be disposed of, then current profits are available for distribution purposes.

Obviously, such a policy could not be pursued by a continuing company which had to face the necessity of renewing its assets, but there are instances of companies, such as those engaged in gold mining, where it is realised that the capital has been sunk in a wasting asset and when this has been exhausted, the company has no purpose for continuing to exist. The distribution of profits in such cases, which might otherwise seem excessive, are then looked upon as not only including the current profits, but an element of return of capital, which will ultimately be written off on liquidation, although in normal circumstances no reduction of the capital of the business would be allowed.

20. Losses on current assets. The courts do, however, maintain a very different attitude with respect to losses sustained on current assets, since these must always be provided against, as was stated by the judge in the extract given from the *Verner* v. *The General and Commercial investment Trust Ltd.* (*See* **14**.)

This distinction between fixed and current assets the court will decide in accordance with the circumstances of the particular case and in conjunction with the provisions contained in the company's Memorandum and Articles. (The expressions, *floating* or *circulating* assets often used in the cases quoted are merely the earlier designations of *current* assets.)

21. Bond v. The Barrow Haematite Steel Co. Ltd., 1902. Although still concerned with mining, in this case there was the important distinction of the company not being an actual mining company but it purchased certain mines to supply raw material for its manufacturing purposes. It was held here that the mines owned must be regarded as floating assets and therefore depreciation must be provided.

The judge stated:

"I think that the money invested in those items (mining leases) is properly regarded as circulating capital. Suppose the company had bought enormous stocks of ore sufficient to last for ten years, it could hardly be said that the true value of so much of this as remained from time to time ought not to be brought into the Balance Sheet, and I can see no difference for the purpose of the account between ore *in situ* and ore so bought in advance."

22. Companies Act requirements. The *Companies Act, 1967*, is quite clear in its requirement as to the auditor reporting that the balance sheet gives a true and fair view of the company's affairs as well as requiring that the following specific matters be shown:

(a) The amount charged to revenue by way of provision for depreciation, renewals or diminution in the value of fixed assets, para. 12(1)(a).

(b) The amounts charged for provision for renewal of assets for which there has *also* been a depreciation charge.

(c) Where the depreciation charge has *not* been determined by reference to value of assets shown in the balance sheet, this must be stated.

(d) The method of providing for depreciation, if other than by a depreciation charge or provision for renewals, or the fact that it is not provided for.

PROGRESS TEST 8

1. What is depreciation? (1)

2. In what way does depreciation differ from other charges against profits? (2)

3. What is the auditor's responsibility regarding depreciation? (3)

4. In what way is the difficulty arising on the replacement of assets at inflated prices overcome? (4)

5. Where reserves are created on revaluation, why do accountants advocate that these should be considered *capital* reserves? (6)

6. Enumerate the various methods of providing depreciation.

7. Which method of calculating depreciation is advocated by the Institute of Chartered Accountants and why? (7)

8. Is it a legal necessity to write off depreciation on fixed assets before distributing profits? (15)

9. Is business policy always in accord with legal considerations regarding depreciation of fixed assets? (19)

10. Where losses are sustained on current assets, may profit distributions be made despite the excess of current expenditure over receipts? If not, why not? (19, 20)

SPECIMEN QUESTIONS

1. Draft your reply to the following letter which, as auditor of XY Co. Ltd., you have received from the Secretary of the company:

"At the last meeting of the Board one of the directors proposed that the heritable properties and plant should be shown in the financial accounts at their present-day values in order to present to the shareholders a fair statement of the worth of the company. My Board would be glad to have your views on this proposal before considering it further." *C.A.*

2. Discuss the statement that "The balance Sheet of a company as it is normally drawn up in accordance with the Companies Acts, is inadequate as a guide to the value of the share capital in a period of fluctuating money values." In your solution deal in particular with the relevancy or otherwise of the above statement in relation to fixed assets. *C.C.A.*

3. State the principal considerations to be borne in mind by the auditor of a manufacturing company in determining the adequacy or otherwise of the provisions made in the annual accounts for depreciation of plant and machinery. *C.A.*

4. Discuss:

 (a) The main advantages and disadvantages of the principal methods of providing for depreciation of the plant and machinery of a manufacturing concern.

 (b) The matters to be considered in determining whether the depreciation provided is adequate. *C.A. (E.W.) (Inter.)*

5. Discuss the considerations which should guide the auditor of a manufacturing concern in deciding whether the provision for depreciation on plant and machinery is, or is not, adequate.

Your answer should be in the form of an essay and should indicate the main features of the principal methods of providing for depreciation. *C.A. (E.W.) (Inter)*

CHAPTER IX

VALUATION OF ASSETS

VALUATION

1. Difficulties of valuation. In times when price levels were stable, it was not a difficult task for the auditor to ascertain whether correct valuations had been placed upon the majority of assets, the cost figure was vouched on acquisition, and thereafter, an amount for depreciation was deducted each year. Fluctuating price levels, and continuous inflation have made the task much more difficult.

The matter of depreciation and appreciation of assets was purposely dealt with in the previous chapter before proceeding to consideration of the various aspects of valuation.

2. Recommendations of the Institute of Chartered Accountants. To assist the auditor in the problems arising, two publications have been issued by the Institute of Chartered Accountants. The first to consider is *Recommendation N.15*: "Accounting in relation to changes in the purchasing power of money."

Unless and until a practicable and generally acceptable alternative is available, the Council recommends that the accounting principles set out below should continue to be applied:

(a) Historical cost should continue to be the basis on which annual accounts should be prepared and, in consequence, the basis on which profits shown by such accounts are computed.

(b) Any amount set aside out of profits in recognition of the effects which changes in the purchasing power of money have had on the affairs of the business (including any amount to finance the increase in the cost of replacements, whether of fixed or current assets) should be treated as a transfer to reserve and not as a charge in arriving at profits. If such a transfer is shown in the profit and loss account as a deduction in arriving at the balance for the year, that balance should be described appropriately, since it is not the whole of the profits.

(c) In order to emphasize that as a matter of prudence the amount so set aside is, for the time being, regarded by directors as not available for distribution, it should normally be treated as a capital reserve.

(d) For balance sheet purposes fixed assets should not be written up, especially in the absence of monetary stability.

The Council also recommends to members who are directors or officers of companies or who are asked by clients for advice, that they should stress the limitations on the significance of profits computed on the basis of historical cost in periods of material changes in the purchasing power of money; and that they should draw attention to the desirability of:

(a) Setting amounts aside from profits to reserve in recognition of the effects which changes in the purchasing power of money have had upon the affairs of the business, particularly their effect on the amount of profit which, as a matter of policy, can prudently be regarded as available for distribution.

(b) Showing in the directors' report or otherwise the effects which changes in the purchasing power of money have had on the affairs of the business, including in particular the financial requirements for its maintenance and the directors' policy for meeting those requirements, either by setting aside to reserve or by raising new capital.

(c) Experimenting with methods of measuring the effects of changes in the purchasing power of money on profits and on financial requirements. If the results of such experiments are published as part of the documents accompanying the annual accounts, the basis used for the calculations and the significance of the figures in relation to the business concerned should be stated clearly.

It is apparent, therefore, that the provision of depreciation on the historical cost basis is still acceptable, but that the rise in price levels should be acknowledged and dealt with by the setting aside of additional sums to meet subsequent higher costs of replacement.

3. Fluctuations in value. With the same matter of rising price levels in mind, due to various factors, not only of an inflationary nature, where assets have materially changed in value since the balance sheet date, the auditor may experience some difficulty in satisfying himself as to the value to be set upon an asset. He may even be under pressure to accept a certain figure which it is held is more reasonable to show due to the subsequent change in value. The other publication is *Recommendation N. 17*: "Events occurring after the balance sheet date."

> Events which, at the time of preparing annual accounts, are known to have occurred after the Balance Sheet date, should not normally be taken into account in preparing accounts unless:
>
> (a) They assist in forming an opinion as to the amount properly attributable, in the conditions existing on the Balance Sheet date, to any item the amount of which was subject to uncertainty on that date, or,
>
> (b) They arise from legislation affecting items in the accounts, for example changes in taxation, or are required by law to be shown in the accounts, for example appropriations and proposed appropriation of profits.

TYPES OF ASSET

We now consider some specific types of asset under the following various headings to which they refer:

(a) Fixed assets.
(b) Investments.
(c) Current assets.
(d) Fictitious assets.

4. Fixed assets. Inflationary price increases are most obviously felt on assets retained for lengthy periods of use and they are likely to cause the most difficulty in valuation. The need for providing sufficient finance for replacement of assets at increased prices is not of concern to the auditor, although he should ensure that where assets are depreciated at a greater rate than is justified in order to effect the setting aside of profits for replacement purposes, that such excess depreciation is properly shown as a replacement reserve.

Where assets on the other hand increase in value it is the auditor's duty to see that any new value placed upon them is justified, and that the excess on revaluation is placed preferably, though not necessarily, to a capital reserve. The latter, of course, excludes depreciation written off which may be transferred back to the appropriation section of the profit and loss account, or to a reserve.

(a) *Freehold and leasehold land and buildings.* Appreciation in value has been a feature of this type of asset. The remarks as to transfer to a capital reserve made above apply particularly here.

The auditor should request that a certificate by a competent valuer be produced, especially in view of the fact that frequently very large sums are involved.

With the idea of retaining a hidden reserve on the balance sheet in the form of the non-revaluation of such assets, some businesses prefer to maintain such assets at their cost or written down figure. The auditor has no right to insist on re-valuation, but he should point out the dangers of undervaluation of assets, such as take-over bids, lower valuation of shares, etc., and also mentioning that the *Companies Acts* forbid by implication the maintenance of secret reserves in company's affairs. Should his advice be ignored and the sum involved warrant it, he should qualify his report accordingly.

In the case of leaseholds, the auditor should ascertain that the amortisation charge is adequate, bearing in mind the life of the lease.

(b) *Plant and machinery.* The cost of such assets will have been vouched on acquisition, but the auditor will not be in a position to know the expected life of such an asset, he may therefore request a certified assessment be supplied by a responsible official of the organisation. Such certification may be shown on each folio sheet giving details of the plant or machinery in the plant register. Where some time has elapsed since the last certification, he may request that this be brought up to date.

Obsolescence may intervene with expensive machinery, and any material sudden losses in value should be checked, with exceptional depreciation being shown apart from the normal annual charge.

Frequently, the company's own employees may be engaged on erection of machines, in which case their wages may properly be charged to the cost of the asset, together with the value of any parts supplied. In confirming the asset value, the auditor should check the original documents arising, such as time sheets, etc., and the costing records maintained in respect of any capital project.

(c) *Furniture and fittings.* No real difficulty should exist in the valuation of such assets which the auditor may ascertain when verifying their existence.

Whilst furniture will be written off at an agreed annual rate, fittings may be of varying types, and where changes are frequently made in installations for advertising purposes, *e.g.*, in reception rooms for companies selling various types of office machinery, it may be necessary to write off such fittings over a short period.

(d) *Office machinery.* The more usual types of office machinery may be valued, as mentioned above, for furniture and fittings, but where expensive punched card, or even computer systems are involved, the auditor should endeavour to obtain an authoritative valuation figure from an outside source. Usually the suppliers are helpful in supplying details regarding their machines, although the temptation may exist for them to quote a higher figure than might be justified by the wear and tear, or obsolescence factor, involved. However, the auditor has the original cost and an expected life estimate should be obtainable.

5. Investments. This type of asset is shown here separately as it may be classified as either a fixed asset or a current asset. Where investments are obtained with the purpose of holding them continuously, such as in the case of an investment company, they should be viewed as fixed assets, whereas if it is not intended to retain them but rather to set aside surplus funds for a short period in view of earning a higher interest rate, or as in the case of a finance company, their resale at a profit is envisaged, then they should be treated as current assets.

The Companies Acts require that there shall be shown under separate headings the company's trade investments and other investments, with the aggregate amounts respectively of the company's quoted and unquoted investments.

Where investments may be properly viewed as fixed assets, there is no legal necessity to provide for their diminution in value, but whilst this is the *legal* position, the Institute of Chartered Accountants have stated in their publication,

Treatment of Investments in the Balance Sheet of Trading Companies:

> "Provision should be made for the diminution in the value of investments:
>
> (i) where the market value at the date of the Balance Sheet of investments which are current assets is lower than cost;
> (ii) where the value to the business of investments which are fixed assets appears to have decreased permanently below cost.
>
> Provision for diminution in value should not exceed the amount required to reduce cost to market value at the date of the Balance Sheet in the case of investments which are current assets or to long-term value in the case of investments which are fixed assets."

6. Trade investments. These may be considered as such where the investment has been made in order to secure some trading advantage, such as in the case of vertical integration. It follows that the investment to afford some advantage has to be of such an amount proportionately that the company must be able to gain some effective power in the company concerned. Such investments will be shown normally at cost, but to quote again (*see* 5):

> "Exceptional circumstances may arise in which an undertaking, wherein an important trade investment is held, has retained and accumulated profits on such a scale that the income which reaches the investor company and the amount at which the investment is carried in the accounts are a wholly inadequate reflection of the value of the investment, although this fact is not apparent from the trade investments item in the Balance Sheet or from the accounts as a whole. In such circumstances consideration should be given to the question whether the relative importance of the matter is such that without some explanation in the accounts they would fail to show a fair view."

7. Investments in subsidiary companies. Investments in subsidiary companies and indebtedness to and by subsidiaries must be shown separately in the holding company's balance sheet (*Companies Act, 1948, 8th Schedule, Part 2*), and therefore, in order to ensure that a true and fair view is given, the auditor must satisfy himself that the values shown are true. This will involve examination of the balance sheet and accounts of the subsidiaries, and if, after enquiry, he is not satisfied, he should qualify his report accordingly.

The auditor should ensure that dividends received after acquisition of controlling interests, if paid out of pre-acquisition profits, are credited against the cost of the shares, so reducing their value, as the holding company has since received part of the value which it originally purchased.

8. Quoted and unquoted investments. In the case of quoted shares, the Stock Exchange official list should be consulted and the value fixed at the mid-market price, *i.e.*, the figure between the quoted buying and selling prices.

To obtain a valuation figure where investments are made in companies whose shares are not quoted, it will be necessary to obtain past final accounts and balance sheets, and to request the secretary of the company to give information as to the value at which recent share transactions have taken place. Some idea of the valuation may also be obtained by computation on a dividend yield basis, as compared with companies of a similar nature.

The *Companies Act, 1967*, requires that the matters referred to in the following heads shall, if not otherwise shown, be stated by way of note or in a statement or report annexed (in the case of investments consisting in equity share capital other than any whose values as estimated by the directors are separately shown).   Sch. 2, para. 5A:

(a) "the aggregate amount of the company's income for the financial year that is ascribable to the investments;
(b) the amount of the company's share before taxation, and the amount of that share after taxation, of the net aggregate amount of the profits of the bodies in which the investments are held, being profits for the several periods to which accounts sent by them during the financial year to the company related, after deducting those bodies' losses for those periods (or vice versa);
(c) the amount of the company's share of the net aggregate amount of the undistributed profits accumulated by the bodies in which the investments are held since the time when the investments were acquired, after deducting the losses accumulated by them since that time (or vice versa);
(d) the manner in which any losses incurred by the said bodies have been dealt with in the company's accounts."

9. Current assets. The valuation of current assets are more often of an obvious nature, such as liquid funds. Book debts should be dealt with on their verification as to any bad debts to be written off or provision against such to be made.

Stock in trade and work in progress are dealt with in Chapter X.

10. Intangible and fictitious assets. Because an asset is intangible, it does not signify that it may be of no value; goodwill is an example of this.

(a) *Goodwill.* There is no legal liability to write off goodwill, and if this is done, there is nothing against writing it back at a fair value so making the profits originally written off available for distribution: *Stapley* v. *Read Bros. Ltd.* (*1924*). It is usual to show goodwill at its cost value until written off, however, and as in such circumstances as where goodwill has been paid on acquisition of a branch since disposed of, it would be misleading to leave such an asset on the balance sheet. The auditor should use his discretion in considering whether goodwill shown at cost is really of the value shown, and would be wise to comment in his report if he considers such is misleading to any degree.

(b) *Preliminary expenses, discount on issue of debentures and other fictitious assets.*

Fictitious assets such as these should be written off as soon as possible for they are of no value. In any case, they should not be left on the balance sheet at the same time as the inclusion of reserves, since the true excess of assets over liabilities cannot be said to be represented in part by such fictitious assets.

PROGRESS TEST 9

1. What one main cause has made valuation from the auditing point of view more difficult in recent years? (1)

2. State briefly the Institute of Chartered Accountants' recommendations with regard to changes in the purchasing power of money. (2)

3. Summarise the recommendations with regard to events taking place after the balance sheet date. (3)

4. Where it is decided to revalue freehold properties, what is the auditor's duty regarding this? (4)

5. Where the company's own employees are engaged on work

in erection of machines, how should the expenditure involved be treated? **(4)**

6. How may such expenditure as in Question 5 above be vouched? **(4)**

7. Under what heading should investments be shown on the balance sheet? **(5)**

8. If investments are considered as fixed assets, is there any necessity to provide for their diminution in value? **(5)**

9. How should investments in subsidiary companies be valued? **(7)**

10. At what value is it usual to show goodwill? **(10)**

SPECIMEN QUESTIONS

1. To what extent, if any, do you consider that an auditor should take into account events which happen after the balance sheet date but before the completion of the audit? Reasons and examples should be given of your explanations. *C.C.A.*

2. Discuss the extent to which an auditor should have regard to events occurring after the balance sheet date when auditing the following items in a company's balance sheet:

(a) Fixed assets.
(b) Debtors.
(c) Stock-in-trade. *C.A. (E.W.)*

3. To what extent should an auditor have regard to events that take place between the balance sheet date of a client's business and the date of the completion of his audit? *C.A. (E.W.) (Inter.)*

CHAPTER X

VERIFICATION AND VALUATION OF STOCK AND WORK IN PROGRESS

The verification of stock in trade and work in progress held and their proper valuation is of the utmost importance to the auditor.

The case of *The Kingston Cotton Mill Co. Ltd., 1896,* is taken as exemplifying the governing principle regarding the auditor and his general responsibility thereto. In this case it was held *not to be the duty of the auditor to take stock, and that he is not guilty of negligence if he accepts the certificate of a responsible official in the absence of suspicious circumstances.* This does not absolve the auditor from his responsibility to exercise his professional skill in ascertaining that stocks are what they are stated to be. The defalcations arising by means of the manipulation of stocks and the moneys expended upon them have been numerous and the auditor must apply the utmost care in investigating the procedures governing these and the true position with end of period stocks on hand.

VERIFICATION

1. Auditing difficulties. In the first instance where raw materials or other goods are purchased the procedures operating must be sound. These have been dealt with (*see* p. 58), covering the ordering of goods and the subsequent receipt of invoices. But to illustrate the difficulties which may arise it may be mentioned that where collusion took place in a business, sums of money were paid away to a fictitious company having its own bank account and for which invoices were specially printed, while stocks were purported to be held in various outside warehouses for which certificates were supplied. Such a case as this is exceptional and difficult to discover but does serve to emphasise the necessity of sound audit procedures to ascertain that not only are payments made on properly authenticated documents but also that goods are duly received.

Furthermore, the double entry book figures which are normally available to the auditor may not be applicable in the case of stocks since the figures are in effect introduced into the system after verification and valuation of the physical stocks. This fact is sufficient to make it possible to manipulate the amount of profits or losses shown in a business by inflation or deflation of the figures for stocks held.

2. The auditor and physical stock-taking. Although it is not part of the auditor's duty to take stock, the application of auditing in depth has caused attention to be given to the physical aspects of control of stock. In recognition of this the I.C.A. have issued *Recommendation U.9* in which it is advocated that in examining the effectiveness of the internal control of stock the auditor should observe personally how the procedures involved are carried out, not completely but on a test basis. Measures to ensure efficient stock control within the business are mentioned and suggested audit procedures are outlined, including the following:

(a) *Before stock-taking.* The client's stock-taking instructions should be examined. After familiarising himself with the procedures the auditor should discuss any weaknesses with the client.

(b) *During stock-taking.* In order to ensure efficient stock-checking counts or recounts should be made in the employees' presence of certain items by selecting mainly objects of high value and checking these back from records to warehouse or vice versa. Notes should be taken of any important matters, such as slow-moving stocks, for later examination.

(c) *After stock-taking.* The "cut off" should be checked especially with regard to any movements of stock near the end date.

Where physical attendance is not possible, the auditor should exercise his skill to obtain additional evidence such as independent confirmation, but in any case responsibility rests with management to provide stock figures and the auditors should make it clear that they are not attending for the purposes of taking stock but to examine the effectiveness of the client's procedures.

3. Cut-off procedures. *Cut-off* procedures are those arrangements made in order to ensure that at a particular point of time, *e.g.*, the end of the financial period, there will be agreement between the physical stock in trade and work in progress and the figures shown in the accounts, as obtained from the records of purchases, sales, debtors and creditors.

Briefly, the relevant considerations are:

(a) The linking of sales and stock records to ensure goods sold but not dispatched are excluded from stock.

(b) The linking of purchases and stock records to ensure all invoices are included for stock held wherever situated.

(c) Where physical stocktaking is at a date other than the balance sheet date that the movements of stock in or out are properly added or deducted as required.

(d) That stocks held on others' behalf are excluded from stock figures.

4. Auditing procedures. In *Recommendation U.11* the Council of the I.C.A. have pointed out that in order to satisfy themselves as to the validity of the amount attributed to stock it will be necessary for the auditors to check the soundness of the procedures adopted and to test the competence of their execution. However, responsibility still rests with the directors to ensure that stock is properly recorded and that the physical quantities and condition of stock are ascertained, and that the amount shown on the balance sheet has been properly determined by suitable methods.

Audit procedures, in addition to attendance at stocktaking, should cover:

(a) General scrutiny of stock records and comparison with the previous year, attention being given to the possibility of material omissions or inclusion of items, such as loose tools which should appear elsewhere in the accounts.

(b) Where applicable, tests by reference to statistical information covering matters such as yields which may be expected from given quantities and normal losses or gains by evaporation or absorption of moisture.

Where stock is defective or is obsolete or slow-moving, these factors must be taken into account. Audit tests of the company's procedure for judging the physical condition will normally include:

(a) Scrutiny of stock records to ascertain what information as to condition and slow-moving stocks has been recorded and what action has been taken on that information.

(b) Comparison with the stock records relating to the previous balance sheet date.

(c) Examination by reference to normal experience of wastage due to rejects and deterioration.

(d) Examination of the relationship between stocks and turn-over, including consideration of current trading conditions and any changes in sales or stock-piling policies.

(e) Discussion with the management.

5. Amount at which stock is stated. Valuation of stock is dealt with hereafter but further procedures mentioned in U 11 are as follows.

After examining the principles adopted by the management, the audit procedure to test the application of those principles will normally include:

(a) Test of the stock sheets or continuous stock records with relevant documents such as invoices, costing records and other sources for the ascertainment of "cost."

(b) Examination and testing of the treatment of overhead expenses.

(c) Tests of "net realisable value" (or, as the case may be, "replacement price").

(d) Careful enquiry of responsible officials and examination of evidence supporting the assessment of net realisable value, with particular reference to defective, obsolete or slow-moving stock, and consideration of the reasonableness of the replies from officials to the enquiries made.

(e) Tests of the arithmetical accuracy of the calculations.

(f) Tests of the consistency, in principle and in detail, with which the amounts have been computed.

(g) Consideration of the adequacy of the description applied to stock-in-trade and work in progress in the accounts.

6. Work in progress. Costing records, work tickets attached to unfinished work, relevant contracts, and, in fact, any financial or statistical data likely to be of help, should be examined, as often it is not possible to identify physical quantities of stock in work in progress.

Where such difficulties arise the auditor will wish to ascertain.

(a) The nature and reliability of the costing records.

(b) The extent to which checks are made by reference to statistical information concerning outputs of main products and of by-products (if any) which ought to be obtained from materials used.

(c) The system of inspection and reporting thereon to enable allowance to be made in the costing records for scrapping and rectification.

(d) The basis upon which overheads and profit elements are dealt with (*see* pp. 152 and 156).

7. Overall tests.   Audit tests which may often be appropriate by way of overall assessment of the reliability of the records will include, according to circumstances:

(a) Reconciliation of changes in stock quantities as between the beginning and end of the financial year with the records of purchases, production and sales.

(b) Comparison of the quantities and amounts of stocks in the various categories with those included at the previous balance sheet date and with current sales and purchases.

(c) Consideration of the gross profit ratio shown by the accounts and its comparison with the ratio shown in previous years.

(d) Consideration of the rate of turnover of stocks and its comparison with previous years.

(e) Consideration of the relationship of the quantities ready for sale and in course of production with the quantities shown in operating and sales budgets.

(f) Where applicable, examination of standard costing records and consideration of the variances shown thereby and their treatment in the accounts.

8. Independent stock-takers.   The auditors should ascertain direct with the stock-taking firm the basis of valuation used, and assure themselves that proper cut-off procedures have been operated.   Although it may be that the stock count and valuation are virtually one operation, nevertheless the auditors must still accept their own responsibility in forming an opinion.

9. Inventory letters.   It is usual and desirable to obtain from a director or other responsible official a written statement outlining in detail stock quantities and bases of valuation. This constitutes both a record of action taken by management and a reminder of their responsibility, but this in no way relieves the auditors of their own responsibility to form their own opinion as to the stock being reported upon and presented in the accounts.

F

VALUATION

10. Recommendations of the I.C.A. The Council of the Institute of Chartered Accountants have made recommendations (N. 22) as to "The treatment of stock-in-trade and work in progress in financial accounts" which merit careful study in the original. The quotations in the remainder of this chapter are from that source.

The basis for valuation of stock-in-trade and work-in-progress may be stated briefly as being that of cost, net realisable value or replacement price, whichever is the lowest, but it is in computing cost and the amount, if any, to be written off, that practical difficulties arise. The elements making up the cost of stock are:

    (a) Direct expenditure on the purchase of goods bought for resale, and of materials and components used in the manufacture of finished goods.

    (b) Other direct expenditure which can be identified specifically as having been incurred in acquiring the stock or bringing it to its existing condition and location; examples are direct labour, transport, processing and packaging.

    (c) Such part, if any, of the overhead expenditure as is properly carried forward in the circumstances of the business instead of being charged against the revenue of the period in which it was incurred.

11. Overhead expenditure. Overhead expenditure is recognised as a necessary cost of production and of bringing goods to the market, such overheads being classified as either factory overheads, administration overheads, and in fixing selling prices these expenses are taken into consideration. But when valuing stock, whether in a finished or partly finished state, upon which such overheads have been expended, opinions differ as to the wisdom of increasing the direct costs of labour and material by the overheads incurred.

In some cases no overhead is included, this is a conservative policy and keeps stocks down to their direct cost value.

Where the "marginal" cost of stock in included, only those expenses directly concerned with production of the actual stock remaining is included, *i.e.*, all other overheads, such as depreciation, are written off in the accounts of the period concerned, as it is considered they would have been incurred irrespective of the stock remaining.

Where overheads, based on normal production costs, are included, a proportion of the total overheads incurred, whether directly or indirectly concerned with the stock on hand, is added.

12. Consistent valuation. It is generally accepted that although production overheads may be added to stock values, it is not always prudent to add overheads in respect of administration or selling and distribution costs. Whichever method is decided upon, however it is essential that it should be applied consistently.

13. Overheads: deciding factors. In deciding the method to adopt with regard to the inclusion or omission of overheads, the nature of the business would normally be the deciding factor. The following serve to illustrate the matters to be taken into consideration:

(a) *Fluctuating production and sales levels.* Where a smooth flow of production and sales takes place, profits may not be greatly influenced by the inclusion of overheads, but where wide fluctuations take place profits may be made to fluctuate unduly by their addition.

(b) *Risks of subsequent losses arising.* Where sales are of a nature which is not easily predictable, it is prudent to keep stock values as low as practical, as in the case of certain fashion trades.

(c) *Work of a protracted nature.* Building and other contractors often have their work spread over periods of years, and to exclude overheads would cause the profits of such businesses to be unduly low in early years of a contract and abnormally high on completion.

(d) *Where stocks are held over long periods.* Fixed costs may be proportionately high in the case of businesses holding maturing stocks, so to add continuing overheads to stock values would cause heavy risks to be incurred in respect of future sales.

(e) *The extent of the variation in fixed or standing charges.* "The less the fixed or standing charges vary in amount with variations in the volume of output, and the more they accrue on a purely time basis, the greater is the justification for their exclusion."

14. Exclusion of fixed overheads. In **11** (e) the recommendations mentioned have been quoted as it is of the utmost importance to ensure that overheads incurred purely on a time basis should be excluded from stock variations. To increase the value of stocks merely because fixed overhead charges are incurred by the passage of time would be unwise policy. For example, a slowing down in sales might cause an increase in quantities of stocks held and also increase the time for which they are held. To add further charges to their value due to expense incurred in having to retain such goods in stock, which in any case is due to a lack of demand, would be most unwise.

15. Methods of computing cost. The methods of computing cost are varied, and where a number of different lines is dealt in, more than one method may be employed. The following are most frequently used:

(a) "*Unit*" *cost.* The total cost of stock is computed by aggregating the individual costs of each article, batch, parcel or other unit. The method is not always capable of application, either because the individual units lose their identity (notably where stocks are bulked or pass through a number of processes) or because it would involve undue expense or complexity to keep individual records of cost particularly where these necessitate allocations of expense.

(b) "*First in, first out.*" Cost is computed on the assumption that goods sold or consumed are those which have been longest on hand and that those remaining in stock represent the latest purchases or production.

(c) "*Average*" *cost.* Cost is computed by averaging the amount at which stock is brought forward at the beginning of a period with the cost of stock acquired during the period; consumption in the period is then deducted at the average cost thus ascertained. The periodical rests for calculating the average are as frequent as the circumstances and nature of the business require and permit. In times of rising price levels this method tends to give a lower amount than the cost of unsold stock ascertained on a "first in, first out" basis and in times of falling prices a higher amount.

(d) "*Standard*" *cost.* A predetermined or budgeted cost per unit is used. The method is particularly convenient where goods pass through a number of processes or are manufactured on mass production lines; but it will not result in a fair approximation to actual cost unless there is a regular review of the standards with appropriate adjustment and revision where necessary.

(e) *"Adjusted selling price."* This method is used widely in retail businesses. The cost of stock is estimated by calculating it in the first instance at selling prices and then deducting an amount equal to the normal margin of gross profit on such stocks. It should be appreciated that where the selling prices have been reduced the calculation will bring out cost only if appropriate allowance for price reductions is included in fixing the margin to be deducted; if no such allowance is made it may bring out amounts which approximate to replacement price as defined below. The calculations under this method may be made for individual items or groups of items or by departments.

16. Net realisable value and replacement price.

The Institute of Chartered Accountants Recommendations quoted above also mention various methods of valuation which briefly are:

(a) *Reduction to net realisable value.* Where it is known that part or all of the cost incurred on stocks held will be irrecoverable, provision must be made for the losses arising. Such calculations may be made on:

(i) Each individual article.
(ii) Articles in certain categories.
(iii) The total cost value in relation to its total net realisable value.

The loss sustained is considered as being the difference between its cost ascertained and the net realisable value as estimated. In arriving at the net realisable value all information available should be used, even that arising after the close of the accounting period.

(b) *Reduction to replacement price.* Reduction of cost values to replacement price would normally be applied in special circumstances, and even then would not exclude the addition of certain overheads to the reduced basic price if such overheads were usually applied.

The special circumstances might be those of:

(i) *Uncertainty of net realisable value.* If the lengths of production times are long or proportionately large stocks are held in comparison with turnover, then selling prices at the balance sheet date may be unreliable for fixing net realisable values.

(ii) *Selling prices based on current replacement prices.* If it is desired to reflect current replacement prices in selling prices, subsequent profits would be adversely affected where replacement prices have already fallen; in this case valuation should be adjusted to cover the fall in value in the current period.

(iii) *Adjusting for losses sustained due to inefficient buying.* To obviate the carrying forward of losses already sustained, stock values would be reduced to replacement price.

To quote the Recommendations:

"Replacement price" for this purpose means an estimate of the amount for which, in the ordinary course of business, the stock could have been acquired or produced either at the balance sheet date or during the latest period up to and including that date. In a manufacturing business this estimate would be based on the replacement price of the raw material content plus other costs of the undertaking which are relevant to the condition of the stock on the balance sheet date. In all cases the prices used should be a fair reflection of the ordinary course of business; a depression which has passed before the accounts are completed would generally be disregarded."

17. Special bases of valuation. In some businesses special bases of stock valuations are used, *e.g.*:

(a) *Stocks at selling prices.* Such cases are very rare and apply to such companies as those of tea or rubber, or sometimes mining companies, or by manufacturing companies in respect of by-products.

(b) *Long term contracts.* These have been mentioned previously. Due to length of time over which contracts are spread profits may be added to work-in-progress on a conservative basis.

(c) *Base stock.* This rather unrealistic basis is sometimes applied whereby a basic amount of stock is considered to be purchased, and all purchases thereafter are treated as renewing the basic amount. If the base stock is large this could lead to the portrayal of an unusually small figure for stock held on the balance sheet and cause in effect a secret reserve to arise.

(d) *Last in, first out.* Under this system the last delivery of goods in is accounted to be the first to be disposed of (*see* "First in, First out, p. 152).

18. F.I.F.O. and L.I.F.O.

(a) *Effect on profits.* To illustrate the effect of the systems of *F.I.F.O.* (First in, First out) and *L.I.F.O.* (Last in, first out) respectively, the following trading accounts where only one particular commodity is dealt with may clarify the effect on trading profits in conditions where prices are rising.

(i) *F.I.F.O.*

Trading account

Purchases (in chronological order)

	£	£		£	£
200 @ 20s.	200		Sales 360 @ 40s.		720
200 @ 25s.	250		Closing stock		
200 @ 30s.	300		40 @ 25s.	50	
		750	200 @ 30s.	300	
Gross profit		320			350
		£1,070			£1,070

(ii) *L.I.F.O.*

Trading account

	£	£		£	£
Purchases					
200 @ 20s.	200		Sales 360 @ 40s.		720
200 @ 25s.	250		Closing stock		
200 @ 30s.	300		40 @ 25s.	50	
		750	200 @ 20s.	200	
Gross profit		220			250
		£970			£970

(b) *Economic effects.* It will be observed that in a time where prices and profits are rising the effect of the L.I.F.O. method of valuation is to have a neutralising effect on profits. In the illustration given the effect is actually to reduce profits but the further complication of possible increases in sale prices where inflationary tendencies are in operation cannot be ignored, in this case the profits would still be lessened, although not to such a marked degree.

As the opposite effect of that shown above would operate in a period of falling prices, *i.e.*, that profits would tend to increase, economists are much in favour of the L.I.F.O. method of stock valuations since if applied on a national scale a lessening of purchasing power would apply in times of inflation, and conversely, greater profits might be distributed in times when the economy is running down.

(c) *Accountancy standpoint.* Viewed, however, from the accounting standpoint, the application of the L.I.F.O. method presents recording and pricing difficulties and is not very practical unless applied to special types of business where purchase orders may be easily allocated to particular contracts.

19. Recommendations of the Institute of Chartered Accountants (N. 22).

It is recommended that the following principles be applied by every industrial and commercial enterprise.

Appropriate amounts for all stock-in-trade (including raw materials and partly finished or finished stocks) and all work in progress, wherever situated and whatever their nature, should be included in the financial accounts and should be computed in accordance with the recommendations below. There is no justification for the omission of stock nor for stating stock at an amount which is higher or lower than the amount so computed; to use a higher amount would be to overstate profits (or understate losses) of the period and reduce the profits (or increase the losses) of the next period, whilst to use a lower amount would be to create a reserve which should be so described and disclosed and should not be treated as a charge against revenue.

A profit should not be anticipated unless this is justified by the special bases used in some businesses but provision should be made to the full extent of expected losses.

The amount carried forward for stock and work in progress should be computed on a basis which, having regard to the nature and circumstances of the business, will enable the accounts to show a ture and fair view of the trading results and the financial position. In most businesses the basis should be the cost of the stock held, less any part thereof which properly needs to be written off at the balance sheet date.

The circumstances of each business should determine the basis which is appropriate and the method of computation which should be adopted in determining cost and the part thereof, if any, which should be written off. In most businesses the choice lies between writing off any excess of cost over either (a) the net realisable value of the stock, or (b) the lower of net realisable value and replacement price, these terms having the meanings attributed to them below. In some businesses it may be appropriate to use special bases, including some which depart from the rule that profit should not be anticipated.

The basis adopted and the methods of computation should be used consistently from period to period. A change of basis or method should not normally be made unless the circumstances have changed in such a way that its continued use would prevent the accounts from showing a true and fair view of the position and results. When a change is made the effect, if material, should be disclosed as an exceptional item in the profit and loss account or by way of note.

The following are the meanings attributed to "cost," "net realisable value" and "replacement price" in this Recommendation:

(a) "Cost" means all expenditure incurred directly in the purchase or manufacture of the stock and the bringing of it to its existing condition and location, together with such part, if any, of the overhead expenditure as is appropriately carried forward in the circumstances of the business instead of being charged against the revenue of the period in which it was incurred.

(b) "Net realisable value" means the amount that it is estimated, as on the balance sheet date, will be realised from disposal of stock in the ordinary course of business, either in its existing condition or as incorporated in the product normally sold, after allowing for all expenditure to be incurred on or before disposal.

(c) "Replacement price" means an estimate of the amount for which in the ordinary course of business the stock could have been acquired or produced either at the balance sheet date or in the latest period up to and including that date. In a manufacturing business this estimate would be based on the replacement price of the raw material content plus other costs of the undertaking which are relevant to the condition of the stock on the balance sheet date.

Where the amount carried forward for stock is material in relation to either the trading results or the financial position, the accounts should indicate concisely the manner in which the amount has been computed. If this is not practicable the accounts should contain a note to the effect that a concise statement of the bases and methods used is not practicable but that the amount has been determined for the whole of the stock at the balance sheet date on bases and by methods of computation which are considered appropriate in the circumstances of the business and have been used consistently. The use of the term "market value" should be discontinued.

Goods purchased forward do not form part of the stock-in-trade or work in progress on the balance sheet date but where they are not covered by forward sales, provision should be made in the accounts for the excess, if any, of the purchase price over the net realisable value (or over replacement price, where lower than net realisable value, if stock is stated at the lowest of cost, net realisable value, and replacement price)   Similarly, where goods have been sold forward and are not covered by stocks and forward purchases, provision should be made in the accounts for the excess, if any, of the expected cost over their net realisable value.   Such provisions should not be deducted from the amount at which stock is stated.

INTERNAL CONTROL QUESTIONNAIRE
STOCKS AND WORK IN PROGRESS

(A) *General*.   Note that certain aspects of the Internal Control Questionnaire in respect of receipt and issue of stocks are dealt with in sections covering Purchases and Trade Creditors and Sales and Trade Debtors.
  1. Has a list of all warehouses and stores been received or prepared and duly certified by a responsible official?
  2. Is stock efficiently handled as to storage and packing and properly safeguarded?
  3. Is a continuous stocktaking maintained or annually? List centres if partially applied as to which is in operation.
  4. Do all goods pass through stores or are some delivered direct to customers or sites?

(B) *Documentation*
  5. Are goods only released on authorised requisitions?
  6. Who has authority to authorise these?
  7. Are Returned to Stores dockets completed when stores are returned?
  8. Are proper bin cards maintained in respect of all goods?
  9. Are the warehouse records maintained in quantity and value?
  10. Are stock records maintained by
      (a) storekeepers,
      (b) persons independent of those handling stores?
  11. From what sources are entries made in respect of
      (a) receipts,
      (b) issues?
  12. Is any system of internal check operated to ensure that

only authorised transactions and documents are entered
on stock records?

13. Are control accounts maintained in respect of stocks,
and are these compared and reconciled with warehouse
records?

14. Are the staff who prepare and check control accounts
independent of those maintaining stock records?

15. Are all inter-company sales clearly recorded for later
identification on valuation?

(C) Work in progress

16. Is an efficient system of costing in operation?

17. Are costing figures reconciled with financial accounts or
is a fully integrated system in operation?

18. If reconciliations are made, how regularly is this done?

19. Is it possible to trace the amount of expense involved on
jobs at any given time, i.e., direct costs and indirect
expenses?

20. By what method are overheads charged to jobs?

21. Are overheads divided into fixed and variable?

22. What system is operated to ensure charges to works
orders are properly allocated?

23. If standard or predetermined costs are used
    (a) At what intervals are variances compiled?
    (b) How often are standards revised?
    (c) How often are variances written off?
    (d) Whose responsibility is it to deal with this?

24. What records are compiled when materials and labour
are transferred between jobs or between departments?

25. What system is applied to ensure the accuracy of work
in progress values and existence, *e.g.*, physical verification
or otherwise?

(D) Scrap and by-products

26. What types of these arise?

27. What control is exercised over these and what documentation arises?

(E) Stocktaking

28. Is a responsible official in charge of stocktaking at each
centre? (list names and centres).

29. Are detailed written instructions given to staff as to
method, recording, teams, marking off completed bins,
etc.

30. Are stock checkers
    (a) independent of those maintaining the stores,
    (b) never less than two working together?

31. Are specially printed and numbered stock sheets issued and checked for continuity on return?

32. By what method are stock quantities entered:
    (a) By stock checkers, or
    (b) Previous to stock-taking from continuous stock records?

33. Is comment called for as to condition or movement of stock?

34. By what method is work in progress counted:
    (a) As having reached a certain stage in production?
    (b) As a complete job less certain parts?
    (c) As an assembly of various parts?

35. Are all stock sheets signed by those taking stock and countersigned by the official in charge.

36. What system is in operation to ensure that, purchases returns, sales returns, transfers between departments, are recorded in the correct accounting periods?

37. What arrangements have been made to ensure that where liabilities for goods in transit are accepted the goods are included in the stock figures?

38. Are certificates obtained from third parties where goods are held by them, and how often are these obtained?

39. (a) Are stock sheets compared with stock records)
    (b) Are the stock records adjusted to agree with physical stock-taking?
    (c) Are material differences investigated?
    (d) Whose responsibility is it to carry out (c) above?

(F) Stock valuation

40. Is stock valued on the basis of the lowest of
    (a) cost,
    (b) net realisable value,
    (c) replacement price?
    If cost, state method applied, *e.g.*, F.I.F.O., L.I.F.O., average or standard.

41. Are any stocks consistently valued below cost?

42. Are any stocks valued on an estimated basis below cost, if so, by whom is the estimate made, and for what reason?

43. Work in progress—*see* (c) 16–25 above.

44. If profit is taken on uncompleted contracts,
    (a) On what basis is this calculated?
    (b) Is such profit authenticated by a responsible official?

45. Is provision made against unrealised profit on inter-company sales made on a cost plus basis?

46. On what basis are
    (a) by products,
    (b) scrap,
    (c) obsolete stocks valued,
    and who is responsible for this?
47. From what sources are prices on stock sheets obtained?
    Are these independently checked?
48. If forward purchases or sales are made,
    (a) What system is operated to ensure that such
        contracts are recorded in the accounting records?
    (b) Are forward profits and/or losses brought in or
        provided against in the current period. If so, on
        what basis are stocks valued?

STANDARD AUDIT PROGRAMME

STOCK AND WORK IN PROGRESS

(A) *General*

1. Obtain a copy of any instructions to staff as to method
   of stock-taking and examine as to adequacy.
2. Ensure that issue of stock sheets has been properly
   controlled—where prenumbered, test for complete
   sequence, noting that all have been signed and countersigned.
3. If final stock sheets are supplied, request originals and
   test these enquiring into any relevant differences.
4. If continuous stock records are maintained, test the
   stock sheets with the records, noting that the records
   are adjusted and that the cards have been marked as to
   the physical check amounts. Enquire into any material
   differences, and examine authority for writing off
   differences.
5. If the continuous stock records are used for the year end
   figures, ensure that a physical check has been made at
   least once during the year and that the records have been
   marked accordingly.
6. Enquire as to method dealing with work in progress,
   ascertain whether physical inspection takes place. If
   not, check how the company verifies its existence. Test
   check records of some of the larger items.
7. Check that stock in transit is received after closing date.
8. Examine stock sheets to ensure that items other than
   stock are excluded, *e.g.*, capital items, property of third
   parties.
9. Ensure that the cut-off procedures are properly operated
   by testing items of sales, sales returns, purchases and

purchases returns, to ensure that items are excluded or included as necessary. (*See* p. 148.)

(B) Valuation

1. Test prices shown as cost value with suppliers' invoices or other evidence. Where net realisable value or replacement prices are less than the cost figures shown, ensure that stocks are of normal production requirements and that a profit may still be made on the finished product.

2. Where base stock is valued, ascertain the reason for the application and that the valuation is consistently applied. Ascertain that the fact of such valuation has been notified to the Inland Revenue authorities.

3. Ascertain the method of valuation of any scrap or by-products.

4. The value of work in progress should be checked with the costing records (*see* I.C.Q. Section (*c*)).
   - (*a*) noting that individual cost records are in agreement with control accounts,
   - (*b*) comparing overhead rates with those used in the current period,
   - (*c*) examining a number of items to ensure that with estimated future costs a profit may still be made in view of the ultimate sale or contract price.

5. Ensure that any inter-company or inter-branch unrealised profit on stock or work in progress is eliminated. (This may be traced back from the type of stock or work in progress concerned.)

6. Where contracts are outstanding, ensure that any profit taken is calculated on a consistent basis (see I.C.Q.) and investigate the possibility of losses of retention moneys or penalties arising.

7. Investigate slow moving or obsolete stocks, ensure that the system is such as to reveal these, and that the method of valuation is satisfactory and duly certified.

8. If standard or predetermined costs are used, ensure that
   - (*a*) The method of overhead recovery is satisfactory.
   - (*b*) The standards applied are in accordance with current conditions.
   - (*c*) The variances arising are properly accounted for so far as stock is concerned.

9. Investigate overall stock position as compared with previous year, check with previous gross profit, and if possible, account for any material changes. Check stock to turnover ratio.

10. Obtain a stock certificate from chairman or managing director.

PROGRESS TEST 10

1. What is the governing principle with regard to the auditor's duty concerning the verification and valuation of stock in trade? (1)

2. What peculiar difficulties are experienced in the verification and valuation of stock in trade? (1)

3. Enumerate the auditing procedures in verification of stock in trade. (3)

4. What are "cut off" procedures? Why is their efficient operation of importance to the auditor? (4)

5. How may work-in-progress be verified? (5)

6. What audit procedures should be applied regarding finished goods? (6)

7. Is the certificate of an expert valuer sufficient evidence of the existence and value of stock for audit purposes? (7)

8. What, in brief, are the main methods of valuation of stock recommended by the Institute of Chartered Accountants? (8)

9. What are the deciding factors regarding the inclusion of overheads in stock valuation? (9)

10. Why should fixed overheads be excluded from stock values? (12)

11. In what circumstances may special bases of stock valuation be appropriate? (15)

12. Explain the effect of F.I.F.O. and L.I.F.O. and summarise the recommendations of the Institute of Chartered Accountants in connection with them. (16, 17)

SPECIMEN QUESTIONS

1. As auditor of Exwy Ltd., a manufacturing company, you are required to state concisely what audit tests you would apply in relation to the ascertainment of the physical quantities and ownership of stock-in-trade, excluding work in progress.

You may assume that the company maintains continuous stock records and that all stocks are held at the factory. *C.A. (E.W.)*

2. Write an essay on the auditor's duties in relation to the verification (but not the valuation) of stock-in-trade and work-in-progress of a manufacturing company. *C.A. (E.W.)*

3. The stock-in-trade of a limited company as on the balance sheet date has been based on a physical count made ten days

previously and valued at cost, the total being adjusted for transactions subsequently arising.

State what steps you would take to ascertain that the proper
amount has been included in the balance sheet.

You are not required to discuss the basis of valuation.

C.A. (E.W.) (Inter.)

4. After completion of the general routine audit of the accounts
of Russell Ltd., you find that, although the books appear to be in
order, the rate of gross profit on sales appears to be unduly high.
You suspect that profits have been deliberately inflated.   What
steps would you take to satisfy yourself on the matter?   *C.C.A.*

5. The accounts of a firm of wholesalers disclose an unexpected
increase in the rate of gross profit on sales.   You suspect that the
profits may have been overstated.

State the steps you would take to satisfy yourself of the
accuracy of the accounts.   *C.A. (E.W.)*

6. State four methods of valuation which might be applied to
quantities of similar stock, purchased at various times and prices
during the year, and state the advantages and disadvantages of
each.   *C.C.A. (Inter.)*

7. In a year when the value of sales of a wholesale grocery
business has increased substantially, you find that the net profit
has been considerably reduced.   How would you satisfy yourself
as to the accuracy of the accounts and in what particular respects
would you investigate the transactions during the year?   *C.C.A.*

8. (a) For what purpose, and in what circumstances would you
consider it desirable for the auditor of a limited company
to attend at stocktaking?

(b) To what extent is the auditor affected by the employment by the company of independent stock-takers and
valuers?

(c) What overall audit tests may be appropriate when
assessing the reliability of records of stock-in-trade and
work in progress?   *C.A. (E.W.)*

9. What enquiries and tests should be made by an auditor to
satisfy himself that at the date of the balance sheet:

(a) the balances on continuous stock records can be relied upon
to prove accurate figures of stock quantities;

(b) the cost figures appearing in stock sheets are correct; and

(c) the values placed on by-products can be accepted?   *C.A.
(E.W.)*

CHAPTER XI

RETENTION AND DISTRIBUTION OF PROFITS

NATURE OF PROFITS

The recognised object of any business is that of earning profits, but what constitutes profits is a matter not easily established.

1. Definition of profits. Profits may be defined as "the increase in the net value of the assets of a business over their net value at the commencement of a given period which has arisen other than by capital adjustment."

Whilst this definition has the advantage of brevity, due to the many difficulties which have arisen in practice it is necessary to have a more exact description, and the following is that given by the Court in the case of the *Spanish Prospecting Co. Ltd., 1911*:

". . . If the total assets of the business at the two dates be compared, the increase which they show at the later date as compared with the earlier date (due allowance, of course, being made for any capital introduced into or taken out of the business in the meanwhile) represents in strictness the profits of the business during the period in question. . . . The strict meaning of the word 'profit' is rarely observed in drawing up the accounts of firms or companies . . . . Certain assumptions have become so customary in drawing up balance sheets and profit and loss accounts that it may almost be said to require special circumstances to induce parties to depart therefrom. For instance, it is usual to exclude gains and losses arising from causes not directly connected with the businessof the company. . . . The value assigned to trade buildings and plant is usually fixed according to arbitrary rule, by which they are originally taken at their actual cost and are assumed to have depreciated by a certain percentage each year, though it cannot be pretended that any such calculation necessarily gives their true value either in use or exchange. . . . It is better to under-rate than to over-rate the profits, since it is impossible for you to see all the risks to which a business may in future be exposed. . . . But though there is a wide field for variation of practice in these estimations of profit, this liberty ceases at once when the rights of third parties intervene. . . . In the absence of certain stipulations to the contrary, 'profits,' in cases where the rights of third parties come in, mean actual profits, and they must be calculated as closely as possible, in accordance with the definition to which I have referred."

It is in the *distribution* of profits, or the charges to be set against them, that most of the difficulties mentioned have arisen, but before proceeding to these matters, the *retention* of profits for various purposes will be considered.

2. Ploughing back of profits. In dealing with the subject of depreciation it has been pointed out that to distribute profits without making adequate provision for the replacement of assets is an unwise policy to pursue. In the case of sole traders and partnerships they are free to pursue any course of action in this respect which they may desire to do, and even with limited companies it is not legally required that fixed assets shall be depreciated. Nevertheless, to ignore depreciation of the fixed assets of a business, save in isolated cases, would tend towards ultimate failure. Furthermore, assets have now often to be replaced at figures higher than cost. Therefore any efficiently run business will normally "plough back" profits either for specific purposes or for the general strengthening or expansion of the organisation.

When considering the amount of profit available for "ploughing back" purposes, the auditor must first satisfy himself that the sums to be appropriated are available, not only after having provided against all known liabilities but also after having checked that provisions have been made against any liability likely to arise which are uncertain as to amount.

3. Provisions.
(a) *Definition.* At this stage it is apposite to consider the relevant definitions of provisions and reserves as given in the *Companies Act, 1967 (Second Schedule, Part IV)*:

"For the purpose of this Schedule, unless the context otherwise requires:

(*a*) The expression 'provision' shall . . . mean any amount written off or retained by way or providing for depreciation, renewals or diminution in value of assets, or retained by way of providing for any known liability of which the amount cannot be determined with substantial accuracy.

(*b*) The expression 'reserve' shall not, subject as aforesaid, include any amount written off or retained by way of providing for depreciation, renewals or diminution in value of assets or retained by way of providing for any known liability or any sum set aside for the purpose of its being used to prevent undue fluctuations in charges for taxation;

and in this paragraph the expression 'liability' shall include all liabilities in respect of expenditure contracted for and all disputed or contingent liabilities."

Where:

(*a*) any amount written off or retained by way of providing for depreciation, renewals or diminution in the value of assets. . . .

(*b*) any amount retained by way of providing for any known liability;

is in excess of that which in the opinion of the directors is reasonably necessary for the purpose, the excess shall be treated . . . as a reserve and not a provision.

The definitions are not so obscure as might at first appear, since, once a provision has been defined, any other amounts provided fall clearly under either of the headings of a reserve—an appropriation, or a liability—a specific amount.

(b) *Auditor's duty*. From the auditor's point of view a provision requires careful attention. As no actual sum constituting the liability exists, which would be indisputable, and since a reserve is an appropriation of ascertainable profit, a provision not being of such a certain nature may cause difficulty in assessment as to whether it is adequate or otherwise.

(c) *Provision for bad debts*. The provision for bad debts has on occasions been the cause of controversy. The debtors shown on a balance sheet form part of the current assets and it is of importance to ensure that they come within the requirement of showing a "true and fair view," therefore if there is the likelihood of bad debts arising, they must be provided against.

(d) *Auditing case law*. There are certain cases having a bearing on the subject of amounts to be provided against bad debts, for example:

(i) *Verner* v. *General and Commercial Investment Trust Limited,*
1894. This case has already been mentioned with regard to
the depreciation of fixed assets, (*see* p.130) and although
book debts are current assets the case is relevant in that
the judge stated that:

> "Floating or circulating capital must be kept up, as
> otherwise it will enter into and form part of such excess, in
> which case, to divide such excess without deducting the capi-
> tal which forms part of it, will be contrary to law. . . .
> That is, if a profit is shown without provision having been
> made for the fall in the value of current assets an illegal
> distribution of capital would ensue.

(ii) *Re London and General Bank, 1895.* Where the auditor
reported to the directors, but not to the shareholders, the
unsatisfactory state of the company's book debts which, as
the company was a bank, consisted of "Loans to customers
and other securities," and he was held liable. (*See also*
Chapter XIV.)

(iii) *Arthur E. Green & Company* v. *Central Advance and Discount Corporation Ltd., 1920.* The auditor accepted from
the Managing Director and the Board a schedule of the
amounts to be written off for bad and doubtful debts each
year. The auditor knew of the retention of old debts on
the books but accepted the explanation of the Managing Director that such debts would eventually be paid
as the debtors would return for further loans.

The auditor here was held to have failed in his duty, not
only by not making proper enquiries where these seemed
necessary, but also in that he at no time reported the
state of affairs to the members.

(e) *Summary.* The foregoing cases serve to emphasise the
importance of ensuring that book debts must be shown at their
true value, and if this is not done, and if adequate provision is
not made against bad debts, the auditor must report thereon.

4. Provisions for the extinction of goodwill. One further
provision which might cause difficulty to the auditor is that
made in order to write down the value of goodwill.

As goodwill is considered a fixed asset there is no necessity
in normal circumstances to write this off: *Wilmer* v. *McNamara
& Co. Ltd., 1895.* (*See* **10** (a) (iii) 3.)

Where, however, goodwill has been lost in such circumstances as, for example, where a business is acquired and retained as a branch which is subsequently closed down to

retain an asset of goodwill would be untrue and not complying with the requirements of the *Companies Act, 1948*, necessitating the showing of a true and fair view of the company's affairs. In this case the goodwill should be written off.

5. Reserves. Various types of reserves and the distinction between capital and revenue are dealt with in Chapter VII.

DISTRIBUTION OF PROFITS

6. Right to distribute profits. Definitions of profits have been given at the commencement of this chapter and as the object of any business is the earning of these when any profits arise it would appear that they may be distributed to the proprietors without any question as to their rights to do so.

Such is the case with respect to sole traders and partnerships, the proprietors have subscribed the capital of the business concerned and those who deal with them should act under the principle of *caveat emptor*. (Literally—"let the buyer beware" but as a principle for creditors and others, "let those who deal with them look to their own interests.")   As in the case, however, of limited companies, the wider field of the public at large and shareholders are more particularly concerned, the courts are prepared to ensure that the rights of the various parties are protected. Creditors and other third parties, as well as minority interests, have sought the aid of the courts quite frequently when they have considered their rights to be infringed by acts in which the distribution of profits have been concerned.

7. Governing factors. The overall governing factors as to profit distribution are those laid down in decided cases and as specified in the Memorandum and Articles of the companies concerned.

There is some conflict of view as to that which may be considered legally distributable and that which prudent business policy dictates should be distributed. Profit may legally be distributable, but it has already been mentioned that to run down the main assets of a business without making any provision for future trading is unwise. This has, however, been dealt with above, so we proceed to the legal position which it is the auditor's responsibility to ensure is complied with.

8. Capital profits. Profits may arise during the course of the life of a business other than that directly concerned with its actual trading, for example, in connection with disposal of its fixed assets. Such profits may be realised or take the form of book figures only brought about by such matters as revaluation.

(a) *Realised capital profits.*

(i) *Lubbock* v. *British Bank of South America Ltd., 1892.* This case was brought by a shareholder against the company in order to ascertain the legal position with regard to the proposal to distribute certain capital profits. These had arisen on the sale by the bank of its assets and liabilities in Brazil, agreeing as it did so to discontinue operating there. It subsequently re-purchased rights to operate its original branch and a profit arose on the whole transaction of some £205,000. The Articles of the company permitted the carrying of such profits to the profit and loss account and the distribution of dividends subject to passing a necessary resolution.

It was held that the profit was a sum in excess of the capital and not part of the capital itself and as the articles so permitted it was distributable.

(ii) *Foster* v. *The New Trinidad Lake Asphalte Co. Ltd., 1901.* The company had taken over a debt on its formation, which at the time was deemed to be valueless. Subsequently the debt was paid together with interest which had accrued. The directors proposed to distribute the sum arising as dividends.

The interest arising was not brought into question but the sum received in payment of the orginal debt was considered by the judge to be a capital profit.

Taking into consideration the decisions of the cases *Lubbock* v. *British Bank*, etc., mentioned above and the *Verner* v. *General and Commercial Investment Trust, 1894,* Byrne, J. stated: "If I rightly appreciate the true effect of the decisions, the question of what is profit available for dividend depends upon the result of the whole accounts fairly taken for the year, capital, as well as profit and loss, and although dividends may be paid out of earned profits, in proper cases, although there has been a depreciation of capital, I do not think that a realised accretion to the estimated value of one item of the capital assets can be deemed to be profit divisible amongst the shareholders without reference to the result of the whole accounts fairly taken."

To summarise from the foregoing cases the position with regard to distributable capital profits, should fulfil the following requirements:

1. They must be realised.
2. They must exist after taking into consideration the value of the total assets and liabilities of the business at the same time.
3. The Memorandum and Articles must permit such a distribution.

(b) *Unrealised capital profits.* When we turn to the subject of unrealised capital profits the difficulty becomes immediately apparent as we have stated above that, *inter alia*, capital profits must be realised before being available for distribution, then the question of distributing unrealised capital profits should not arise.

The summary given above has been accepted as the rules governing the distribution of capital profits but two more recent cases have caused some doubt as to the restriction of distributions of profits only when realised.

(i) *Dimbula Valley (Ceylon) Tea Co. Ltd.* v. *Laurie*, 1961. In this case the preference shareholders raised objections to the capitalisation of unrealised reserves, submitting that the case of *Westburn Sugar* mentioned below was relevant.

(ii) *Westburn Sugar Refineries Ltd.* v. *I.R.C.*, 1960. In this Scottish Court of Sessions case it was held that an unrealised capital profit was not a "distributable sum," Lord Sorn categorically stating that in his view capital profits were not distributable until they were realised.

However, in the *Dimula case* this restriction on the right of a company to distribute unrealised profits was rejected by Buckley, J., who stated that:

(i) "If the reserve fund arising from a revaluation of capital assets could not be distributed, it likewise could not be capitalised, and such a result conflicted with the generally accepted view of the law. As a general rule only that which could be distributed in dividends can be capitalised, the exception to this general rule being the share premium account or a capital redemption reserve fund which never at any time were distributable, being governed by sections 56 (1) and (2) and 58 (1) and (2) of the *Companies Act, 1948.*

(ii) The fact that the reserve in question, being an unrealised profit, was dependent for its existence upon a valuation should not (provided the valuation was itself not open to criticism) be allowed to prejudice the foregoing conclusion.

Since trading concerns having an opening and closing stock relied to a varying extent upon the valuation placed upon such stock in arriving at their profit and loss account, it was a difference of degree rather than of principle to calculate capital profits by comparing their estimated with their book value."

With the frequent revaluation of assets, due to the influence of continued inflation, it is likely that companies will put much weight behind the decision in the *Dimbula case*, but as the position as to the distribution of capital profits, whether realised or unrealised, is now not settled decisively, no doubt some further legislation may be expected on this subject.

9. Profits prior to incorporation. As a company comes into existence on the date of its incorporation, any profits earned by a business taken over are considered to be part of the capital assets taken over and not revenue earned by the new company.

The usual diffidence to distribute profits of a capital nature applies with regard to such revenue, but legally it seems that no objection can be raised, provided that the Memorandum and Articles permit such distributions.

It would appear advisable rather to set off such profit earned against any payment made for goodwill. Likewise, where interest is payable to vendors, the interest may be set off against the profits arising. Conversely, if a loss is sustained between the date of takeover and the incorporation date, this may be added to goodwill.

The auditor should be careful to ascertain that the calculations arising are made up to the date of incorporation of the company and not to the date from which the certificate to commence business operations, as any transactions between the incorporation date and the commencement of business date can always be back-dated.

10. Distributable profits. In the case of sole traders and partnerships, the distribution of sums to the partners, provided it is in accordance with any agreement is immaterial whether paid out of capital or revenue.

In the case of limited companies, however, any payment of dividends other than out of profits is illegal and constitutes a breach of *Section 66* of the *Companies Act, 1948*. Table "A" likewise specifies that "no dividend shall be paid otherwise than out of profits," but should the Table "A" clause be excluded, any such distribution would come under the jurisdiction of *Section 66* mentioned above.

From the point of view of sound financial policy, losses should always be made good before taking funds from the business in the form of dividends unless there are adequate reserves, but this is not the legal position.

The following principles with regard to the distribution of dividends have been dealt with in the cases shown.

(*a*) Dividends may be paid before losses sustained on fixed assets are made good.   This is so provided:

  (i) There is an excess of current income over current expenditure.
  (ii) The regulations of the company so permit.
  (iii) Sufficient assets are retained to meet current liabilities.

Examples of this can be seen in:

1. *Lee* v. *Neuchatel Asphalte Co. Ltd.* (See p. 131.)
2. *Verner* v. *General and Commercial Investment Trust Ltd.* These cases have been dealt with earlier in Chapter VIII regarding depreciation.
3. *Wilmer* v. *McNamara & Co. Ltd.*, 1895.   (*See* **4**).   Although depreciation had been written off adequately in former years, without writing off any depreciation for the current year, a resolution was passed to distribute the profit shown as a dividend to the preference shareholders. The ordinary shareholders sought the aid of the court to restrain the directors from carrying out the terms of the resolution.
   The court refused to grant the injunction desired.

(*b*) Directors are entitled to place profits to reserve.   They may do this before recommending the payment of preference dividends.

Cases which exemplify this are:

  (i) *Fisher* v. *Black and White Publishing Co., 1901,* and
  (ii) *Burland* v. *Earle, 1902.*   In the first of these two cases the court would not interfere where directors were given discretion to determine how much profit should be put to reserve before recommending the payment of a dividend, even though this would obviate the payment of a dividend on founders' shares.   In the second case, the court acted similarly and would not compel the distribution of total

profits as it was considered right and lawful for a company to carry forward a proportion of current profits.

(iii) *Bond* v. *Barrow Haematite Steel Co., 1902* This case has already been dealt with in detail. (*See* p. 133.) Here it may be mentioned that the profit shown on the profit and loss account was carried forward, depreciation on assets, which a valuation had revealed to be apparently worth considerably less than shown, not having been written off. After refusing to allow an application for reduction of capital on the grounds that the losses sustained on the assets were not proven, certain preference shareholders sought the court's aid to compel the payment of the dividend on their shares out of the profit and loss account. The court refused to do so in accordance with the principle stated above.

(c) Debit balances. A debit balance on profit and loss account consisting of accumulated losses of previous years need not be written off prior to the payment of dividends out of current profits.

A case which exemplifies this is *Ammonia Soda Co.* v. *Chamberlain, 1918* The company, having sustained losses on revaluation of its land, created a reserve account and wrote off a proportion of its adverse profit and loss account, the remaining proportion was written off subsequently out of current profits.

Preference dividends were paid, but it was contended that in so far as the whole of the debit balance on the profit and loss account had not first been written off out of current profits, there had been a payment of dividends out of capital.

The Court of Appeal rejected this contention, Swinfen, L. J., stating:

The *Companies Acts* do not impose any obligation upon a limited company nor does the law require it, that it shall not distribute as dividend the clear net profit of its trading unless its paid-up capital is intact, or until it has made good all losses incurred in previous years.

But the words of Warrington, L. J., are important, as they emphasise the fact that such cases will be judged according to their own particular circumstances.

The nature of the business and the amount of the loss may be such that no honest and reasonable man of business would think of paying dividends without providing for it. In such a case, I apprehend the court would take the view that a payment which no honest and reasonable man of business would think it right to make could not properly be made by directors.

(d) Goodwill written off in past years. This may be written back to profit and loss account and a dividend paid from it.

An example of this can be found in the case of *Stapley* v. *Read Bros. Ltd., 1924.* Having written off goodwill against a reserve account created out of profits, the company subsequently sustained losses which caused the profit and loss account to show a debit balance. Thereafter, a profit was made, but it was not sufficient to pay a dividend with arrears to the preference shareholders. The directors proposed to restore the profit and loss account and to utilise the reserve to write off the debit balance on profit and loss account, and to appropriate the sum remaining, plus the profit, earned, to pay the preference dividends.

An injunction was sought to restrain the directors, but this was refused, Russell, J., stating:

> If they had retained goodwill as an asset in their balance sheet, and if, instead of writing off its value out of profits, they had carried those profits to a goodwill depreciation reserve fund, they would have been at liberty at any time to distribute those profits, at all events to the extent by which the amount of such a reserve fund exceeded the amount of the actual depreciation.

11. Table "A" clauses. While the *Companies Act* itself lays down no rule as to the distribution of profits in the form of dividends, Table "A" does contain certain clauses affecting profit distribution. Table "A", being the first Schedule to the *Companies Act, 1948*, is a model set of rules which are taken to apply as governing the internal matters of a company unless they are excluded in whole or in part, and if completely excluded, a company is required to register its own Articles of Association.

The clauses referring to the payment of dividends are as follows:

Clause 114: The right to declare dividends shall be vested in the members in general meeting, but no dividend may be declared at a rate exceeding that recommended by the directors.

Clause 115: The directors may pay such interim dividends as appear to be justified by the profits.

Clause 116: No dividend shall be paid otherwise than out of profits.

Clause 117: Before recommending any dividend the directors may transfer to reserve such sums as they deem desirable.

The foregoing clauses are in accord with the legal decisions outlined in **10** of this chapter, and where Table "A" is modified, no article may be introduced which would alter the over-riding legal requirements.

12. No dividends out of capital. No dividend may be paid out of capital and directors who knowingly pay dividends out of capital are personally liable to make good the amount of such dividends to the company: *Re London and General Bank, 1895.* This does not, of course, exclude the payment of dividends out of capital profits, as explained above, but if members receive dividends knowing them to have been paid out of capital, then the directors have a right of indemnity against them: *Moxham* v. *Grant, 1910.* From the foregoing it is abundantly clear that the courts will not tolerate any reduction of capital unless it take place under their own supervision.

13. Declaration and payment of dividends. The following matters affect the declaration and payment of specified kinds of dividend:

(a) *Scrip dividends.* Unless there is a specific agreement to the contrary, shareholders are entitled to receive these dividends in cash: *Hoole* v. *Great Western Railway Company, 1868.* Where, however, there is express agreement, then dividends may be paid in kind, *e.g.*, in the form of shares, debentures or assets.

(b) *Preference dividends.* Whether preference dividends are to receive simple or cumulative dividends is a matter to be ascertained from the Articles. Where cumulative dividends are in arrears, it is required that:

> There must be shown as a note or in a statement or report annexed to the accounts the amount of any arrears of preference dividends before deduction of income tax, and the period for which the dividends or, if there is more than one class, each class of them are in arrear. When the dividends are payable free of income tax, the free of tax amount of the arrears will be shown, and this fact stated (8*th Sch. Companies Act, 1948*).

There is an implied power in every company to pay dividends but this is not to state that a company is legally required to do so. Furthermore, if the Articles require the payment of dividends in a particular manner, then profits must be applied only in the manner specified: *Oakbank Oil Co.* v. *Crum (1883).*

The wisdom of clauses of Table "A", and of the decisions as mentioned above (*see* **10**) are apparent, for often revenue reserves may indicate the prosperity of a company, but if its resources are tied up in assets not readily realisable, it may not be possible to utilise such reserves for the payment of dividends without putting the company into a difficult position regarding working capital.

It is with this latter point in mind that care has to be exercised with regard to the payment of interim dividends.

14. Interim dividends. Whilst the responsibility for the declaration and payment of interim dividends is not that of the auditor but of the directors, nevertheless he may often be consulted as to the desirability of declaring an interim dividend, in which case the following matters have to be borne in mind:

(*a*) If the Articles permit, the directors may declare interim dividends before the end of the company's financial year, and where Table "A" is in operation, *Clause 115.*

(*b*) If an interim dividend is declared and the company's accounts subsequently show a loss for the year, there is the possibility of the dividend having been paid out of capital. It is essential, therefore, that adequate interim accounts be prepared in order to give a true position of the company's financial state, from which the justification mentioned in the Table "A" *Clause 115* may be obtained. Where a receipts and payments account was prepared which incorrectly showed a surplus, a bonus issue was deemed to have been improperly declared on the strength of the account, and a director who benefited was ordered to refund the amount received by him. *Rance's case*, 1871 stipulates that directors may from time to time pay to the members such interim dividends as appear to the directors to be justified by the profits of the company.

(*c*) Where shares are quoted, to declare an interim dividend at a certain rate, and then to have to declare a final dividend at a lower rate, would be regarded as a sign of financial weakness, with subsequent effect on share prices. Every care should be taken to estimate carefully the course of the company's trading when deciding upon the rate of an interim dividend, or whether to pay one at all.

(*d*) The effect on the liquid resources of the company must be taken into consideration. If profits are tied up in assets other than in a liquid state, the drain on immediate resources might cause embarrassment in an otherwise prosperous company.

(e) Unlike a final dividend, which is sanctioned by the shareholders in general meeting, and after declaration becomes a debt due, an interim dividend if declared by the·directors does not constitute a debt, and consequently a shareholder cannot claim payment thereof. (*Lagunas Nitrate Co.* v. *Schroeder* 1901.)

PROGRESS TEST 11

1. Give a brief definition of profits. (1)
2. For what reason is it advisable to plough back profits into a business? (2)
3. What is a provision and how does it differ from a reserve and a liability respectively? (3)
4. Why must the auditor pay particular attention to provisions? (3)
5. Have any decided cases had any bearing upon the provision for bad debts? If so, what is the main principle involved? (3)
6. How may the auditor ascertain whether profits are available for distribution or not? (6)
7. Give a summary of the principles maintained in decided cases with regard to the distribution of capital profits. (8)
8. Recently, the governing principle regarding the distribution of capital profits changed. In what way has it changed? (8)
9. It is legally possible to distribute pre-acquisition profits. Is it to be advocated, however? (9)
10. Enumerate the main principles regarding the distribution of dividends. (10)
11. In certain circumstances it is forbidden to distribute profit. What are they? (11, 12)
12. What is the principle governed by *Rance's case (1871)*? (14)
13. When distributing interim dividends, what factors should be borne in mind? (14)

SPECIMEN QUESTIONS

1. (a) Define the following terms used in the *Companies Act, 1967*:

(i) Capital reserve.
(ii) Provision.
(iii) Revenue reserve.

(b) State, giving your reasons, in which of the above three categories you consider each of the following items should be placed:

(i) The surplus arising on a professional revaluation of the company's properties.

(ii) The estimated cost of maintaining, for the remaining period of guarantee, machines sold during the year.

(iii) An amount, transferred from profit and loss account, equal to the reduction in taxation in respect of initial allowances.

(iv) An amount, appropriated from profits, to provide for the increased cost of replacement of fixed assets.

(v) A sum, set aside from profits, towards a special publicity campaign which the directors are considering starting in the following year. *C.A. (E.W.)*

2. Write an essay, of not more than three pages, upon the general principles underlying the availability for distribution to members of the profits of a company limited by shares.

C.A. (E.W.)

3. A limited company has asked you, as auditor, to advise as to the treatment in the accounts of the following:

(a) Surplus on revaluation of leasehold property, £8,000.
(b) Surplus on sale of freehold property, £5,000.
(c) Excess of valuation over cost of investments, quoted on the Stock Exchange, held in respect of Leasehold Redemption Fund, £7,000.

Write a letter to the Company explaining the principles applicable to the distribution of capital surpluses and advising them on the treatment of the above three items. *C.A. (E.W.) (Inter.)*

4. Where a limited company has declared and paid a dividend "out of capital profits," bearing in mind case law on the subject, discuss the considerations which an auditor should take into account in deciding whether or not the payment was *intra vires*. *C.A.*

5. Discuss briefly the factors governing distribution of the profits of a limited company. The directors of a limited company, of which you are the auditor, seek your advice as to the distribution of surplus following a professional revaluation of their shop premises. Draft a report to them and include therein your opinion of the uses to which the surplus might be put.

C.C.A. (Inter.)

6. In ascertaining the profits of a company which are legally available for dividend, consider the following points and state, giving your authority where possible, whether:

(a) Depreciation of fixed and wasting assets must be made good before current income is to be distributed.

(b) Depreciation of current assets must be made good before dividends out of current income.

(c) A debit balance on Profit and Loss Account brought about by losses in past years must be made good before dividends are paid out of current profits.

(d) Goodwill written off in past years may be brought back to the credit of Profit and Loss Account and a dividend paid thereout.

(e) Directors are entitled to place profits to reserve before recommending payment of preference dividends. *C.C.A.*

7. You are the auditor of a Limited Company which has made a profit which the directors intend distributing, notwithstanding that the balance of the Profit and Loss Account is in debit. Write a letter to the directors outlining your views on the matter. *C.C.A.* (*Inter.*)

8. You are auditor of XY Ltd. The directors produce the following profit and loss account:

	£	£
Trading profit		5,000
Less Depreciation	4,000	
Directors' Remuneration ..	6,500	
Auditor's Remuneration ..	500	
		11,000
Net loss		6,000
Income Tax Recoverable		2,000
		4,000
Gain on sale of premises	2,500	
Gain on revaluation of other assets	6,500	
Balance brought forward from last year	2,000	
		11,000
		7,000
Dividend		5,000
Balance carried to balance sheet ..		£2,000

The company has no revenue reserves apart from the balance on profit and loss account. Comment on the accounts and the provisions therein. *C.C.A.*

CHAPTER XII

SPECIALISED AUDITS

1. Varieties of audit. Neither for practical purposes, nor for answering examination questions, is it possible to have had personal experience of every type of audit for which information is required. It is necessary, therefore, in compiling an audit programme to use knowledge and experience gained on similar types of audit, and to augment this with imagination of procedures involved.

(a) *Application of experience.* Thus, if a programme for the audit of a cinema is required, then if the box office is brought to mind, the checking of daily takings with ticket numbers of various denominations should be apparent; thereafter, the procedures with regard to daily banking and the proper segregation of takings from disbursements and so forth, should come to mind.

(b) *Examination requirements.* It may be mentioned that in answering questions on specialised audits, the routine procedures attaching to all audits need not be listed.

In the following examples, for the sake of brevity, only the main points have been given. If time allows in an examination, additional specialised points might be added which may be indicated by the main items mentioned here.

2. Building Societies. *The Building Societies Act, 1962,* is the culmination of a number of changes affecting Building Societies brought about by the need for a more rigid legal control over their affairs.

(a) *Report of auditors.* Auditors now have to report specifically as to:

(i) The keeping of records of the valuation of the security on which advances are made: *Section 27.*

(ii) The keeping of proper books of account, the maintenance of a system of control of the books and transactions and the safe custody of deeds and documents of title: *Section 76.*

(iii) The revenue and appropriation account and balance sheet giving a true and fair view . . . : *Sections 77* and *78.*

In effect, the auditor is now required by statute to carry out such a complete audit as will enable him to report on all the foregoing.

(b) *Form of accounts.* The Chief Registrar of Friendly Societies has, under the *Act,* prescribed the form the balance sheet and revenue and appropriation account shall take, stating certain matters which must be shown therein: (*Building Societies (Accounts) Regulations, 1962.*)

Furthermore, the auditors have also to report on the annual return, stating:

(i) Whether in their opinion the return is properly drawn up in accordance with the requirements of the *Act* and regulations made under these requirements.

(ii) Whether the return gives a true and fair view of the matters to which it is addressed (other than those with which the auditors are not required to deal).

(iii) Whether the return is in agreement with the books of account and records of the society.

(c) *Disclosure of advances to officers.* Regarding (a) above, where advances are made to any director or the manager or secretary, or to companies in which any person is interested, these must be disclosed (*Section 89*). The importance of this requirement to the auditor is obvious.

3. Suggested audit procedures for Building Societies. In order to offer guidance regarding the new phase in the audits of building societies, the Institute of Chartered Accountants have issued in the "Statements on Auditing" series, *Audits of Building Societies,* from which the following quotations on matters of outstanding importance are taken:

TESTING THE SYSTEM OF INTERNAL CONTROL

The auditors should compile and maintain an up-to-date record of the system of internal control, obtaining copies of rules, standard forms, internal instructions and any publications showing terms of business. This record should cover each aspect of the society's activities (such as advances, shares, deposits, custody of assets, handling of cash). . . . (Para. 27.)

MORTGAGE ADVANCES

The auditors will have to decide upon the nature and extent of the tests which they should apply to the new advances on mortgage, including such tests " in depth" as may be appropriate. Some may find it expedient to do this work during the year of account, concurrently with the transactions. The auditors' procedures will be governed by their assessment of the system in the light of the considerations referred to in the following paragraphs. (Para 34.)

The proper control of advances on mortgage is of fundamental importance in the operations of a building society. A sound and effective system of internal control is vital. The system must take into account the provisions of the Act relating to "special advances"; these are defined in Section 21 and Section 22 (1) provides specifically that a society "shall so conduct its business as to secure that special advances are not made by it except as authorised by this section". When the Act of 1960 came into force an essential step for every building society was to identify existing advances which fell within the definition of "special advances". (Para. 35.)

SAFE CUSTODY OF DEEDS

The directors must, in order to comply with subsections (3) and (4) of Section 76, establish and maintain a system to ensure the safe custody of all documents of title belonging to the building society and of the deeds relating to property mortgaged to the building society. Subsection (4) provides specifically that a society shall not be taken to have established a proper system unless, under the system, on each occasion on which any such document of title or deed is released from the custody of the officers of the society, the consent is obtained of the board of directors of the society, or of a person authorised by the board to give such consent. (Para. 43.)

The auditors have a statutory duty (Section 87 (4)) to carry out such investigations as will enable them to form an opinion whether the foregoing requirement has been complied with. (Para. 44.)

Prior to the Act of 1960 the auditors of a building society were required by law to examine all deeds relating to each property in mortgage to the society at the balance sheet date. This obligation has now been superseded by the more important obligation to form an opinion on the system of control throughout the year and on the view of the state of the society's affairs as presented in the annual accounts. The number of deeds to be examined is a matter for the judgment of the auditors of each society in the process of examining the soundness and effectiveness of the system. Deeds which are not available for inspection will call for special enquiries, to be pursued until the auditors are satisfied with the explanation. (Para. 45.)

CASH

The handling of cash is always accompanied by possibilities of error and misappropriation, concealed by "teeming and lading", manipulation of dormant accounts and other devices. This problem is of special importance to auditors of building societies because of the large extent of the cash transactions, but it does not involve audit considerations which differ in principle from those encountered in many other businesses. In assessing the system and testing its effectiveness the auditors will need to apply rigorously their professional techniques. Discrepancies revealed by surprise cash counts or by searching tests "in depth" will call for exhaustive investigation. (Para. 59.)

INTEREST AND OTHER AMOUNTS PAID BY BORROWERS

The prescribed form of revenue and appropriation account requires separate disclosure of "interest on mortgages" and "other amounts paid by borrowers as consideration for advances". The auditors will therefore need to satisfy themselves that the records are maintained in such a way that this important distinction is properly made in the revenue and appropriation account. (Para. 61.)

PROVISION FOR MORTGAGE LOSSES

The provision for anticipated losses on mortgages is required to be stated separately in the balance sheet as a deduction from the total amount outstanding on mortgages. The auditors will need to be satisfied that where repayments are in arrear a realistic provision is made if the security is not adequate; and even if the account is dormant, interest should be accrued and the provision for mortgage losses augmented accordingly. Where arrears have been satisfied by the granting of additional advances the soundness of the debts will need special examination, including a review of transactions with those borrowers subsequent to the balance sheet date. (Para. 66.)

"WINDOW DRESSING"

Auditors should examine transactions which have the effect of showing as on the balance sheet date a state of affairs (particularly the society's liquidity) which is materially better than it was during the year and shortly after.   Items requiring particular attention are:

   (a) large deposits received shortly before the year end and repaid shortly after

   (b) large mortgage repayments received shortly before the year end and readvanced on the same property shortly after

   (c) unusual delay until after the year end in making payments in accordance with applications received before the year end for withdrawals of shares or deposits

   (d) an abnormal year end accumulation of commitments for advances followed by the making of the advances shortly after the year end

   (e) the significance of the items in bank reconciliation statements.   (Para. 70.)

AUDITOR'S REPORT

Where the auditors have no reservations to make in respect of any of the matters specified in Section 87 a suitable form of report would be:

Report of the auditors to the members of the . . . . . . Building Society
The foregoing balance sheet and revenue and appropriation account are properly drawn up in accordance with the requirements of the Building Societies Act 1962 and the regulations made thereunder.   In our opinion they give respectively a true and fair view of the state of the society's affairs as on . . . . and of its income and expenditure for the financial year ended on that date.   (Para. 73.)

4. Banks.

(a) The efficient working of a system of internal control is vital here, and this should be investigated thoroughly on commencement and checked in part regularly thereafter.

(b) Ascertain that the system of internal check is not only reduced to writing, but continually applied.   Such matters as the changing of machine operators, cashiers not having access to customers' ledgers, etc., should be carefully checked.

(c) Verify balances with other banks and the Bank of England.

(d) Examine investments and bills, care being taken to obviate the possibility of substitution.

(e) Check the market value of securities, ascertaining that provision is made against any material losses.

(*f*) Verify the existence and adequacy of securities given for loans and overdrafts.

(*g*) Check the amount of secret reserves, as the exemption afforded by the *Companies Act, 1948*, allows of their use, but it should be ascertained that those in authority have full details of them.

5. Clubs.

(*a*) The regulations of the club should be studied, noting the extent of activities and requirements as to accounting matters.

(*b*) Entrance fees and members' subscriptions should be checked with minutes of meetings in which applications for membership are passed and resignations noted, and also with lists of members.

(*c*) The receipt of cash for membership fees should be checked with counterfoil receipts.

(*d*) Where the club's activities include the running of a hotel or restaurant, the audit will follow that as stated in that of a hotel (*see* **8**).

(*e*) The auditor should ensure that any honorarium paid to any officer is properly voted and minuted.

(*f*) Petty cash balances held by any club officers should be checked as well as careful vouching of their petty cash books.

6. Contractors.

(*a*) Normally, it is necessary for such businesses to prepare accounts in respect of each contract or of each section of certain contracts undertaken. This necessitates the maintenance of records which will facilitate the efficient allocation of expenses. The system of cost accounting should be carefully examined, as the auditor may have to make considerable use of such records.

(*b*) The internal check system governing the payment and allocation of wages should be examined.

(*c*) Wages sheets should be tested exhaustively with employees' records, time cards, etc., as due to the payment of wages on sites and the frequent turnover of certain staff, the system may leave itself open to easy manipulation.

(*d*) The system governing the recording of stores issues, and transfer of plant to various sites, should be checked.

(*e*) Control accounts should be carefully checked, or if not kept, should be compiled in order to verify the allocation of the total wages and stores issued to various contracts.

(*f*) Liabilities to sub-contractors at the close of the period should be carefully checked.

(*g*) Receipts on account of contracts should be vouched with architects' or engineers' certificates, retention moneys being ascertained.

(*h*) Stocks of raw materials should be verified carefully as well as value placed upon work-in-progress. The value placed upon the latter should be considered in conjunction with architects' or engineers' certificates, the possibility of losses arising being provided against.

(*i*) Where credit is taken for profit on uncompleted contracts, the auditor should satisfy himself that this is justified and calculated on a conservative basis (methods of bringing in such profits are outlined in costing textbooks).

(*j*) Frequently, work of a capital nature is undertaken by the company's own staff. The allocation of such work to capital as opposed to revenue expenditure should be checked.

7. Executors' and trustees' accounts.

(a) *Executors' accounts.*

  (i) The will should be examined, noting points of interest as to disposition of property, creation of trusts, investment of estate funds, distribution of residue, etc.

 (ii) To ensure all the estate is brought in, access should be obtained to private books of account, tax returns, etc., checking the information obtained with the estate duty account.

(iii) Dealings in estate properly should be verified by auditing in normal manner, including the disposal of property in form of investments or otherwise.

(iv) All interest, rents, or other regular payments should be checked to ensure their due receipt. Apportionments should be checked in accordance with the *Apportionments Act, 1870.*

 (v) Receipts for payment of estate duty and legacies should be vouched.

(vi) Where the estate is not fully distributed, the auditor should verify the actual holding of the assets.

(b) *Trustees' accountants.* This type of audit is similar to that in respect of executors' accounts. The trust deed should be examined, notes being taken of the instructions contained in it. The payments made should be checked to see that they are in accordance with the deed, and where the trust is in respect of an infant, the auditor should ensure that payments are properly authorised and appear reasonable in the light of the provisions contained in the deed.

8. Hotels.

(a) It is essential in this type of business that a sound system of internal check be operated. This should be examined in particular with regard to:

   (i) Receipt of cash and accounting for it by waiters.

  (ii) The requisitioning for wines and spirits and the maintenance of adequate stock records, and the checking of stocks on hand with balances shown.

(b) The visitors' ledger should be examined, care being taken to ensure that all charges against visitors are duly entered against them. The daily totals should be checked to the summary, and from thence to the ledger account.

(c) The depreciation rates applied to fixtures, furniture and fittings should be checked.

(d) The internal check system with regard to restaurant services should be checked, especially with regard to the full accountability in respect of bills issued to residents and outside customers for meals. All bills should be serially numbered and accounted for.

(e) The method of valuation applied to expendable assets, such as crockery, should be examined.

(f) The payment of wages to outside staff and casual workers should be carefully checked.

9. Insurance Companies.

(a) Insurance companies are governed by the *Companies Acts* of *1948* and *1967* and also by the *Insurance Companies Act*, *1958*, as amended by the *Companies Act*, *1967*. Such companies (which include life assurance companies) must prepare a revenue account and a balance sheet and, save where only one type of business is carried on, a profit and loss account, annually. The form of such accounts being prescribed by the *Insurance Companies (Forms) Regulations, 1958*.

(b) The internal control and check systems should be examined in depth, as this type of business is highly specialised. The systems prevailing regarding post opening and the recording of cash and maintenance of ledger accounts should be thoroughly checked.

(c) Premium income should be vouched with new policy books, renewals register and lapsed policies.

(d) Commission paid and due to agents should be compared with agents' receipts and with their returns and accounts.

(e) Where policies are surrendered those should be checked with receipts and the endorsed policies.

(f) Claims paid should be tested with documents and correspondence arising. Claims made but not settled should be examined to ascertain that adequate provision is made against these.

(g) Re-insurance and recoveries on re-insurance and provision for all amounts outstanding should be checked.

(h) The premium reserve carried forward should be checked to ensure its adequacy.

(i) It should be ascertained that, where separate funds are kept, no part of any such fund has been applied directly or indirectly for any purpose other than the class of business to which it is applicable. The auditor is required to certify this fact.

10. Publishers.

(a) *Book publishers.* The following points must be noted:

 (i) Ascertain system of accounting regarding publications. This would normally involve the debiting to a separate account for each book published the expenses involved.

 (ii) Check values of stocks of publications on hand which should be at cost of publishing divided by the number produced.

 (iii) Note whether stocks nave been held over a protracted period with little or no movement, for writing down of value or otherwise.

 (iv) Ensure that books sent on "sale or return" are properly shown as stock at a figure not in excess of cost.

 (v) Check system maintained whereby the volume of sales is recorded in order to credit authors with royalties due. Ascertain that all those due have been properly credited within the period. Vouch a number of authors' contracts noting rates payable.

 (vi) If it is desired to carry forward certain costs of publication on books of a popular nature, ascertain that such costs are those which would be saved on subsequent editions.

(b) *Journal publishers.* Where weekly or monthly journals are published, the outstanding matters to be dealt with are:

(i) Ascertain that an advertising journal is properly maintained, showing advertising bookings over each edition.

(ii) Ascertain that where advertisements are to appear over a number of editions, that the advertising revenue in advance is properly carried forward to the next period.

(iii) Vouch a number of the advertisements with the journals published.

(iv) Check the advertising journal with the advertisers' accounts.

(v) Ensure that all outstanding amounts due to contributors are brought into account.

(vi) Vouch a number of contributions in the publication with the contributors' journal.

11. Share transfer audit. As the accounts of the company are not affected by share transfers it is not part of normal audit procedure and, if to safeguard itself against losses arising through fraudulent transfers or otherwise, the company requests that such an audit be carried out, the auditor may charge an additional fee for such work.

The programme should be on the following lines:

(a) Examine the Articles for relevant clauses.

(b) Each transferor should have been notified of the lodgment, and it should be seen that no objections have been received. Where any calls due have not been paid, the transfer should have been refused if the Articles so require.

(c) Check that the transfer is properly stamped, that the distinctive numbers (if any) of the shares are shown and that the consideration is stated.

(d) Note whether the consideration appears adequate. If not, enquiry should be made unless the document has already been stamped by the Revenue Stamp Office.

(e) Check the particulars on the old certificates to the transfer deeds and see that the old certificates are cancelled.

(f) Vouch the transfer deeds with particulars in the transfer register.

(g) Check the transfer ledger postings to the share ledger.

(h) See that work done by registration clerks is duly initialled.

(i) Vouch receipt of transfer fees.

(*j*) See that the directors' minute is passed in respect of the transfers.

12. Solicitors.   Whilst a normal audit may be carried out, special rules have to be observed by solicitors as required under the *Solicitors' Act, 1965* and the *Solicitors' Accounts Rules, 1967*, the *Solicitors' Accounts (Deposit Interest) Rules, 1965*, the *Solicitors' Trust Accounts Rules, 1967*, and the *Accountants' Report Rules, 1967*.   The object of the enactment and rules are to ensure adequate bookkeeping and recording systems are maintained, with particular concern to obviate the confusion of clients' monies with those of the solicitor.

With such a number of relevant acts and rules the position might appear to be somewhat confusing.   This, however, is not the case.   The Law Society publish a handbook clarifying the necessary requirements.

The general effect of the legislation concerned is to

(*a*) require the keeping of books of account and separate bank accounts for solicitors' and clients' monies respectively,

(*b*) require the solicitor to state annually when applying for his practising certificate whether or not the Solicitors' Account Rules apply to him, and

(*c*) provide for the compulsory examination each year of the solicitor's accounts by a duly qualified accountant for the delivery to the Law Society of an Accountant's Report as to his compliance with the Solicitors' Account Rules.

With regard to actual examination and report by the accountant, the following are points of outstanding interest:

(*a*) The Accountant's Report is to refer to an individual solicitor whether he is a member of a firm of solicitors or not.   So if there are a number of partners in a firm of solicitors a Report is necessary for each.

(*b*) Save in exceptional circumstances the place of examination should be at the office of the solicitor and not of the accountant.

(*c*) Any partner of a firm of accountants may sign the Report, but whoever signs is deemed by the Council of the Law Society to accept responsibility for the accuracy of the Report.

The rules are quite specific as to the work that shall be carried out by the accountant in order to enable him to give the Report, these include such matters as:

(a) Examination of the bookkeeping systems in each office of the solicitor's office to ensure that separate ledger accounts are maintained for each client with distinction being kept between clients' or other monies.

(b) The test checking of postings and castings of clients' ledger accounts.

(c) Comparison of lodgements and payments from clients' accounts as shown on the bank statements with the solicitors' records.

There follow various other matters which accountants would normally carry out during an audit of this kind.

It is required that the accountant shall not extend his enquiries beyond the information contained in the relevant documents relating to clients' matters supplemented by the information and explanations given by the solicitor. He need not also enquire into securities or documents of clients held by the solicitor.

There is the discretion allowed to the accountant, however, that if after having carried out the examination as specified in the rules, he may carry out such further examination as he deems necessary to complete his report with or without qualification.

13. Statutory report.

(a) Examine the Prospectus and Articles as to terms of the issue, etc., and see that these have been complied with.

(b) Vouch the application and allotment sheets with application forms and check cash received per the application and allotment sheets with the Bank pass book; usually a special one is maintained.

(c) Check the "numbers of shares allotted" with the directors' minutes of allotment. Ascertain that provisions as to minimum subscription have been complied with, and that the allotments do not exceed the amount of the authorised capital, or the amount offered for subscription.

(d) Check the "amount payable on application and allotment" column and "balance due on allotment" column on the application and allotment sheets, check cash received on allotment with the pass book and vouch any amounts returned as excess applications with receipts, or returned paid cheques, and counterfoils of "letters of regret"; the last named being sent where applications are refused and application moneys are refunded; check the amounts returned with pass book.

(e) Check particulars of members, the numbers of shares allotted, and balances payable and unpaid on shares, from application and allotment sheets to the register of members and share ledger.

(f) Ascertain that return of allotments has been filed with Registrar of Companies within one month.

(g) Test counterfoils of share certificate books with the share ledger and the application and allotment sheets. See that receipts for certificates have been duly returned to the company.

(h) Check casts of application and allotment sheets, seeing columns agree in total (i.e., shares allotted agree with cash columns). Check postings of totals of cash to main and cash book, and vouch journal entries for the issue of capital and agree the balances on share ledgers with the balance on share capital account in nominal ledger. Similar work will be necessary in regard to instalments paid or calls made before the date of the statutory report.

(i) If there are various classes of shares, they should be dealt with separately, i.e. with separate pass sheets, etc.

(j) Check the main cash book with bank pass sheets and reconciliation statement and obtain bank certificate.

(k) Vouch any capital expenditure and check to the ledger accounts concerned.

(l) Check entries with the statutory report.

PROGRESS TEST 12

1. Under the Building Societies Act, 1962, what is the auditor required to report upon? (2)

2. In what form should a building society's accounts be prepared? (2)

3. What important aspect regarding building societies' advances is of concern to the auditor? (2)

4. With what particular aspects of building society activities should the auditor concern himself? (3)

5. What is an essential feature necessary in the audit of a bank? (4)

6. What aspect of a contracting business is particularly liable to manipulation? (6)

7. What is the first matter to which the auditor should pay attention when acting as auditor in respect of executors' or trustees' accounts? (7)

8. To what should the auditor pay particular attention in hotel audits? (8)

9. Why is the system of internal control of vital importance in the audit of insurance companies? (9)

10. Is it essential that the auditor should carry out a share transfer audit on the occasion of each annual audit? (11)

11. Mention the particular statutory requirements affecting the audit of solicitors' accounts. (12)

12. What aspect of the audit of solicitors' accounts requires special attention? (12)

13. Enumerate the procedures necessary for the conduct of the audit of a statutory report. (13)

SPECIMEN QUESTIONS

1. Indicate the special points to which your attention would be directed in verifying the income of a sports and social club.

C.A. (E.W.)

2. As Auditor of a licensed non-residential Country Club, owning its own Golf Course and Squash and Tennis Courts, outline the steps which you would take to verify the income of the Club. C.A.

3. In auditing the accounts of a large company of Public Works Contractors state the uses which you would make of the costing records and the extent to which you would consider yourself entitled to rely upon the figures appearing therein. C.A.

4. Outline a programme for the audit of estate accounts for the first two years from the date of death when there is a life interest. The assets include leasehold properties and shareholdings in private companies and quoted public companies. C.A. (E.W.)

5. Outline the audit procedure you would adopt to verify the amounts included in the balance sheet of a builder and contractor for work in progress and materials on sites. C.A. (E.W.)

6. Draft your programme for a Share Transfer Audit. State the objects of such an audit. C.A.

7. What are the principal matters to which the auditor of a building society should have regard when examining the deeds of properties in mortgage to the society? C.A. (E.W.)

8. (a) State the underlying objects of the Solicitors' Accounts Rules and describe in outline the requirements.

   (b) What work is the accountant required by the Accountants' Certificate Rules to do with a view to signing the certificate? C.A. (E.W.)

CHAPTER XIII

INVESTIGATIONS

INVESTIGATIONS AND REPORTS

1. Definition of an investigation. An investigation may be defined as an examination of the accounts and balance sheet of an organisation and their supporting documents for the specific purpose of obtaining information to be submitted to an interested party. An audit is a form of investigation but the term is more usually applied to all work of an interrogatory nature other than that of an audit.

2. Events necessitating an investigation. Such work may be undertaken on request of interested parties for such matters as:

(*a*) The purchase of a business.

(*b*) Admission of a partner into a business.

(*c*) Investing money in a concern by way of loan or otherwise.

(*d*) Ascertaining the extent of a known fraud or negligence, or investigating whether such has taken place.

(*e*) Reporting on profit forecasts for take-over or merger purposes.

3. Statutory investigations. Investigations may be necessary to satisfy some legal requirement under statutory authority, such being the case in respect of:

(*a*) The report required by a company's promoters for prospectus purposes.

(*b*) An investigation by inspectors appointed by the Board of Trade in accordance with the provisions of *Sections 164 and 165 of the Companies Act, 1948, and Section 38 of the Companies Act, 1967* (see p. 203).

(*c*) *An investigation under the Public Trustee Act 1906* on application of a trustee or beneficiary.

(*d*) An investigation by the liquidator of a company where

directors are suspected of fraud or misfeasance regarding
the affairs of the company.

(e) An investigation by a trustee in bankruptcy where the
bankrupt is suspected of having acted fraudulently in the
past.

4. Liability of investigating accountant. In conducting an
investigation and submitting his report on it, the accountant is
exercising a professional skill and expressing his opinion as an
expert.   It is necessary, therefore, to exercise particular care
in the conduct of such work and to be guarded in the expression
of any opinions in his report.   He may be generally liable to
anyone who, having employed him to do such work, puts
money into a business and subsequently suffers loss due to the
negligence of the accountant in not discovering the true state
of affairs.

In *Short and Compton* v. *Brackett, 1904,* it was held that the
investigating accountants were entitled to assume that the
figures appearing in the defendants' books were correct, when
in fact an employee had defrauded the company by defalcation
of the wages sheets, so there was no negligence on their part.

On the other hand, where a loss was suffered due to the
negligence of the investigating accountants, despite extenuat-
ing circumstances, which were taken into consideration in the
damages awarded, the accountants were held liable (*Colmer* v
Merrett, Son and Street, 1914).

In a later case, *Regina* v. *Wake and Stone, 1954,* where it was
admitted that stock and work-in-progress had been valued at a
figure considered to be false, deceptive and misleading, having
accepted an explanation by the managing director of various
alterations in stock sheets without making any independent
investigations, the auditor was convicted in respect of his
having signed the report recklessly and was fined £200 (with
the alternative of six months' imprisonment).

It behoves the accountant, therefore, in undertaking any
investigation work to obtain explicit instructions, and to
exercise great care both in his method of working and in
his report.

5. The purchase of a business.

(a) *Accounting aspects.*

(i) Obtain details of nature of business and of current trend
of trade generally.

(ii) Ascertain whether book-keeping is satisfactory and properly audited and examine auditors' reports for any reservations.

(iii) Ascertain whether adequate stock records maintained.

(iv) Set out accounts in columnar form for comparative purposes, showing percentages to turnover, as relevant. Investigate material differences.

(v) Pay particular attention to gross profit ratio. This may tend to rise in latest years as stocks may be inflated to increase profits.

(vi) Examine sales figures, note that no goods on sale or return included and that sales cover only periods referred to. In particular, check last period to note whether sudden fall in sales after last balance sheet date.

(vii) Obtain analysis of customers, if possible, noting any proportionately large buyers and ascertaining whether any fall in sales recently.

(viii) Examine purchases records. Check with stock records. Note whether any very slow moving stocks still maintained at cost.

(ix) Examine the columnar analysis of profit and loss accounts. Note any material changes. Adjust profit figures for exceptional items either of income or expenditure. If income shown on assets is not to be taken over, e.g., investments, this should be eliminated.

(x) Examine variations in assets held and note adequacy or otherwise of depreciation. Note any exceptional profits or losses arising on disposal of assets. Losses may signify inefficient management.

(xi) Prepare percentage balance sheets and note any material changes. Accounting ratios, in particular, with regard to liquid position, should be noted.

(xii) Make enquiries as to any outstanding contracts likely to affect the business.

(b) *Profits available*.

(i) Using the adjusted profits as mentioned in (ix) above, note the percentage return on capital employed.

(ii) Calculate any super profits arising as compared with similar businesses. From this figure capitalised at the percentage rate of return on similar businesses, a figure for goodwill may be obtained to be added to a net tangible assets figure. This may then be compared with the price demanded.

(iii) Consider the effect of retirement of any partner or of the sole proprietor. Ascertain whether any agreement to be given as to non-competition within a stated area.

(iv) Ascertain whether any important professional or technical

staff are likely to be leaving in the near future.   Examine
service agreements, if any.

6. Admission of a partner into a business.   An investigation
may arise, either on behalf of a person intending to bring in
capital and to become a partner, or for the existing proprietors
who intend to take in a partner.

The investigation would be somewhat similar either way, as
in the case of the purchase of a business, but with the additional requirements to ascertain the rights and responsibilities
which will arise under the agreement.   Here the investigating
accountant would have to examine the proposed agreement to
ensure that nothing detrimental would arise in respect of his
client.

7. Investigation in the event of fraud or negligence.   The
nature of the work to be carried out in either the event of fraud
or negligence, or in order to ascertain whether such have taken
place, will depend on the type of fraud or negligence, and on the
instructions received by the accountant.

If the fraud should concern only a section of the work, such
as the entry of dummy workmen on a wages sheet by one
clerk, then the extent of the investigation would be restricted.
On the other hand, a fraud of the nature mentioned at the
beginning of Chapter X (1) involving collusion between
responsible officials, would necessitate work of an extensive
nature.

Whilst the normal audit procedure would still apply, the
following matters should receive particular attention:

(a) *Misappropriation of cash.*   All cash received would have
to be checked in detail, and this would involve the following
steps:

    (i) The rough cash book should be checked with the cash book
       and bank paying-in slips obtained from the bank.

    (ii) Where receipts are issued, the copies of these should be
       checked with the cash book.

    (iii) Statements should be sent to debtors who have paid
       amounts asking for notification if they do not agree with
       any details shown on them.

    (iv) Payments should be vouched with returned cheques and
       original documents, checking authorisation for payment

signatures on the documents concerned. If vouchers are missing, copies should be requested.

(v) Payments to directors or partners should be confirmed.

(vi) Petty cash should be vouched and any I.O.U.'s outstanding checked with those who have received them.

(vii) All balances should be counted—production of them being at one and the same time—and all other balances confirmed direct with banks and duly reconciled after checking the pass sheet entries.

(b) *Wages defalcations.*

(i) The internal check system should be investigated and any loopholes noted.

(ii) The original documents from which the wages sheets are compiled should be checked. This would include such matters as changes in wage rates, as well as original notifications of staff taken on.

(iii) Every care should be taken to ensure that all those shown as employees are actually in the employ of the business, or have been so. (Dates of cessation of employment being important in the latter case.)

(iv) Payments out in respect of deductions should be checked, such as those in respect of National Insurance stamps.

(v) Casts and cross-casts should be checked and wages control accounts compiled where these have not been kept.

(vi) The system operated with regard to unclaimed wages should be checked.

(c) *Manipulation of stock figures.* Matter affecting stocks and work-in-progress have been dealt with in detail (*see* X). It is emphasised that the original stock sheets should be obtained and checked, and items shown in the sales and purchases day books at the end of financial periods should be checked with the goods outwards and inwards books respectively.

Again, fraud (*see* p. 145) reveals the need to investigate stocks held at outlying branches and personal inspection may be necessary.

Quite recently the over-valuation of stocks has been discovered despite the checking of stock records by the company's auditors. This involved the pricing of various lots of steel by a director. The difficulty in checking such stocks of a specialised nature is emphasised, and the investigating accountant should do all within his power to obtain confirmation of prices from outside sources, such as market reports or trade associations.

(d) *Defalcation of sales and purchases*. The defalcation of sales is not so likely to be met as this requires the creation of fictitious debtors. If such arose, the details regarding the debtors on checking by direct statements would reveal these, or by noting long outstanding debts. The more likely fraud to increase profit figures would be to increase stock figures.

Although concerned with misappropriation of cash, the entering of credit notes in accounts where such misappropriations have taken place may be mentioned. Credit notes, therefore, should be carefully checked, ascertaining that they are properly authorised and initialled.

Fictitious purchases, on the other hand, are more likely than fictitious sales, this might facilitate paying out sums of money and also reducing profits for taxation purposes.

Invoices have been printed (*see* p. 145), and also employees have sometimes submitted invoices received in respect of purchases made in their own private businesses, for payment by their employing organisations.

Such manipulations as these should be revealed by careful vouching in full of documents and also by comparison with the goods inwards book and stock records.

8. Investigations for accountants' reports for prospectus purposes. In accordance with the requirements of the *Companies Act, 1948*, any prospectus issued by a company, or in respect of one to be formed, must contain certain reports specified in *Part II* of the *Fourth Schedule*.

Such reports involve heavy responsibilities for the reporting accountant (*see* p. 196), *Regina* v. *Wake and Stone*, 1954. The Institute of Chartered Accountants has issued its Recommendations (*N*.13 *and N*.16) regarding such reports, from which the following quotations are taken:

ACCOUNTANTS' REPORTS FOR PROSPECTUSES:
ADJUSTMENTS AND OTHER MATTERS.

Adjustments generally

In the preparation of accountants' reports for the purpose of inclusion in prospectuses (which, where appropriate, should be read as including offers for sale and similar documents) it may be necessary to make various adjustments, in addition to giving consideration to the special matters dealt with in Recommendation 13 on *Accountants' Reports For Prospectuses: Fixed Assets And Depreciation.* The reports required under the Third, Fourth and Fifth Schedules to the *Companies Act, 1948* must either indicate by way of note any adjustments as respects the figures of profits or losses or assets and liabilities dealt with by the report which appear necessary to the persons making the report, or must make those adjustments and indicate that adjustments have been made. There is no statutory guidance as to the nature of the adjustments to be made; the accountants making the report must form their own judgment. Where required by *Section 41* (1) of the *Act,* a signed statement, setting out the adjustments and giving the reasons therefor, must be attached to or endorsed on the copy of the prospectus delivered to the Registrar of Companies.

The accountant's report is necessarily confined to past results and does not purport to deal with future prospects. The intending investor is concerned with the future and he will regard the accountants' report, showing the trend of past results, as being submitted to assist him in forming his own assessment of the prospects. It may therefore be necessary, in order that the trend of past profits may be fairly presented having regard to the purposes of the prospectus, either to make appropriate comments thereon or to adjust the figures.

The circumstances in which adjustments to the figures of profits or losses are usually required fall generally under the following headings:

   (a) where there are material facts which should have been taken into account in preparing the profit and loss accounts for the various years covered by the report if those facts had been known at the time when the accounts were prepared

   (b) where there have been material sources of revenue or categories of expenditure which are expected not to recur

   (c) where during the period covered by the report there has been a material change in the accounting principles applied or where accepted accounting principles have not been applied.

In considering whether an adjustment is required it is essential to bear in mind that the accountants' duty is to report on past profits or losses and not to attempt to forecast results in future conditions.

Adjustments or comments may also be necessary in relation to the statement of assets and liabilities shown in the accountants' report. In particular it will be necessary to consider to what extent it is relevant to include notes which appeared on the last balance sheet and to consider the appropriate treatment of matters such as the market value of investments, the accumulated amount of profits tax non-distribution relief, and reserves for future income tax. The accountants' report deals with the assets and liabilities as on the last balance sheet date; but the reporting accountants may have knowledge of events subsequent to that date which may have a material bearing on the conclusions which the intending investor may draw from the prospectus and in such cases the accountants will need to consider their report in the light of that knowledge.

Period covered by the report

Apart from the question of adjustments, the period to be covered by the report requires consideration having regard to the importance of presenting a fair view of the trend of results. At present the Stock Exchange, London, requires the report on profits or losses to cover a period of at least ten years instead of the statutory minimum of five years specified in the *Companies Act, 1948*. A period of ten years ending in 1954 or earlier will include part of the 1939–45 war period, when conditions were exceptional.

Not only has the reporting accountant to consider the statutory requirements of the *Companies Act, 1948*, but also the regulations of the Stock Exchange, regarding which the *Recommendations* (*P.* 8, para. 18, *et seq.*) are relevant, and to which reference should be made.

It is with respect to the "adjustments" to the profit figures that the accountant must exercise care, as stated in *Recommendation N.16: Profits or losses.*

Presentation. The figures relating to profits or losses should be set out in the report in columnar form, accompanied by appropriate definition of the bases on which the figures have been computed. A figure of "average profits" should not be stated.

Adjustments generally. The reporting accountants should make such adjustments to the profits or losses as shown by the accounts as they consider appropriate and the report should state that this has been done. If the amount involved in any adjustment is of special importance in relation to the results disclosed, the nature of the adjustment should be stated. The accountants should consider whether the amount involved in any such adjustment should also be stated.

Adjustments regarding capital expenditure may be properly written back where it has been charged against profits, and as promoters will have every incentive to show profits to be as large as possible, the auditor should be careful in the making of such adjustments as stated in *N*.16:

> *Capital expenditure*. Where an item which has been charged in the accounts has been disallowed for taxation purposes as being capital expenditure, it should not necessarily be adjusted. Moreover no adjustment should be made to write back, as being capital, expenditure which has been charged in the accounts and allowed for taxation purposes, even though some items may be of a kind which might have been regarded as of a capital nature if a different accounting practice had been followed. Where an adjustment is made, it is necessary to consider whether it has a significant effect on the provisions for depreciation.

Where a business is to be acquired, it may be necessary to obtain two certificates, for if the "proceeds of the issue, or any part thereof, are or is to be applied in the purchase of any business, a report must be included, made by named accountants in respect of (a) the profits of the business for each of the five financial years immediately preceding the issue of the Prospectus, (b) the assets and liabilities of the business at the last date to which the accounts of the business were made up." (*Companies Act, 1948, Fourth Sch.*) The two certificates being supplied, one by the accountants of the vendor company, and the other as required by the accountants of the purchasing company.

9. Investigations by inspectors appointed by the Board of Trade. The relevant Sections of the *Companies Act, 1948*, as amended by the *Companies Act, 1967*, are as follows:

> The Board of Trade may appoint one or more competent inspectors to investigate the affairs of a company and to report thereon in such manner as the Board direct:
>
> (a) In the case of a company having a share capital, on the application either of not less than two hundred members or of members holding not less than one tenth of the shares issued.
>
> (b) In the case of a company not having a share capital, on the application of not less than one fifth in number of the persons on the company's register of members.
>
> The application shall be supported by such evidence as the

Board of Trade may require for the purpose of showing that the applicants have good reason for requiring the investigation, and the Board may, before appointing an inspector, require the applicants to give security, to an amount not exceeding one hundred pounds, for payment of the costs of the investigation. (*Section* 164.)

Without prejudice to their powers under the last foregoing section, the Board of Trade:

(*a*) Shall appoint one or more competent inspectors to investigate the affairs of a company and to report thereon in such manner as the Board direct, if

　(i) The company by special resolution; or
　(ii) the court by order;

declares that its affairs ought to be investigated by an inspector appointed by the Board; and

(*b*) May do so if it appears to the Board that there are circumstances suggesting:

　(i) That its business is being conducted with intent to defraud its creditors or the creditors of any other person or otherwise for a fraudulent or unlawful purpose or in a manner oppressive of any part of its members or that it was formed for any fraudulent or unlawful purpose; or

　(ii) that persons concerned with its formation or the management of its affairs have in connection therewith been guilty of fraud, misfeasance or other misconduct towards it or towards its members; or

　(iii) that its members have not been given all the information with respect to its affairs which they might reasonably expect.

Section 38, Companies Act, 1967, amends this in stating after the words "is being" in sub-para. (1) of para. (*b*) shall read as if the words "or has been" were inserted and the Board's powers shall be exercised in the case of a body corporate notwithstanding that it is in the course of being wound-up.

Section 166 empowers such inspectors to investigate the affairs of any other body corporate which has been or is its holding company or subsidiary. The following Sections give the inspectors wide powers to examine an oath officers and agents of the company, and where he has no such power, he may apply to the court.

Section 167 of the original *Act* is also amended by *Section 39* of the *1967 Act* to give even wider powers to inspectors whereby attendance before the inspectors may be required as well as production of books and documents.

Such investigations would leave the method of working to the discretion of the inspector and would, no doubt, include work such as is included in a detailed audit, as well as the exercise of powers exceeding those of a statutory auditor.

10. Reports on investigations. The report submitted in respect of *any* investigation should cover the following points:

(a) Reference to instructions given and summary thereof.
(b) Reference to basic documents covering information obtained. Copies attached if necessary.
(c) General outline to work done.
(d) Summary of information obtained.
(e) Recommendations in accordance with information obtained. In dealing with matters affecting investigations, the reporting accountant should be most careful to avoid making unwarranted assumptions or giving forecasts, *e.g.*, of prospective profits.

ACCOUNTANTS' REPORTS ON PROFIT FORECASTS

11. I.C.A. Recommendations. The Council of the Institute of Chartered Accountants has proferred its guidance for auditors and consultant accountants with reference to any independent accountants' review of profit forecasts, having particular regard to the City Code on take-overs and mergers (Section 15).

The Council has pointed out that, although normally for internal use, such forecasts may be disclosed to outsiders. Owing to inherent uncertainties both numerous and substantial, profit forecasts are not capable of verification by reporting accountants and cannot be audited in any sense, even though the reporting accountants may also be the company's auditors. It is important, therefore, that reporting accountants should make this clear when they accept instructions to review profit forecasts, and in the wording of their report they should take care to avoid giving any impression that they are in any way confirming, underwriting, guaranteeing or otherwise accepting responsibility for the ultimate accuracy and realisation of forecasts. They can, however, within limits (*see* below), properly undertake a critical and objective review of the assumptions on which profit forecasts are based, and can verify that the forecasts have been properly computed, on a basis consistent with the company's previous accounting principles, from the underlying assumptions and data.

In guidance as to preliminary consideration, the Council point out the following:

(*a*) The time allowed for the compilation of the report should not be such as to make it impossible for the accountants properly to exercise their professional judgment.

(*b*) That the accountants' instructions and responsibility under the Code should be concerned with accounting bases as opposed to commercial matters.

(*c*) The forecast should cover normally only the current accounting period or the next following year.

(*d*) Although the accountants may give some reassurance by the nature of their review, they cannot relieve the directors of their responsibilities.

The main points to be considered, briefly stated, are as follows:

(*a*) The nature and background of the company's business.

(*b*) The accounting practices normally followed by the company, *i.e.* such matters as the methods of dealing with overheads in stock valuation, profit on long-term contracts, depreciation, etc.

(*c*) The assumptions on which the forecasts are based. If a circular includes profit forecasts, *Rule 15* of the Code requires the assumptions, including the commercial assumptions, upon which the directors have based their profit forecasts to be stated. It is fundamental that the reporting accountants should report whether or not the forecasts are consistent with the given assumptions, economic, commercial, marketing and financial, which underlie them.

(*d*) In carrying out their review of the accounting bases and calculations for forecasts, and the procedures followed by the company for preparing them, the main points which the reporting accountants will wish to consider include the following:

(i) Whether the profit forecasts under review are based on forecasts regularly prepared for the purpose of management, or whether they have been separately and specially prepared for the immediate purpose.

(ii) Where profit forecasts are regularly prepared for management purposes, the degree of accuracy and reliability previously achieved, and the frequency and thoroughness with which estimates are revised.

(iii) Whether the forecasts under review represent the management's best estimate of results which they reasonably believe can and will be achieved, as distinct from targets which the management has set as desirable.

(iv) The extent to which forecast results for expired periods are supported by reliable interim accounts.

(v) The extent to which the forecasts are built up from detailed forecasts in respect of the main divisions or lines of activity of the business, distinguishing where possible between those which may be regarded as showing a proved and consistent trend and those of a more irregular, volatile or unproved nature.

(vi) How the forecasts take account of any material exceptional items, their nature, and how they are presented.

(vii) Whether adequate provision is made for foreseeable losses and contingencies.

(viii) Whether working capital appears adequate for requirements as shown by properly prepared cash flow forecasts; and, where short-term finance is to be relied on, whether the necessary arrangements have been made and confirmed.

(ix) Whether the forecasts have been prepared and presented on acceptable bases consistent with the accounting principles and practices adopted by the company in previous years, and, if not, whether the fact and effects of any material change of basis are made clear.

Under the heading "*The main matters to be stated in the accountants' report*" (para. 14), it is stated:

"The accountants' report under the Code will be addressed to the directors and will normally include statements dealing with the following matters, so far as appropriate:

(a) The fact that the reporting accountants have carried out a review of the accounting bases and calculations on which the profit forecasts have been based.

(b) Specific identification of the forecasts and documents to which the report refers.

(c) If, as will usually be the case, the reporting accountants have not carried out an audit of estimated results for expired periods, a statement to that effect.

(d) Whether in the opinion of the reporting accountants the forecasts have been properly compiled on the basis of the assumptions made by the board of directors, as set out in the circular, and are presented on a basis consistent with the accounting practices normally adopted by the company."

Again, it is emphasised that if the reporting accountants have not been able properly to exercise their professional judgment they should qualify their report.

12. City Code on Take-overs and Mergers. The following extracts are from the Rules as contained in *The City Code on Take-overs and Mergers* (1969) issued by the City Working Party. Paragraphs 14 and 15 are quoted in full as they are of particular interest to reporting accountants.

"13. Any document or advertisement addressed to shareholders under these headings must be treated with the same standards of care with regard to the statements made therein as if it were a prospectus within the meaning of the *Companies Act, 1948*. This applies whether the document or advertisement is issued by the company direct or by an adviser on its behalf. . . .

14. Shareholders must be put into possession of all the facts necessary for the formation of an informed judgment as to the merits or demerits of an offer. Such facts must be accurately and fairly presented and be available to the shareholder early enough to enable him to make a decision in good time. The obligation of the offeror company in these respects towards the shareholders of the offeree company is no less than its obligation towards its own shareholders.

15. Without in any way detracting from the imperative necessity of maintaining the highest standards of accuracy and fair presentation in all communications to shareholders in a take-over or merger transaction, attention is particularly drawn in this connection to profit forecasts and asset valuations.

Notwithstanding the obvious hazard attached to the forecasting of profits, profit forecasts must be compiled with the greatest possible care by the Directors whose sole responsibility they are.

When profit forecasts appear in any document addressed to shareholders in connection with an offer, the assumptions, including the commercial assumptions, upon which the Directors have based their profit forecasts, must be stated in the document.

The accounting bases and calculations for the forecasts must be examined and reported on by the auditors or consultant accountants.

Any Merchant Bank or other adviser mentioned in the document must also report on the forecasts. The accountants' report and, if there is an adviser, his report, must be contained in such document and be accompanied by a statement that the accountants and, where relevant, the adviser, have given and not withdrawn their consent to publication.

Wherever profit forecasts appear in relation to a period in which trading has already commenced, the latest unaudited profit figures which are available in respect of the expired portion of that trading period together with comparable figures for the preceding year must be stated. Alternatively, if no figures are available, that fact must be stated.

When revaluations of assets are given in connection with an offer the Board should be supported by the opinion of independent professional experts and the basis of valuation clearly stated."

PROGRESS TEST 13

1. For what reasons are investigations conducted? **(1, 2)**
2. How do investigations differ from normal audits? **(1)**
3. Under what statutory provisions may investigations take place? **(3)**
4. Why should the investigating accountant take every care when conducting an investigation? **(4)**
5. Enumerate the matters to receive attention when conducting an investigation regarding the purchase of a business. **(5)**
6. Enumerate the procedures to be adopted when investigating the affairs of a business, when fraud has taken place or is suspected. **(7)**
7. When conducting an investigation (as in Question 6 above) is it necessary to completely investigate the affairs of the business on all occasions? **(7)**
8. When making an investigation for the accountant's report to be included in a prospectus, what matters should be attended to and what should be avoided? **(8)**
9. Under what conditions will the Board of Trade appoint inspectors to investigate the affairs of a company? **(9)**

10. Specify the general matters to be included in an investigating accountant's report. **(10)**

SPECIMEN QUESTIONS

1. A client of yours is contemplating the purchase of an interest in a partnership and requests you to make an investigation of the firm's accounts. There are three partners in the firm, one is full-time and has intimated that he intends retiring in two years, the other two are part-time. Outline the procedure you would follow, illustrating your answer with assumed figures where desired. *C.C.A.*

2. Outline the points to which you would give attention when carrying out an investigation on behalf of a client who is considering the purchase of a retail business. You may assume that the books have been properly kept and that the accounts have been audited. *C.A. (E.W.)*

3. Your client, Mr. Jones, a building contractor, is contemplating the purchase of a competitor's business and instructs you to examine and report on the accounts.

Your client considers that the amounts appearing in the last accounts for stock-on-hand and uncompleted contracts are unduly high and asks you to devote special attention to these assets.

Describe the matters to which you would direct attention when considering these two items. *C.A. (E.W.)*

4. You are asked by the secretary of an incorporated trade association to investigate an apparent cash deficiency. The cashier's duties included the payment of wages to the weekly-paid employees.

List, in tabular form, the steps which you would take to determine the extent of the deficiency. *C.A. (E.W.)*

5. A client is considering the purchase of a retail drapery store and has requested you as his accountant to carry out an investigation. In particular, he is concerned about the considerable variation in the ratio of gross profit to turnover disclosed by the accounts of the business for the past five years.

Outline the procedure you would follow and suggest possible reasons for the variation in gross profit ratios. *C.C.A.*

6. When conducting the audit of a manufacturing company, you suspect that fraud has been committed in connection with wages.

(a) Outline the investigation you would carry out.

(b) Indicate three different ways in which fraud might have occurred. *C.A. (E.W.)*

7. Mr. Rich proposes to invest a substantial sum in a private company by acquiring a holding of ordinary shares which will not give him control. He asks you to carry out an investigation and

to advise him whether the price to be paid for the shares is reasonable.

Set out the matters to which you would direct your inquiries.

C.A. (E.W.)

8. The City Code on Take-overs and Mergers requires, *inter alia*, that the calculations and the bases for any profit forecasts must be examined and reported on by the auditors or consultant accountants. Answer either (*a*) or (*b*).

(*a*) What are the main points to be considered in the reporting Accountant's Review?

(*b*) What are the main matters to be stated in the Accountant's Report? *C.C.A.*

CHAPTER XIV

THE AUDITOR

TERMS OF OFFICE

1. Private audits.

(a) *Written instructions.* Where the auditor undertakes work which is other than of a statutory nature, he should always ensure that he receives his instructions in writing. He need not always wait for his client to supply these as it is more than likely the client would not have the professional knowledge required. The auditor should set out what he considers necessary properly to conduct the work which his client desires him to undertake, and can then request his client's agreement in writing thereto.

(b) *Notification to retiring auditor.* The necessary notification to the retiring auditor, where there is such, has already been mentioned (*see* II), and terms affecting notice of termination of agreement by either the client or the auditor should be settled.

2. Statutory audits.
Where the auditor is appointed under statute he should ascertain that his client complies with any statutory requirements before he officially takes office. This is most important and the auditor may have to advise his client of the procedures involved. We now consider the matters affecting the terms of office of the auditor under the following statutes:

(a) *The Companies Acts, 1948 and 1967.*
(b) *The Building Societies Act, 1962.*
(c) *The Friendly* and *Industrial and Provident Societies Act, 1968.*
(d) *The Public Trustee Act, 1906,* and *Trustee Act, 1925.*

3. The Companies Acts, 1948 and 1967.
Under the *1948 Act* the following matters are relevant. The Act itself is quoted subject to adjustment for the sake of brevity.

(a) *Appointment of auditors (Section 159).* Every company shall at each annual general meeting appoint an auditor or auditors to hold office from the conclusion of that, until the conclusion of the next, annual general meeting.

At any annual general meeting a retiring auditor, however appointed, shall be reappointed without any resolution being passed unless:

(i) He is not qualified for reappointment.
(ii) A resolution has been passed at that meeting appointing somebody instead of him or providing expressly that he shall not be reappointed.
(iii) He has given the company notice in writing of his unwillingness to be reappointed.

Where at an annual general meeting no auditors are appointed or reappointed, the Board of Trade may appoint a person to fill the vacancy.

The first auditors of a company may be appointed by the directors at any time before the first annual general meeting, and auditors so appointed shall hold office until the conclusion of that meeting:

Provided that:

(i) The company may at a general meeting remove any such auditors and appoint in their place any other persons who have been nominated for appointment by any member of the company and of whose nomination notice has been given to the members of the company not less than fourteen days before the date of the meeting.
(ii) If the directors fail to exercise their powers under this subsection, the company in general meeting may appoint the first auditors, and thereupon the said powers of the directors shall cease.

The directors may fill any casual vacancy in the office of auditor, but while any such vacancy continues, the surviving or continuing auditor or auditors, if any, may act.

(b) *Remuneration of auditors, (Section 159* contd.) The remuneration of the auditors of a company:

(i) In the case of an auditor appointed by the directors or by the Board of Trade, may be fixed by the directors or by the Board, as the case may be.
(ii) Subject to the foregoing paragraph, shall be fixed by the

H

company in general meeting or in such manner as the company in general meeting may determine.

For the purposes of this subsection, any sums paid by the company in respect of the auditors' expenses shall be deemed to be included in the expression "remuneration".

(c) *Resolutions concerning appointment and removal of auditors (Section 161).* A person shall not be qualified for appointment as auditor of a company unless either:

(i) He is a member of a body of accountants established in the UK and for the time being recognised for the purposes of this provision by the Board of Trade (at present this comprises the three Institutes of Chartered Accountants in the UK, and the Association of Certified and Corporate Accountants).

(ii) He is authorised by the Board of Trade as (*a*) holding similar qualifications overseas or (*b*) having obtained adequate knowledge and experience in the course of his employment by a member of a recognised UK accountancy body.

(d) *Disqualifications for appointment as auditor (Section 161,* contd). None of the following persons shall be qualified for appointment as auditor of a company:

(i) An officer or servant of the company.
(ii) A person who is a partner of or in the employment of an officer or servant of the company.
(iii) A body corporate:

Section 13 (i) of the *Companies Act, 1967,* allows that where an auditor of a formerly exempt private company comes under the category of (i) and (ii) above, but was in office on 3rd November, 1966, and was in practice on his own account for the previous twelve months, he may continue as auditor for a further three years from the date of the *Act,* provided:

(*a*) that no shares or debentures of that company, or of its holding company, have been quoted on a stock exchange;
(*b*) that no shares or debentures of that company, or of its holding company, have been offered to the public for subscription or purchase.

References in this subsection to an officer or servant shall be construed as not including references to an auditor.

Appointment of a person other than the retiring auditor and the retiring auditor's rights are dealt with later (*see* **9**).

4. The Building Societies Act, 1962.

The relevant sections regarding the terms of office of the auditor are covered in *Sections 84, 85* and *86*.

The appointment and removal of auditors under *Sections 84 and 85* are similar to those applicable to the *Companies Act, 1967*.

Regarding, however, eligibility, the provisions covering qualifications and independence are more stringent. Under Section 86 a person is not eligible for appointment as auditor if he is:

(a) An officer or servant of the building society.
(b) A partner of, or in, the employment of, *or if he employs,* an officer or servant of the building society.

It is the section in italics above which narrows the requirement as compared with the Companies Act, 1948 provision.

5. Friendly and Industrial and Provident Societies Act, 1968.

(a) *The I.C.A. Recommendation U.13.* This deals in detail with this specialised area of the auditor's work to which reference is advocated. Briefly, it may be stated that any "society" as registered under the former separate Acts is now required to keep proper books of account, to prepare a revenue account and balance sheet and to appoint a qualified auditor or auditors (Sections 1, 3 and 4).

Under Section 4 a qualified auditor is such as is recognised for appointment under the Companies Acts; but an "exempt" society need not comply with this provision, but must appoint two or more persons who are not qualified, though the Registrar has power to require the appointment of a qualified auditor. An "exempt" society is a society which is not a collecting society (*i.e.* a friendly society which carries on industrial assurance business) and in respect of which all three of the following conditions are satisfied:

(i) The aggregate of receipts and payments in respect of the preceding year did not exceed £5,000.
(ii) The number of members at the end of that year did not exceed 500.

(*iii*) The aggregate value of the assets at the end of that year did not exceed £5,000.

On the same conditions a registered branch can be "exempt." In the case of a registered branch condition (*iii*) above is treated as fulfilled if at the end of the preceding year of account the branch had transferred at least 75 per cent of its assets for investment either to its parent society or to another registered branch of the society which has appointed qualified auditors and the value of the assets not so transferred did not exceed £5,000.

Section 9 requires the auditors to report to the society on the accounts and the revenue account and balance sheet examined by them. The necessity is laid upon the auditor to state that a true and fair view is shown and where the auditor's report is silent it is accounted as a positive report that the auditors are satisfied as to the maintenance of proper books of account by the society, that a satisfactory control has been exercised over its transactions, and that its revenue account(s) and balance sheet are in agreement with the books of account.

(*b*) *Form of report*. The provisions of the 1968 Act and of the other relevant registration Acts relating to accounts, audit and annual returns are to the effect that, while it is open to a society to prepare its annual accounts and balance sheet in any form provided that they give a true and fair view of the matters specified in Section 3, societies remain under an obligation to send to the Chief Registrar annual returns in such form and containing such particulars as he prescribes.

If societies find it convenient to prepare their annual accounts in the form required for the annual return, one form of auditors' report, suitably worded, will cover both the annual accounts required by Section 3 and the annual return.

If, however, a society prepares the accounts and balance sheet required by Section 3 in a form which differs from that required for the annual return, the auditors will have to report on both documents in similar terms, even if they write two separate reports.

6. The Public Trustee Act, 1906, and Trustee Act, 1925. On application in prescribed manner by any trustee or beneficiary, the condition and accounts of any trust shall be investigated and audited by a solicitor or public accountant as agreed between the applicant and trustees or in default of agreement, by the Public Trustee.

The remuneration and expenses are determined by the Public Trustee.

Under the *Trustee Act, 1925*, trustees at their absolute discretion may employ an independent accountant to audit the accounts—but not more than once in three years—unless for special reasons it is desirable more frequently.

RIGHTS AND RESPONSIBILITIES

7. Rights generally. In the case of private audits, the auditor's rights will be accorded him in agreement with the contract drawn up, covering such matters as his method of remuneration, notice to be given on either side, etc. In addition to such contractual rights, one important matter covering all work done in connection with audits, whether private or under statute, is that of the right of lien.

8. Right of lien on client's books and papers.

(a) *Contractual variation.* Whilst the right of lien may be varied contractively or by necessary implication, the accountant may exercise a right of lien over the books and documents of his client for the due payment of his fees.

(b) *Relationship with client.* The Institute of Chartered Accountants has dealt with this matter in *Recommendation P.5.* Briefly, it may be stated that the accountant may exercise such a lien in respect of audit and accountacy work where the relationship is that of professsional man and his client, (*re Hill Ex parte Southall, 1848*), but that where he acts in the capacity of an agent, as in the case settling a client's income tax liability with the Inland Revenue, then the documents arising are the property of his principal: *Leicestershire County Council* v. *Michael Faraday and Partners Ltd., 1941.*

(c) *Registered companies.* A doubt arose as to the exercise of such a right in respect of the books of a registered company, but provided the necessary rights of access is allowed in accordance with *Section 14* (5) of the *Companies Act, 1967*, the right still exists.

The I.C.A. has pointed out in *Recommendation P.5* that where an accountant acts on behalf of the company's directors while at the same time being the auditor of the company, no right of lien exists over the books or papers of the company in relation to any dispute arising on his having acted for a director in his private capacity. This is a quite obvious recognition of the principle that a company is a separate legal entity.

(d) *Liquidations.* On a summons by the liquidator of a company, the Registrar ordered that the auditor should produce the books and papers of the company in his possession without prejudice to his lien, and that the liquidator should pay fees due to the auditor for all work done before the liquidation, prior to his own remuneration, but after all creditors ranking above the liquidator: *D. M. Carr and Company Ltd., 1961.*

9. Rights under the Companies Acts, 1948 and 1967.

(a) *On appointment.* The appointment of the auditor has already been mentioned above (**3** (a)), and regarding such appointment, important rights exist where it is proposed to appoint a person other than the retiring auditor.

Special notice is required of such an intention and if the retiring auditor so desires, he may make representations to the company and request their notification to the members. If such representations are not sent to members, he may require that they be read out at the meeting, without prejudice to his being heard at the meeting: *Section 160, Companies Act, 1948.*

These are valuable rights and have already been used to good effect where it has been proposed to re-appoint someone other than the retiring auditor.

(b) *Access to all material information.* The auditor is entitled under *Section 14, Companies Act, 1967,* to access at all times to the books, accounts and vouchers of the company. It will be observed that while this gives complete access to the records of the company, not only of double entry accounting records, at the same time it confers an added responsibility in that, if material information is available other than under the normal double entry system, the auditor would be expected to have made proper use of it in the event of any dispute affecting the auditor. This would include such matters as minute books, costing records and internal audit records.

(c) *Explanations from officers.* Likewise, under *Section 14*, the auditors have the right to require form the officers of the company such information and explanations as they think necessary for the performance of their duties.

(d) *Attendance at general meetings.* The auditor is also entitled to attend any general meetings and to receive all notices and other communications relating to any general meetings and to be heard on any part of the business which concerns him as auditor: *Section 14, Companies Act, 1967.*

10. Duties of the auditor.

(a) *Report to members.* Whilst every facility is afforded to the auditor by statute to enable him to carry out his duties properly, under contract he should ascertain that his rights in this respect are preserved. Nevertheless, as a professional person, a number of onerous responsibilities are laid upon him both under Common Law and under Statute.

Dealing in the first instance with his duties under the *Companies Acts, 1948* and *1967*, we shall thereafter consider the broader aspects of his responsibilities.

Under the *Companies Act, 1967*, Section 14:

(1) The auditors of a company shall make a report to the members on the accounts examined by them, and on every balance sheet, every profit and loss account and all group accounts laid before the company in general meeting during their tenure of office.

(2) The auditors' report shall be read before the company in general meeting and shall be open to inspection by any member.

(3) Here, briefly, it is required that the report must state whether in the auditors' opinion the company's balance sheet and profit and loss account and (if it is a holding company submitting group accounts) the group accounts have been properly prepared in accordance with the provisions of the *Companies Acts, 1948* and *1967*.

The report must also state whether in their opinion a true and fair view is given

(i) in the case of the balance sheet, of the state of the company's affairs as at the end of its financial year;

(ii) in the case of the profit and loss account (if it be not

framed as a consolidated profit and loss account) of the
company's profit or loss for its financial year;

(*iii*) in the case of group accounts submitted by a holding
company, of the state of affairs and profit or loss of the
company and its subsidiaries dealt with thereby, so far
as concerns members of the company.

(4) It shall be the duty of the auditors . . . in preparing their
report . . . to carry out such investigations as will enable them
to form an opinion on the following matters . . .

(*a*) whether proper books of account have been kept by the
company and proper returns adequate for their audit
have been received from branches not visited by them;
and

(*b*) whether the company's balance sheet and (unless it is
framed as a consolidated profit and loss account) profit
and loss account are in agreement with the books of
account and returns.

The *1967 Act* now simplifies the form of the auditors' report
in that it requires a positive statement on matters (*a*), (*b*)
and (*c*) in sub-section (3) above unless he is unable to report
in the affirmative as to (*a*) and (*b*) in sub-section (4).

A further duty to report to members is laid upon the auditor
under *Section 6* of the *Companies Act, 1967*, with regard to
the disclosure of directors and certain other employees'
emoluments, but in this case the necessity to report only
applies if the particulars required by the *Acts* are not disclosed
in the accounts.   The details required are specified in the
Companies Act, 1948, Section 196 and the *Companies Act, 1967,
Section 6*.

(*c*) *Nature of report.*   In the absence of any qualifications
the I.C.A. Council have recommended the following form of
reports.

(*a*) *Companies not submitting group accounts*

AUDITORS' REPORT TO THE MEMBERS OF . . .

(*See* note (*a*)).   In our opinion, the accounts set out on pages . . .
to . . . (*see* note (*b*)) give a true and fair view of the state of the
company's affairs at . . . and of its profit (or loss) (*see* note (*c*))
for the year ended on that date and comply with the *Companies
Acts, 1948* and *1967*.

(b) Companies submitting group accounts

AUDITORS' REPORT TO THE MEMBERS OF . . .

(See note *(a)).* In our opinion, the accounts set out on pages . . . to . . . *(see* note *(b))* together give, so far as concerns members of the holding company, a true and fair view of the state of affairs at . . . and of the profit (or loss) *(see* note *(c))* for the year ended on that date and comply with the *Companies Acts, 1948* and *1967.*

(c) Banking, discount, insurance and shipping companies

In the case of a company which is entitled to avail itself and has availed itself of any of the provisions of Part III of Schedule 2 to the *Companies Act, 1967,* the auditors are not required to report whether, in their opinion, the accounts give a true and fair view. This dispensation, however, applies only to the consequences of the exemptions from disclosure which are permitted by Part III and does not extend to other matters (for example, the overstatement of assets or the omission of liabilities) which, in the auditors' opinion, prevent the disclosure of a true and fair view in the generally accepted sense. In the absence of qualifications the following form of auditors' report is considered appropriate by the Council:

AUDITORS' REPORT TO THE MEMBERS OF THE . . . BANK
(OR THE . . . INSURANCE CO., ETC.)

(See note *(a)).* In our opinion, the accounts set out on pages . . . to . . . *(see* note *(b))* comply with the provisions of the *Companies Acts, 1948* and *1967,* applicable to (banking or insurance, etc.) companies.

Notes of variations to suit particular circumstances

The following are the notes referred to in the forms of audit report set out in paragraphs *(a)* to *(c)* above:

(a) If it is desired to refer to the auditors' examination, each of the forms of auditors' report may appropriately commence as follows:

We have examined the accounts set out in pages . . . . to . . . . and report that, in our opinion, they . . .

(b) The documents to which the auditors' report relates should be clearly identified by reference to the page numbers, or if the pages are not numbered, the word "accounts" should be replaced by a description, *e.g.* "the annexed balance sheet, profit and loss account and notes." If it is necessary for the auditors to make reference to information included in the directors' report (for example, if the directors have taken advantage of the proviso to *Section 163* of the *Companies Act, 1948* to include in their report certain matters which the *Act* requires to be included in the accounts), the auditors' report should clearly specify the paragraphs of the directors' report which fall within its scope.

(c) In certain circumstances, for example where the consolidated accounts disclose a profit but the holding company incurs a loss, it may be convenient to use the word "results."

(d) If the consolidated accounts incorporate the accounts of material subsidiaries which the auditors of the holding company have not themselves audited, it is usually desirable for them to include a reference to the fact in their report for the information of the members. This may be done by adding an appropriate sentence at the end of the report set out........above. (*See* the Council's Statement on Auditing U.5—*Auditors' Reports on Group Accounts*.)

(a) *Responsibility of the auditor*. To ensure that a true and fair view is provided by group accounts, special problems arise for the auditors of the holding company, since it is still their responsibility to see that the accounts comply with the requirements of the *Acts*. Although they may have not actually audited the accounts of the subsidiary companies, the sentence in italics in the report does not absolve them of their responsibilities as auditors to the holding company.

The Institute of Chartered Accountants have dealt with this matter in the *Recommendation U.5*, but briefly, it may be stated that it is primarily the duty of the directors to obtain such information as will facilitate the proper preparation of the holding company's accounts. The auditor should be able to obtain such information as he deems necessary to satisfy himself that the *Acts* are being complied with.

It is both convenient and helpful if the auditors of the various companies are authorised to confer direct. Such authorisation is necessary due to the professional duty as to confidence which each auditing firm has to its clients.

12. Qualified report. Where the auditor is not satisfied as to any particular matter of importance and feels that the shareholders or others should be made aware of the fact, he may find it necessary to mention the matter in his report. The inclusion of such a statement serves to create a so-called qualified report. The I.C.A. have issued "Auditors' Reports: Forms and Qualifications" U.10 on this subject in which they mention particularly that any matter requiring qualification should be of "material" importance. The report required under the 1967 Act necessitates qualification where the auditor is not satisfied as to various general matters (*see* p. 219), but there are a number of other matters which may justify qualification. These are listed in Recommendation *U.10* and may justify qualification where in the opinion of the auditors the accounts, though otherwise complying with the requirements of Schedule 2 of the *Companies Act, 1967*, fail to disclose a true and fair view, for example:

(a) because in the auditors' opinion they do not conform to accounting principles appropriate to the circumstances and nature of the business;

(b) because they are prepared on principles inconsistent with those previously adopted and without adequate explanation and disclosure of the effects of the change;

(c) because the auditors are unable to agree with the amount at which an asset or liability is stated;

(d) because the auditors are unable to agree with the amount at which income or expenditure or profit is stated;

(e) because the accounts do not disclose information which, though not specifically detailed in the Acts, is necessary for the presentation of a true and fair view;

(f) because additional information given in a note, or in the directors' report, materially alters the view otherwise given by the accounts.

In some instances more than one of the foregoing matters may be applicable—for example, where the internal control is such as to cast doubt upon the reliability of the records so that the auditors cannot satisfy themselves as to the true and fair view having been shown by the balance sheet and profit and loss account.

Normally, points of disagreement or other matters causing dissatisfaction on the part of the auditor may be settled with the management, but, where the auditor is still not satisfied, the Council of the I.C.A. point out that the auditor's duty is inescapable. Where any qualifying statement is found necessary then it should:

(a) be as concise as is consistent with clarity;

(b) be specific as to the items and facts and as far as possible the amounts involved;

(c) within the limits of the information available to the auditors, make clear its effects on the accounts; and

(d) express the auditors' opinions without possibility of misinterpretation.

The Council have given examples of various types of qualified reports which should be taken to serve only as a guide, the specific circumstances applicable being the overriding factor. The following have been selected:

"Some of the detailed stock-taking sheets relating to stocks held at the balance sheet date have been destroyed. In their absence we have been unable to substantiate the basis of computation of stock amounting to £ . . . out of the total of £ . . . at which stock is shown in the balance sheet.

Subject to the foregoing reservation the accounts set out on pages . . . to . . . in our opinion give a true and fair view . . ." (followed by an appropriate form of wording).

"In the absence of adequate analyses of factory wages we are unable to verify the charge for labour and overhead amounting to £ . . . included in the additions of £ . . . to plant and machinery during the year.

Subject to the foregoing reservation the accounts set out on pages . . . to . . . in our opinion give a true and fair view . . ." (followed by an appropriate form of wording).

"Group profits are overstated by £ . . . by the inclusion of unrealised profits on products transferred at selling price between members of the group and remaining in stock at the date of the balance sheet. With this exception the accounts set out in pages . . . to . . . in our opinion give a true and fair view . . ." (followed by an appropriate form of wording).

13. The interpretation of "material" in relation to accounts.

The necessity to qualify reports leads naturally to the consideration as to the circumstances where such definitive action is required. The word "material" signifies "of relative importance," and in this sense it devolves on the auditor to decide when a matter is of such outstanding importance as to justify his qualifying his report. In U.10 the illustration is given of the fact that £100 in a small firm might be material, whereas £1 million may not be significant in classifying expenditure in a very large undertaking, especially as much elaboration might obscure the true and fair view.

The nature of the item concerned may determine the importance attaching to any variation. Shareholders are most concerned with such matters as directors' emoluments, auditors' fees and investment income, whereas depreciation, which might be based upon an arbitrary assessment, may cause no concern. The following constitutes a brief extract from U.10 of items likely to affect the auditors' decision as to an item being considered of material importance or otherwise.

"*Degree of approximation.* The degree of estimation or approximation which is unavoidably inherent in arriving at the amount of an item may be a factor in deciding on materiality. Examples include contingency provisions, stock and work in progress, and taxation provisions.

"*Losses or low profits.* The use of the profit figure as a point of comparison tends to be vitiated when the profits are abnormally low or where there is a loss; when judging the materiality of individual items in the profit and loss account in such cases, the more normal dimensions of the business have to be considered.

"*Critical points.* The view given by accounts may sometimes be affected by the trend of profit, or turnover, and of various expense items. An inaccuracy which might not otherwise be judged to be material could have the effect of reversing a trend, or turning a profit into a loss, or creating or eliminating the margin of solvency in a balance sheet. When an item affects such a critical point in accounts, then its materiality has to be viewed in that narrower context.

"*Disproportionate significance.* An item of small amount may, nevertheless, be of material significance in the context of a company's particular circumstances, especially if the context would lead the reader to expect the item to be of substantial amount."

14. Liabilities. The liability of an auditor may arise under civil law or he may be held criminally liable. Where an action is brought against him under civil law, he will be required to make good any loss suffered by his client due to his negligence, on the other hand if he has been negligent, but his client has suffered no loss, he will not be liable in damages.

Briefly, an auditor may be held liable in any of the following circumstances:

(a) *In civil actions.*

   (i) *Under Common Law (Negligence).* As a professional person employed as an agent, a high standard of care, skill and diligence may be expected of him. If it is considered that he has not brought such to bear on his work, he may be held liable for any loss arising to his client (*see* **14**).

   (ii) *Under Statute (Misfeasance).* Under *Section 333 of the Companies Act, 1948,* as an officer of the company, if he has been guilty of misfeasance, he may be required, on the winding-up of the company, to contribute a sum to the assets of the company by way of compensation in respect of the misfeasance (*see* **15**).

(b) *In criminal prosecutions.*

   (i) *Under the Companies Act, 1948, S. 438.* Under this *Section* he may be liable if he willfully makes a statement false in any material particular, knowing it to be false.

   (ii) *Larceny Act, 1916* for making, circulating . . . any written statement which he shall know to be false in any material particular.

   (iii) *Prevention of Frauds (Investmevt) Act, 1958,* for making any statement, promise or forecast which he knows to be misleading . . . to induce another person to enter into any agreement . . . to invest.

(c) *Liability to third parties in Tort (see* **16***).*

15. Cases of auditors' liabilities: Negligence. A number of legal decisions affecting the auditor have been dealt with (*see* XI) concerning distribution of profits, and (*see* X) regarding stock-in-trade. The following decisions concern the auditor's liability in respect of negligence.

(a) *Wilde & Others* v. *Cape & Dalgleish,* 1897.

The defendants in this case did not discover defalcations which it was contended could have been discovered had the auditors examined the bank pass-books. The defence submitted that it was not part of the original arrangement that the pass-books should be examined, but this was not sustained and it was held an auditor is liable for losses arising due to his negligence.

(b) *Smith* v. *Sheard,* 1906.

Here the defendants maintained that no agreement had been made by them to conduct an audit and they, in fact, gave no certificate. Nevertheless they were held liable for loss arising through their negligence in not discovering certain defalcations.

This case is of importance since the matter of the auditor's report is mentioned, the principle being applied that, despite the weight given to the existence of an audit report, it is not the governing factor as to liability for losses arising due to negligence.

(c) *Fox & Son* v. *Morris Grant & Co.*, 1918.

In a case somewhat similar to (a) above, the accountants were employed to check books and prepare accounts. They maintained that accuracy could be arrived at without reference to the pass-book, and that as no audit was conducted, it was not necessary to refer to this. The court held, however, that as the balance sheet contained the item "Cash at Bank", the accountants should have verified its existence, and so were held liable.

(d) *Irish Woollen Company* v. *Tyson and Others*, 1900.

Various inaccuracies arose in the accounts of the company regarding its stock, book debts and trade liabilities, due to falsification. The work carried out by the auditor's staff was inadequate, and although the auditor was not held liable in respect of the matters affecting the stock and book debts, nevertheless it was considered it would have been possible to detect the understatement of liabilities had adequate tests been carried out. The fact that he did not carry out the work himself was no defence. He was entitled to employ a deputy but he must still be held responsible to ensure that reasonable care, skill and diligence be exercised.

(e) *London Oil Storage Co. Ltd.* v. *Seear Hasluck & Co.*, 1904.

The secretary of the company had misappropriated petty cash over a number of years. The auditor did not check the petty cash balance, which should have been in the sum of £796 of which in fact, only £30 was on hand.

Although the case was brought against the auditors for negligence, contributary negligence on the part of the directors was held to have been the main factor in causing the loss arising, since they should not have allowed such a large sum to remain in the hands of the petty cashier. The auditors were found liable only in the nominal sum of five guineas, but it was pointed out that it was the duty of the auditor to verify the items on the balance sheet and in this they had been negligent.

(f) *Arthur E. Green and Co.* v. *The Central Advance and Discount Corporation Ltd.*, 1920.

In seeking to recover fees due to them as auditors, the

plaintiffs were met with a counter-claim in respect of the fact
that the auditors had been negligent in their duty.

The auditors had relied upon the word of the managing
director (who was remunerated according to a commission on
profits), when they queried the veracity of a schedule of debtors
which, in fact, contained various statute-barred and bad debts.
It was maintained that they should have brought their dissatisfaction to the notice of the directors, and if still dissatisfied,
to the notice of the members.

(g) *Armitage* v. *Brewer and Knott*, 1932.

The defendants were specifically employed to conduct an
audit in such a way as would obviate the plaintiff from being the
subject of petty frauds.   The auditors gave their assurance to
this effect and were allowed to conduct the audit in any way
they deemed necessary.   It transpired that the audit necessitated a considerable amount of detailed checking work, there
being in effect no internal check.

The defendants submitted that the frauds, which had been
perpetrated by an employee, could not have been discovered by
the exercise of reasonable care, but the Judge pointed out that
though the work involved in detecting such a fraud might
necessitate the minute examination of a large number of documents, this was exactly what the auditors had undertaken to
do.   The auditors were found to be liable for damages to the
extent of £1,200.

16. Cases of misfeasance.   Misfeasance may be described as
the "wrongful performance of a fiduciary duty"; damages
will only be awarded against the tortfeasor, however, if actual
loss has been suffered arising out of the breach.

The auditor is an officer of the company for the purpose of
Section 333 of the *Companies Act, 1948*, and in that capacity
may be held liable in damages in the event of winding-up
provided his misfeasance has been the cause of damage arising
to the company.

(a) *In re The London and General Bank, 1895*.   The auditor
in this case had reported to the directors the serious position
of the company due to loans having been made on insufficient
security and also his opinion as to their being doubtful.

The directors refused to take any action so the auditor
qualified his report by stating that "the value of the assets is
dependant upon their realisation."

Although the wording of the report was such that it might

have led to further enquiry on the shareholders' part, nevertheless the auditor was held to have been negligent, for to give shareholders such information as may induce them to ask for more is not discharging his duty.

The following statements by the Judge are reproduced as they constitute fundamental principles covering the duty of the auditor.

> He (the auditor) must be honest—that is he must not certify what he does not believe to be true and he must take reasonable care and skill before he believes that what he certifies is true. . . . His business is to ascertain and state the true financial position of the company at the time of the audit, and his duty is confined to that. But then comes the question: How is he to ascertain such position? The answer is: By examining the books of the company. But he does not discharge his duty by doing this without inquiry and without taking any trouble to see that the books of the company themselves show the company's true position. He must take reasonable care to ascertain that they do.

(b) *In re The Kingston Cotton Mill Company Ltd., 1896.* This case has already been mentioned (*see* p. 145) in particular reference to stock in trade. By over-valuation of stocks for a number of years, profits had been inflated by a manager who received a commision on them.

The famous phrase referring to the "watch dog and bloodhound" are referred to in the following extract from the words of Lopas, L. J. in the course of his judgment, however, the important point to observe is the principle laid down that the auditor should apply reasonable care and skill and that he should not undertake his work with suspicion and the foregone conclusion that something is wrong.

> It is the duty of an auditor to bring to bear on the work he has to perform that skill, care and caution which a reasonably competent, careful and cautious auditor would use. What is reasonable skill, care and caution must depend on the particular circumstances of each case. An auditor is not bound to be a detective, or, as was said, to approach his work with suspicion or with a foregone conclusion that there is something wrong. He is a watch dog, but not a bloodhound. He is justified in believing tried servants of the company in whom confidence is placed by the company. He is entitled to assume that they are honest, and to rely upon their representations, provided he takes

reasonable care. If there is anything calculated to excite suspicion he should probe it to the bottom, but in the absence of anything of that kind, he is only bound to be reasonably cautious and careful.

(c) *In re City Equitable Fire Insurance Co. Ltd., 1924.* The auditors in this case were held to be guilty of misfeasance, but due to a protecting clause in the company's Articles that, directors and officers should not be answerable for any loss occurring in the execution of their offices or trusts or in relation thereto, the auditors were able to escape any damages against them. Such clauses are now no longer effective as laid down in the *Companies Act, 1948,* nevertheless the case is important as it reveals the auditor's negligence in accepting a certificate from the company's stockbrokers in respect of securities purporting to be held by them for safe custody which did not exist, or if they did, they had been pledged by them. Such a certificate should be accepted at the auditor's discretion only from a person who deals with, and holds, securities in the normal course of business, and who he considers is a trustworthy person to give such a certificate.

(d) *In re Westminster Road Construction and Engineering Co. Ltd., 1932.* The liquidator brought this action against the directors and auditors of the company in order to recover a dividend which had been paid when the profits for the year were stated to have been £3458 while they were, in fact, £297. The profit figure had been arrived at by understating liabilities and over-valuing the company's work-in-progress. The directors were not held liable as they believed the balance sheet on which the auditors had reported. The auditors, however, were held to be guilty of misfeasance on two counts:

(i) They had failed to detect the omission of liabilities which normal enquiries during the course of an audit would have revealed.

(ii) They had failed to ascertain the true valuation of the work-in-progress when there was ample evidence, from which they might have ascertained this.

17. Liability to third parties for negligence. We have considered (*see* **14**) the liability of an auditor to his *client* for negligence in the performance of his duties. We must now consider a new form of liability for negligence, *i.e.* liability *to persons other than clients* for negligent mis-statements. (This form of liability is new since it did not exist until the ruling of the House of Lords in *Hedley Byrne & Co. Ltd.* v. *Heller & Partners Ltd., 1963*.)

(a) *Former Law.* Negligence, as a form of tortious liability, arises where the defendant owes a duty of care to the plaintiff and commits a breach of that duty which occasions harm to the plaintiff. Liability has always been imposed for *negligent actions*, but it used to be held that there could be no liability for *negligent statements;* however harmful they might be. The two cases below show the law in operation as it was before the *Hedley Byrne* ruling.

(i) *Candler* v. *Crane, Christmas & Co., 1951.* Accountants employed by the company prepared accounts at the request of the managing director, knowing that they were intended for the guidance of a prospective investor. The accounts were certified by the accountants as the company's auditors, and were subsequently shown to have been prepared negligently. The plaintiff was induced to invest in the company and lost his money.

It was held that (i) *he had no claim against the auditors in contract since they were employed by the company, and not by him*, and (ii) *he had no claim in tort for negligence since the law did not recognise tortious liability for negligent mis-statements*.

ii) *De Savary* v. *Holden Howard & Co. 1960.* Plaintiff was managing director of a company receiving substantial financial assistance from a bank, and requested the bank to provide further advances. The bank requested that an investigation should be made by an independent firm of accountants on their behalf, the costs of which were to be paid by the plaintiff. The accounts prepared showed a profit of £14,000 (due to inclusion of incorrect figures for stocks and work in progress), though they should have showed a loss. Later the plaintiff made use of the accounts himself and sustained loss.

It was held that the accountants were employed by the bank, and had no contractual relationship with the plaintiff even though he had paid their costs. Applying the two rules in the *Candler Case*, the plaintiff had no claim against the accountants.

(b) *Present Law.* The House of Lords ruled in 1963 that

liability can now be imposed in tort for negligent mis-statements (thus over-ruling the second rule in *Candler* v. *Crane, Christmas*). The position now is that *if a person supplies information or advice to the plaintiff, knowing that it may be relied on, he owes a duty of care to the plaintiff and is liable in negligence for any breach of such duty, if the breach of duty occasions actual loss.*

Hedley Byrne & Co. Ltd. v. *Heller and Partners Ltd., 1963.* Before entering into a transaction with X, the plaintiffs sought a reference as to X's standing from X's bankers. The bankers provided the reference (but stated therein that they accepted no responsibility for its accuracy). The reference proved to be misleading, and the bankers had been negligent. The plaintiffs suffered loss and sued the bankers for damages for negligence.

The House of Lords held (i) that the bankers could be held liable for negligence contained in a reference, but (ii) the dis-claimer of liability in the reference exonerated them from liability on the particular facts of the case.

The case is therefore important since it lays down a general head of liability for negligent mis-statements by professional advisers of all sorts, and in particular means that an auditor could now be liable for negligence to persons who are not members of a company which employs him. An auditor cannot now therefore rely on the protection of the second rule in *Candler* v. *Crane, Christmas*.

18. I.C.A. recommendations. The Institute of Chartered Accountants have now taken legal advice in the light of the foregoing case and have issued its statement S.8 "Accountants liability to third parties—The Hedley Byrne decision."

The reader is referred to the full text but we quote the following paragraphs under the heading "Counsel's advice."

Counsel has advised that the Hedley Byrne decision is much more restricted in its effect than may first appear, and has drawn attention to the development of the law in this sphere overseas, referring particularly to the cases of *Ultramares Corporation* v. *Touche* (255 *N.Y.* 170) in the United States, and *Herschel* v. *Mrupi* (1954 *S.A.* 464) in South Africa. In this connection the *Ultramares* case is of particular interest. There the Court decided that auditors were not liable for negligence to a plaintiff who lent money on the strength of accounts on which the auditors had reported but which they did not know were required for the purpose of obtaining financial assistance or would be shown to the plaintiff. In so deciding the Court recognised that it would be quite wrong to expose the auditors to a potential liability "in an indeterminate amount for an indefinite time to an indeterminate class".

In Counsel's view third parties entitled to recover damages under the *Hedley Byrne* principle will be limited to those who by reason of accountants' negligence in preparing reports, accounts or financial statements on which the third parties place reliance suffer financial loss in circumstances where the accountants knew or ought to have known that the reports, accounts or financial statements in question were being prepared for the specific purpose or transaction which gave rise to the loss and that they would be shown to and relied on by third parties in that particular connection. There is no general principle that accountants may be liable for damages if a report or statement which proves to have been prepared negligently by them is shown casually or in the course of business to third parties who suffer loss through reliance on the report or statement.

The practical applications of the decision have also been dealt with which cover such matters as:

(a) The position of clients' creditors, where clients seek financial assistance—here proof of negligence and knowledge of use for the purpose would be needed.

(b) Shareholders and their judgment of the company's affairs by the use of annual accounts—no action would lie by an individual shareholder but if the company collectively suffered loss due to reliance on accounts negligently prepared the auditors could be liable. The auditors could also be held liable if the accounts were used as an effective part of a document of offer and the auditors knew of or should have known that they were intended to be so used. On the other hand, where an individual shareholder might use them for investment decisions, then the auditors would not be liable as the accounts are not normally prepared for such a purpose.

(c) Where taxation is concerned, although the accountant might know that the accounts would be used for assessment purposes, no action would lie in the case of reliance upon accounts negligently prepared "since in fact any ultimate loss suffered by the Revenue through failure to recover tax lost must be attributed to the death, decamping or insolvency of the taxpayer, not to the negligence of his accountant."

The law relating to principal and client would operate to

the exclusion of the Hedley Byrne principle where an accountant is instructed to agree his client's liability with the Inland Revenue.

The Counsel of the Institute emphasises that it is recognised best practice . . . in the interests of all concerned, the extent to which the accountant accepts responsibility should be made clear beyond possibility of misunderstanding.

To conclude we quote again from Statement in *S.* 8. ". . . Counsel has further advised that where an accountant specifically restricts the scope of his report or expresses appropriate reservations in a note attached to and referred to in the financial statements he has prepared or the report which he has made thereon, this can constitute a disclaimer which will be effective against any action for negligence brought against him by third parties."

PROGRESS TEST 14

1. List the statutes under which an auditor may be appointed. (2)

2. What are the rules governing the actual appointment of the auditor under the *Companies Acts, 1948* and *1967*? (3)

3. In what ways may a company's auditor's remuneration be fixed? Are expenses for these purposes considered as "remuneration"? (3)

4. Specify who may and may not be an auditor of a public company. (3)

5. Does it make any difference with regard to Question 4 above if the company is a private company?

6. In what way does the requirement regarding the qualifications of an auditor differ under the *Building Societies Act, 1962,* from that of the *Companies Act, 1948*? (4)

7. What is an "exempt" society under the *Friendly and Industrial and Provident Societies Act, 1968.*

8. How may an auditor be appointed under the *Public Trustee Act, 1906* and the *Trustee Act, 1925*? (6)

9. In what way are auditors' rights established in the case of private audits? (7, 8)

10. May a right of lien be exercised at all times? (8)

11. How is the auditor's right of lien varied in the event of liquidation? (8)

12. If it is decided by the directors to appoint someone other than the retiring auditor, what rights has the present auditor? (9)

13. The auditor is only entitled to concern himself with the books of account of and documents relevant to a business. Do you agree with this statement? **(10)**

14. Draft an auditor's report sufficient to include the matters that are required to be dealt with under the *Companies Act, 1967*, **(10)**

15. What is signified by a "qualified" report? Give an example of such a qualification. **(12)**

16. Specify the ways in which an auditor may be held liable at law: (a) Civilly. (b) Criminally. **(14)**

17. What is meant by the term "misfeasance"? If misfeasance can be proved, will damages always be awarded? **(14, 15)**

18. If the auditor does not give a certificate, will he be free from any charge of negligence? **(15)**

19. What important principle regarding the auditor's duty was mentioned in the case of *London Oil Storage Co.* v. *Sear Hasluck & Co., 1904*? **(15)**

20. Why did the House of Lords in the case of *Hedley Byrne & Co. Ltd.* v. *Heller and Partners Ltd.* state that the decision in the *Candler* v. *Crane, Christmas* case was wrong? **(17)**

21. Will the auditor now always be liable to third parties when he knows that they may in any way be affected by a statement made by him? **(17, 18)**

SPECIMEN QUESTIONS

1. In what manner does the *Companies Act, 1948*, afford protection to an auditor whom the directors seek to remove from office? *C.A.* (*E.W.*) (*Inter.*)

2. State, giving your reasons, whether or not the auditor of a public company would be disqualified from acting in the following circumstances:
   (a) On the appointment of the firm, in which he is a partner, as Registrars of the company.
   (b) On the appointment of an employee of the firm as secretary of the company.
   (c) On the appointment of one of his partners as financial adviser to the company. *C.A.* (*E.W.*)

3. Discuss the question whether an accountant has the right to retain various types of records with particular reference to:
   (a) working papers;
   (b) correspondence with clients;
   (c) communications with third parties.
   You are not required to deal with lien. *C.A.* (*E.W.*)

4. Discuss the liability of an auditor of a public company incorporated under the Companies Acts in the following circumstances:

(a) Failure to detect omission of liabilities by suppression of several invoices for goods supplied during the last month of the company's financial year.

(b) Omission to verify balance of petty cash where the books showed that during the last two years this had increased from £80 to £700.

(c) Non-detection of serious over-valuation of work-in-progress leading to the declaration of a dividend in excess of the true profits of the company. *C.C.A.*

5. What are the requirements of the *Companies Act, 1948*, in respect of the appointment and removal of the auditor?

What is an auditor's status under the Acts and has he a lien on the company's books for unpaid audit fees? *C.C.A.*

6. As auditor of a holding company with subsidiaries in various countries, you are examining the group accounts and ascertain that:

(a) The directors are of the opinion that the group accounts need not deal with a number of the subsidiaries.

(b) The accounts submitted for one of the foreign subsidiaries are unaudited.

Discuss your position in each of these circumstances.

C.A. (E.W.)

7. Discuss the extent of the liability for negligence of the auditor of a private company, assuming that he has not qualified his report in any way. *C.A.*

ELECTRONIC DATA PROCESSING DEVELOPMENT IN AUDITING TECHNIQUES

As experience gained by auditors widens in the field of Electronic Data Processing, techniques employed tend towards a more rapid assessment of the data involved. At the same time, however, clients' staff also tend to employ short-cut methods to lessen the amount of work involved and obtain information more quickly by the extraction of information at different stages of the "trail" involved. Question 3, set by the I.C.A., shown at the end of this Appendix indicates the awareness of auditors to these trends, the normal outcome of which is to make the "audit trail" more difficult for the auditor to follow through.

Normally it has been possible for the auditor to trace information back by the examination of intermediate print-outs and batch totals from final output to source documents, for up to now there has been plenty of "hard copy" available as used by the client's staff, which has tended to simplify the auditor's work in this respect. Provided with an adequate working knowledge of the computer system, the auditor has been able to ascertain the adequacy of the procedures within the system concerned and, by examination of these procedures and the controls exercised, the auditor has been able to audit "round the computer."

The more recent diminution in the use of "hard copy" by executives has necessitated the auditor having to use the computer, in effect, to audit its own system. The varied procedures involved for the auditor have to be incorporated now in audit programmes.

Owing to the complication of the audit techniques and staff working time involved, as well as the occupation of the client's computer for verification purposes, the auditor cannot operate on a basis of random working as he deems fit at the time. Whilst the auditor will always be seeking to improve the tests he applies, it will be necessary specifically to plan certain computer tests with particular objectives in view whereby he may ascertain the verity of relative information. These tests will, of course, be varied from time to time and in the light of experience, but initially they will have to be specifically planned and reduced to writing within an audit programme.

For example, to employ the computer for such a test, the computer might be used for verification purposes in the case of client's debtor balances. The actual lists of balances might be checked to see if they agree with the debtor control accounts maintained, the auditor then checking various individual accounts selected according to the size of the balance involved, the age of the debts involved, or at random, and also requesting Print-outs for circularisation of debtors (*see* pp. 99–100).

In the case of wages and salaries, print-outs may be requested at differing dates with changes being carefully examined by detailed investigation of any changes which appear at all exceptional.

Where integrated costing systems are employed, overhead charges to various jobs might be tested on an overall basis, so exercising a control effect on the total amount of expenses allocated, such being of particular importance with regard to work-in-progress figures at end-of-period dates where stocks are valued in excess of prime cost.

Computer time is always at a premium and the auditor in the light of experience—where "audit trails" are being obscured—will as explained find it necessary to use the computer for his own investigating purposes. Where the auditor requires such access to the computer it will be necessary for him to draw up an audit programme in order to ensure that he may obtain the information he requires in as short a time as possible, whilst at the same time being able to ensure that the information he receives may be checked with evidence of an adequately substantial nature.

It has been found advisable also for the auditor to attend *during* the period under audit as tests may be made using current information rather than endeavouring to audit historical data, information regarding which has quite often been destroyed. Test packs may still be used, although they have never been regarded very highly as a means of auditing (*see* p. 89); it is preferred rather to put through selected current data containing recognised mistakes and to use such for checking purposes.

Two further points of interest which are being met with in practice are those where clients are changing over to use of computers instead of mechanised accounting systems and where information on any main file is found to be either fraudulently or mistakenly "corrupted."

Where a computer is installed it is essential that the internal control should be absolutely sound. With less documentation for the auditor to examine it is vital to ensure that original data will be processed without the possibility of alteration or substitution. Not only must internal check be seen to be sound but the possibility of its violation in the case of illness, holidays, or otherwise, must be guarded against; the auditor should therefore satisfy himself that definitive rules are established to cover such exigencies. Close examination of the internal control system on and after installation of the computer is essential.

Where so-called "corruption" of a main file takes place the effects may be far-reaching, and it will therefore be necessary for the auditor to trace carefully for what purposes the file has been used. This will indicate the area over which examination of data will be necessary. The extent to which such data will have to be tested will depend upon with what certainty the date can be fixed from which corruption may be established. This will necessitate careful examination of the documentation concerned.

The auditor will need to satisfy himself as to how such incorrect data came to be put upon the file and whether it was done accidentally or fraudulently. The system will have to be examined in order to ascertain how the breakdown occurred, checks being carried out to ascertain whether any established procedures were violated, such as library storage rules or otherwise. The member(s) of staff concerned should be interviewed. If the member(s) of staff was authorised to make the alteration or to put on the incorrect data then a careful investigation should take place, including an interview with the person in authority.

The greatest importance should be attached to any such investigation that it is found necessary to perform, and, as the auditor in certain circumstances may have to report thereon, he must satisfy himself fully as to whether he considers the whole matter has been brought to light and that, in view of the internal control now operating, the possibility of such events taking place in the future is fully guarded against.

SPECIMEN QUESTIONS

1. "The auditor will need to adapt his technique to the conditions of electronic data processing." Discuss this statement. *C.C.A.*

2. Where a system of electronic data-processing is in use:
(a) state in what chief respects the problems likely to be encountered by an auditor differ from those met with in other forms of mechanised accounting;
(b) describe any three important controls or checks that might be found in or around such a system as an essential part of the internal control; and
(c) outline a further independent check that the auditor might carry out to satisfy himself that a programme has been properly prepared and fed into the equipment, and that the internal controls have been properly applied. *C.A. (E.W.)*

3. Where a system of E.D.P. is in operation:

(a) explain how an auditor's choice of approach to his task may be influenced by the current trend towards elimination of batch totals and intermediate print-outs; and

(b) suggest three specific applications for which he might consider employing his own computer programmes for audit purposes. *C.A.* (*E.W.*)

4. Where a business has transferred part of its accounting procedures to a computer, state:

(a) whether in your opinion the work of the auditor becomes less or more important than before, briefly giving your reasons;

(b) how the planning of the auditor's tests in relation to the processing of data will be affected;

(c) the ways in which the ability of the computer to report by exception can be helpful to him;

(d) the principal precautions relating to provision for recovery in the event of a system failure that should be embodied in the instructions manual or other form of permanent documentation; and

(e) the matters that need to be established immediately should a main file be found to have been corrupted. *C.A.* (*E.W.*)

EXAMINATION TECHNIQUE

In examinations two main types of questions are likely to arise, chiefly those covering auditing techniques and, to a lesser extent, those inviting discussion of a subject, such as matters affecting depreciation.

In this very practical subject a wide experience in auditing would be a distinct asset in dealing with examination problems. Unfortunately, however, it is not always possible to have gained this by the time it is necessary to sit for examinations. It is essential, therefore, for the student to *apply his imagination to augment the experience he has already received.*

Examiners are not unreasonable, and it is not expected that a student should have had personal experience of every type of audit, but in attempting a question it is essential to show that he is capable of using sound reasoning in approaching a problem. To facilitate this the student should endeavour to follow through the principles behind the general audit work he undertakes during the course of his training. This can prove invaluable as a background to audit technique questions and obviates the necessity of committing a great deal of procedural work to memory.

Internal Control and its concomitant, *Internal Check*, are of great importance in modern auditing and as there have been clear and practical Recommendations issued by the Institute of Chartered Accountants, questions may be expected on this subject. This type of work requires a knowledge of the flow of work through a business and the proper allocation of duties and responsibilities, *the student should therefore endeavour to see each aspect of the audit work he undertakes as a part, fitting into the whole movement of work through the system.* If this is done conscientiously a valuable background knowledge should be available when dealing with examination problems.

Questions of the essay type on matters arising in the financial sphere and others affected by economic theories, such as depreciation and revaluation of assets, and methods of stock valuation, should be dealt with as essays and the student should bring to play his knowledge gained in other studies. On the other hand, *questions of work procedure* covering pure auditing, *should be answered in a logical manner using succint phrasing*, and wherever possible, *dividing paragraphs into numbered sub-divisions.*

Inevitably, certain *Statutory requirements and legal decisions will have to be committed to memory*, and if when studying kindred subjects, such as Company Law and Mercantile Law, their affect on the auditor and his work, are borne in mind, the study of related subjects may be extended in usefulness and their memorisation for auditing purposes made easier.

For the examination room the following guiding principles should be applied:

(a) Read all the questions over briefly.

(b) Roughly allocate time according to the marks to be awarded.

(c) Attempt the easiest question first.

(d) For the second time read the question to be answered carefully.

(e) List in brief the matters to be dealt with as they come to mind.

(f) Deal with the points listed in a logical order, ticking them off as they are dealt with.

(g) Make answers complete in themselves, *e.g.*,

   "Is it part of the auditor's duty to check the actual stock-in-trade of the organisation he is auditing?"

   should not be answered

   "No, as it has been stated . . . "

   but rather

   "It is not part of the auditor's duty to check stock-in-trade as . . ."

(h) If an essay is requested then such should be submitted, but in other cases be succinct, sub-divide paragraphs and list points wherever this is justified.

(i) Headings, or sub-headings, may be underlined but not words and phrases within the body of the answer. The examiner does not need such unnecessary over-emphasis.

INDEX

A

Accountant, auditor as distinguished from, 2

Accountants reports on profit forecasts, 205

Accruals, S.A.P., 63

Appointment of auditor, 11, 213–4
Board of Trade, 213
Building Societies Act, 1962, 215
Companies Acts, 212
Friendly Industrial Act, 215
Public Trustee Acts, 1906, 216

Approved auditor, 215

Assets
depreciation and appreciation, 123 *et seq.*
valuation, 136 *et seq.*
verification, 92 *et seq.*

Audit
Companies Act, 1967, provisions as to, 219
continuous, 6
classification, 49
definition, 1
final or completed, 5
interim, 6
limited company—on taking up, 12
objects, 1, 2
working papers, 15

Audit, internal, 4, 27, 35
and independent auditor, 35
recommendations of Institute of Chartered Accountants on, 35

Audit file, 14

Audit note book, 15

Audit programme, 14, 15, 19
balance sheet audit, 8
general-specimen of, 16
specialised—*see* Audits

Auditing in depth, 24, 64

Auditor
appointment, 11, 212–3
lien of, 217
qualifications required under:
Building Societies Act, 1962, 215
Companies Act, 1967, 213
report of, 219 *et seq.*
rights and duties of, 218 *et seq.*

Auditor's report
balance sheet on, 219
Building Societies Act, 1962, 182
Companies Act, 1967, 219 *et seq.*
general meeting, must be read at, 219
group accounts, 221
prospectus on, 200
qualification of, 222
Solicitors Acts, under, 191

Audits specialised, 181 *et seq.*
Balance Sheet audit, 8
Banks, 185
Building Societies, 181
Clubs, 186
Contractors, 186
Executors and Trustees, 187
Hotels, 188
Insurance Companies, 188
Publishers, 189
Share Transfer Audit, 190
Solicitors, 191
Statutory Report, 192

B

Bad and doubtful debts
auditor's duty in connection with, 167
provision for, 167

Balance Sheet
audit, 7
auditor's report on, 219
contents, 219
events after date of, 138

243